A Humble Band of People

The Beginnings of Churches of Christ in Franklin and Colbert Counties, Alabama

John Chisholm Church History Series

C. Wayne Kilpatrick

Copyright © 2025 by C. Wayne Kilpatrick

A Humble Band of People: The Beginnings of Churches of Christ in Franklin and Colbert Counties, Alabama

Manufactured in the United States

Cataloging-in-Publication Data

Kilpatrick, C. Wayne (Charlie Wayne), 1943–
A humble band of people: the beginnings of Churches of Christ in Franklin and Colbert Counties, Alabama / by C. Wayne Kilpatrick.
p. cm.
John Chisholm Church History Series
Includes name index.
ISBN: 979-8-89733-003-4 (hdbk); 979-8-89733-004-1 (ebook)
Library of Congress Control Number: 2025936480

1. Churches of Christ—History—Alabama—Franklin County. 2. Churches of Christ—History—Alabama—Colbert County. 3. Churches of Christ—History—Alabama—Tennessee Valley counties. 4. Churches of Christ—History—Alabama—19th century. I. Author. II. Title. III. Series.

286.676191 DDC20

Cover design by Brittany Vander Maas and Brad McKinnon.

Heritage Christian University Press
PO Box HCU, 3625 Helton Drive
Florence, Alabama 35630

www.hcu.edu/publications

All rights reserved.

No part of this book may be reproduced in any form or by any electronic or mechanical means, including information storage and retrieval systems, without written permission from the author, except for the use of brief quotations in a book review.

Contents

Foreword	v
Preface	xi
Introduction	xv
Franklin and Colbert Counties as One County	1
The Abner Hill Era	4
The W. H. Wharton Work	14
Southward in Franklin County to Russellville	28
Post-Civil War Franklin County	39
Churches in Rural Franklin County—Frankfort	61
Pleasant Site	73
Belgreen	79
Forgotten Churches of Franklin County	91
Mount Pleasant	93
Mount Zion	98
Spout Spring—Lost Creek	103
Kimbrough's Chapel—Christian Chapel—Antioch	106
Isbell	109
Later Franklin County Churches	116
Bradley's Chapel	117
Red Bay	124
Spruce Pine	125
Vina	128
Bunker Hill	133
Post War Colbert County	135
Tuscumbia	136
Black Brethren's Work in Colbert County	152
Rock Creek	158
Mountain Mills—Barton Work	181
Christian Chapel—Maud	191

Lyle Academy	197
Cherokee	203
Annapolis Avenue—Sheffield, Alabama	206
Littleville	227
Piney Grove	231
Endnotes	235
Bibliography	255
Name Index	257
Also by C. Wayne Kilpatrick	267
Heritage Christian University Press	269

Foreword

Sunday lunch in the home of Kelby and Martha Smith was where the Harps were first impressed upon by Wayne and Brenda Kilpatrick. After four and a half years in the mission field of New Zealand, my young family made its way to Florence, Alabama, in the winter of 1985–86 to attend International Bible College (now Heritage Christian University). Wayne was to be one of my professors. His expertise is in the fields of History and the Bible. That spring semester, it was my privilege to sit in his World History II class. With every passing day, it was apparent that Wayne's passion was all things historical. On the first day, he said, "We must always stop and pay respects to the bridges we have crossed." And, for the next thirteen weeks, he filled the air with the stories of the past. To Wayne, it was not just information on a page that needed to be shared; it was not just the former things that needed retelling. To him, and ultimately to those of us at his feet, it was our past, our history. Whether talking about John Tetzel's sales of indulgences to build Leo X's St. Peter's Cathedral in Rome, Italy, or the rise of Oliver Cromwell's Parliamentarians in the defeat of

Foreword

Charles I of England, we were led through a maze of factual details that resonated and gave more profound meaning to our lives.

Charlie Wayne Kilpatrick was born on Possum Creek, near Center Hill, Lauderdale County, Alabama, on December 30, 1943. He became a Christian under the preaching of Alden Hendrix, being baptized by him in 1957. After two years of undergraduate studies at the University of North Alabama, Wayne was drafted into the U.S. Air Force. Before his international assignment, he took the opportunity to continue his education by taking courses at the University of Maryland. At the height of the Vietnam War, it was not long before he was stationed in England's R.A.F. Welford in Berkshire, where he was assigned the task of ammunition inspector. During his term of service, he attained the level of sergeant. Being a history lover in an old country like England afforded him a goldmine of antiquity to examine firsthand. Whenever leave was extended, he was either playing his banjo somewhere in a show with some of his friends or striking out on his own in a planned direction to investigate Britain's ancient culture.

Returning to the U.S. after his term of service, Wayne was employed for 18 months by the Tennessee Valley Authority. He married the former Brenda Elaine Chaney of Leighton, Alabama, on December 12, 1970. At the encouragement of his brother-in-law, Milton Chaney, a gospel preacher, Wayne entered the first class of International Bible College (now Heritage Christian University) in the spring of 1972. He was part of the college's first class since transitioning from the older Southeastern Institute of the Bible. After graduating with his Bachelor's Degree in Bible in 1974, Wayne determined to return to England as a missionary. Working primarily with the Wembley church of Christ in Middlesex, just northeast of London, he and Brenda evangelized in that region. Due to a

vi

lack of efficient support, after a year, the family returned to the Shoals area.

Upon his return, he became aware of a need for someone to teach some courses at his alma mater. In the fall of 1975, he accepted the offer to teach World History, Bible Geography, and Church History at Heritage Christian University. Quickly learning the need for more education, he started taking courses at Harding Graduate School of Religion (now Harding School of Theology) in Memphis, Tennessee. While there, he was privileged to sit at the feet of the noted church historian Earl Irvin West. Wayne completed his studies there with a Master of Arts and Religion (M.A.R.) degree. Over subsequent years, he took twelve post-graduate hours at the University of Alabama and six graduate hours at the University of North Alabama.

The summer following my first class in World History, it was my pleasure to travel with Wayne Kilpatrick to Newport, Wales, United Kingdom, where he directed an evangelistic campaign. For a week in the summer of 1986, we knocked on doors, conducted Bible studies in the city during the day, and worshipped with our Welsh brethren in the evenings. One afternoon, we took a break and went about five miles out of town to Caerleon, an ancient Roman city. We walked through the excavated ruins of the amphitheater and the military barracks. A few days following the campaign, we traveled to London, where we had the pleasure of having our own tour guide, C. Wayne Kilpatrick. Whether at the tower of London, Stonehenge, the cathedrals of Winchester, Canterbury, and Salisbury, and just about everywhere in between, the sheer volume of information that seemed to spill freely from this man's mind was nothing short of phenomenal.

Then, there were Kilpatrick's Church History and Restoration History courses. The names, dates, and stories of the past

Professor Kilpatrick's classes were a magnet to students. His kind-hearted and sanguine spirit filled every lecture with meaningful material that could be used in our ministry for a lifetime. Once, while teaching the history of the Restoration Movement, we arrived at class, and he told us to go to our cars and follow him a few miles from the school. He took us over to Chisholm Highway to a little shanty of a house. We followed him to the backyard, where among a few trees was the small Chisholm Cemetery. Wayne had just been lecturing about how Benjamin Lynn came to Madison County, Alabama, as early as 1809 to establish New Testament Christianity there. He had explained that Lynn's daughters had married men with that pioneer spirit, Rachel to Marshall DeSpain and Esther to John Chisholm, Jr. Lynn died in 1814 and was buried somewhere north of present-day Huntsville. After 1816, the family moved into what is now Lauderdale County, the Chisholms to Cypress Creek, north of Florence, and the DeSpains to Waterloo.

As we approached the cemetery, there before our eyes were the graves of John and Esther Chisholm. John's father, John Chisholm, Sr., was also buried there. He had been an agent for Cherokee Indian Chief Doublehead and rented land on his reserve. More importantly, these people were the first New Testament Christians in Lauderdale County, planting a New Testament church on Cypress Creek. Also buried in the cemetery was Dorinda Chisholm Hall, the young wife of Benjamin Franklin Hall, the Christian preacher who came to the region in the fall of 1826, preaching baptism for the remission of sins.

Under his influence came the baptisms of Tolbert Fanning, Allen Kendrick, and others at the hands of James E. Matthews.

History is a science. With this visit to Chisholm Cemetery, pure science—the ideals, the concepts, the people, the facts on a page—became applied science—seeing, touching, experiencing. Pure history became applied history! It was a hands-on examination of the evidence of history. Later that semester, other trips were made, such as to Red River Meeting House in Logan County, Kentucky, where the Second Great Awakening in America's religious history began under the preaching of Presbyterian James McGready in 1799. We also made our way up to Cane Ridge Meeting House in Bourbon County, Kentucky, where the Kentucky Revival reached a crescendo in August 1801. From there, Wayne took us to Bethany, West Virginia, where we witnessed the artifacts, the home, the buildings of Bethany College, and the old mansion that attests to the lives and influences of Thomas and Alexander Campbell. The lectures, the trips, the discussions, and the demeanor made Wayne Kilpatrick the master of his profession.

C. Wayne Kilpatrick is known for his research and journalism. The sheer volume of hours he has spent in front of microfilm and microfiche readers, computer screens, and books in his hands is uncountable. During one Christmas break many years ago, Wayne read the 40 volumes of Alexander Campbell's *Millennial Harbinger*. He has one of the largest book collections of any historian, above 40,000 volumes. He was a staff writer for *The Alabama Restoration Journal*, and his numerous articles appear in many history-related magazines. He has lectured on church history for many churches of Christ, at numerous universities, and other education-based programs across America.

C. Wayne Kilpatrick is an evangelist and successful gospel preacher. He has conducted semi-annual evangelism campaigns through Heritage Christian University in many of the states of the U.S. and other countries. For 20+ years, he traveled annually to teach Bible and church history short courses in the Yucatan, Mexico.

After assisting the History Department at Heritage Christian University for 48 years, he received Emeritus Status in 2022. At the end of 2024, he retired from his position to focus on researching and writing on Alabama restoration history.

This tome is a testimony to the tenacity and pure devotion of the man. After reading it, this writer has been impressed by the voluminous sources gleaned to make this work possible. I fully commend C. Wayne Kilpatrick for this book, as it will be most appreciated by researchers of the future when they attempt to dig where he dug. It will be a much-prized resource of Restoration History in North Alabama for generations to come.

Scott Harp
TheRestorationMovement.com
March 17, 2025

Preface

For many years, there has been a great need for a comprehensive history of the development of the Restoration Movement in Alabama and the Tennessee River Valley in general. Interest began to manifest itself in the early 1900s. In 1903, A. R. Moore presented a historical review to the Alabama State Board of Missionary Society. This was the first work of its kind, but written for the Disciples of Christ—keep in mind that the Disciples were still connected to our movement until 1906. This review was never published. In 1904, John T. Brown included the history of the Alabama work in his book entitled *Church of Christ*. This book was almost like an encyclopedia on our Restoration Movement. This article was written by O. P. Spiegel and was filled with many mistakes. In 1906, J. Waller Henry wrote "Sketches of Pioneer Times" for the *Alabama Christian*—a Disciple Paper. Richard L. James and Donald A. Nunnelly wrote graduate theses on the Alabama Restoration Movement. In 1965, George and Mildred Watson published *History Of The Christian Churches In The Alabama Area*. All of the above-mentioned material dealt with the Disciples of Christ part of the Restoration Movement. Up to this point, there was a dearth of material concerning the Churches of Christ except the information in our brotherhood journals, such as the *Gospel Advocate* and the *Firm Foundation*, and several other lesser-known brotherhood publications. It was not until the 1940s that Asa M. Plyler began traveling over the state and collecting material on the early and then present-day Churches of Christ. He covered every county in the state. His manuscript was finally published upon the request of his family. The book was titled *Historical Sketches of the Churches of Christ in Alabama*, and no date of publication was given. Plyler's book gave us some "personally collected information," but beyond that, it has not been of much help, as most of his sources were very limited. Today, these sources are more readily available, and we have taken advantage of them.

It was needful—yes, even imperative—that lives of devotion to the Lord's Kingdom, such as the men and women in this study, be told. Younger generations need to know what they have. They need to know that these precious servants of the Lord sacrificed so much that we could be where we are today in the Churches of Christ. A generation, now in danger of squandering away the church, needs to appreciate the fact that many of these subjects went without proper clothing and proper medical attention many times, were constantly in need of financial means, and made many other sacrifices in order to establish the Lord's work in so many places. It would be the greatest act of ungratefulness toward the generations of these preaching brethren, who gave so much sacrificial devotion to helping save the lost and dying world, if their story remains in obscurity. We truly are standing on the shoulders of giants, and these—our predecessors—were the giants.

We have undertaken the task of producing a history that

uses only documented sources—such as church records, journal articles, unpublished autobiographies, documented papers written for schools and universities, published and unpublished interviews, courthouse records, and even monuments and cemeteries. We have limited this study to Franklin and Colbert counties. We treat the two counties in one essay because, before the Civil War, they were just one county—Franklin County. This book is written to be used, hopefully, as a resource tool to encourage further research into local church histories and, perhaps, so the lives of these forefathers in the work may inspire us.

Introduction

This portion of Alabama under consideration is taken from 16 counties in what is generally known as North Alabama. They are Blount, Cherokee, Colbert, Cullman, DeKalb, Etowah, Franklin, Jackson, Lauderdale, Lawrence, Limestone, Madison, Marion, Marshall, Morgan, and Winston. Nine of these counties lie along the Tennessee River, which enters Alabama at the extreme northeastern portion of Jackson County and exits Alabama at the extreme northwestern portion of Lauderdale. There are four counties that lie on the north bank of the Tennessee River—Madison, Jackson, Lauderdale, and Limestone. The two westernmost counties that lie immediately below Lauderdale County will be the subject under consideration for this work. In this volume, we will treat Franklin and Colbert Counties chronologically in the order in which the Restoration Movement began.

At first, Alabama was part of the Mississippi Territory, which was ceded by Georgia and South Carolina to the United States. The Mississippi Territory was an organized incorporated territory of the United States that existed from April 7,

1798, until December 10, 1817, when the western half of the territory was admitted to the Union as the State of Mississippi and the eastern half became the Alabama Territory until its admittance to the Union as the State of Alabama on December 14, 1819.

Prior to the War of 1812, many settlers came into what is now Madison and Jackson Counties, Alabama. Alabama was, then, still part of the Mississippi Territory. They could not legally nor safely travel any further into what is presently known as Northwest Alabama because the Indians controlled the land until 1816. Some of these pioneers settled in northeastern Jackson County near modern-day Bridgeport, Alabama. Another group settled 10 miles north of Huntsville, Alabama, and established Meridianville.

In the years that followed the close of the War of 1812, an influx of thousands of settlers came into the northern part of Alabama from Tennessee, North Carolina, South Carolina, Georgia, and Virginia. This was due to the promise of bounty lands to be given to men who had fought in the War of 1812. With each new settler came his own peculiar religious views, resulting in the founding of churches to propagate their views. Along with these settlers from the older states came the views of Barton Stone, James O'Kelly, and, a few years later, Alexander Campbell. Just as with other religious groups, the followers of Stone, O'Kelly, and Campbell founded congregations of believers who were dedicated to spreading the message of the Restoration Movement. Many of these congregations would prosper for a few years and then gradually disappear. Some, however, would weather the storms of time and exist down to the present.

In Northeast Alabama, the Bridgeport (Rocky Springs) and Meridianville pioneers were neither of the James O'Kelly, Barton Warren Stone, nor Alexander Campbell groups. These pioneers began their New Testament churches independent of the other movements. The Rocky Springs congregation was established in 1811 or 1812 by members of the Old Philadelphia church in Warren County, Tennessee, which had been established by a people who came from a mixture of religious beliefs and who wanted to follow the New Testament pattern. They had established their congregation near Viola, Tennessee, in 1808. The Gains and Price families moved shortly afterward to Rocky Springs (1811 or 1812). The Meridianville work was begun by Benjamin Lynn in 1808 or 1809. Both groups had studied themselves out of denominationalism without the influence of any of the three above-mentioned movements.

In Northwest Alabama, one such congregation (Stoney Point, established in 1816) has managed to endure. Tuscumbia work by W. H. Wharton was the first work in the Franklin-Colbert Counties group to be mentioned in a brotherhood publication. It was first mentioned in Walter Scott's *Evangelist* in June 1834.[1] Several other congregations in this area that were established before the Civil War were not so durable. Many of them have faded into obscurity.

Much has been written about the political history of this area, but very little has been written about the religious history. Hardly anything has been written concerning the Restoration Movement in North Alabama. F. D. Srygley's biography of T. B. Larimore, *Larimore and His Boys*, sheds some light upon the history of this area, and George and Mildred Watson's *History of the Christian Churches in the Alabama Area* gives some insight into this part of the state. Several histories of local congregations have appeared, but many times, these works are weighted down by local traditions rather than historical facts. Due to the lack of knowledge on the part of the average church member concerning the Restoration Movement, the purpose of this study is to give a historical account of the North Alabama movement. Our method shall be to discover who established these works and what caused them to grow or die, whichever the case may be. Since every historical work must have a beginning and an end, we have set the date of our study to begin with 1808–1809, the approximate time Benjamin Lynn came to Madison County, Alabama, and ending with the year 1914, the year World War I began. This time span covers a little over a hundred years of Alabama restoration history. It should be remembered, however, that this is in no way a complete history because there are examples of churches, such as Liberty, which appeared in *The Christian Register* of 1848 as being in Lauderdale County, Alabama, having eighty-five members, and possessing their own house of worship, then disappearing from all written records. Such incidents make it impossible to compile a complete history. History, however, does not dwell upon that which has been lost but rather that which can be found. This historical study shall be based upon only that which can be found.

To prepare for such a historical undertaking, many sources have been consulted. Local newspapers of the period under discussion, local courthouse records, journals of historical societies, unpublished histories, and biographical sketches have been valuable sources of material. Many books have been written by our brethren on subjects not related to the Alabama area, yet touching upon it, and literature by other religious groups has proven helpful. There are several historical collections of the brotherhood that have supplied valuable aid in this investigation, but the chief source of material has been found in brotherhood journals, beginning with Campbell's first issue of *The Christian Baptist* in 1823 and through most major journals until the year 2000. Where occasion has demanded and opportunity has afforded, different portions of North Alabama have been visited, and much valuable information has been gained by private conversation. Such were the sources from whence this history is derived. It is hoped that this uncovering of information will give a better understanding of the Churches of Christ in North Alabama.

Franklin and Colbert Counties as One County

EARLY IN THE 19TH CENTURY, white settlers began to trickle into what is now Franklin and Colbert Counties. In the years that followed the close of the War of 1812, an influx of thousands of settlers came into the northern part of Alabama from Tennessee, North Carolina, South Carolina, Georgia, and Virginia. With each new settler came his own peculiar religious views, resulting in the founding of churches in order to propagate their views. Along with these settlers from the older states came the views of Barton Stone, James O'Kelly, and, a few years later, Alexander Campbell. Just as with the other religious groups, the followers of Stone, O'Kelly, and Campbell founded congregations of believers who were dedicated to spreading the message of the Restoration Movement. Many of these congregations would prosper for a few years and then gradually disappear. Some, however, would weather the storms of time and exist down to the present.

In the early Franklin-Colbert County union, one such congregation has managed to endure, having been established prior to the Civil War. This congregation will be thoroughly discussed later in this book. Several other congregations in this area were not so durable. Many of them have faded into obscurity. This portion of Alabama under consideration consists of Colbert and Franklin counties, lying at the extreme west end of the Tennessee River Valley in Alabama; Colbert County lies to the south of the Tennessee River, and Franklin County lies immediately to the south of Colbert. Their histories, both political and religious, have tied them together in times past.

By a legislative act on February 6, 1867, the northern half of Franklin County was organized as Colbert County. Later that year, the county was abolished, but in 1869 it was reestablished with Tuscumbia as the county seat. Thus, we treat the earliest days of the Franklin-Colbert County union as one segment of their history.[2]

Much has been written about the political history of this area, but very little has been written about the religious history. Hardly anything has been written concerning the Restoration Movement in this portion of Northwest Alabama. F. D. Srygley's biography of T. B. Larimore, *Larimore and His Boys*, sheds some light upon the history of this area,[3] and George and Mildred Watson's *History of the Christian Churches in the Alabama Area* gives some insight into this part of the state.[4] Several histories of local congregations have appeared, but many times, these works are weighted down by local traditions rather than historical facts. Due to the lack of knowledge on the part of the average church member concerning the Restoration Movement, the purpose of this study is to give a historical account of the movement in this area. Our method shall be to discover who founded these works and what caused them to grow or die, whichever the case may be.

Since every historical work must have a beginning and an end, we have set the date of our study to begin with 1809, the year Abner Hill came into this area, and to end with 1914, the year World War I began. This time span covers over one hundred years of history in Alabama restoration history. It should be remembered, however, that this is in no way a complete history because there are examples of churches that appeared in *The Christian Register* of 1848,[5] then disappeared from all written records. Such incidents render it impossible to compile a complete history. History, however, does not dwell upon what has been lost, but rather on what can be found. This historical study shall be based upon only that which can be found.

In order to prepare such a historical undertaking, many sources were consulted. Local newspapers of the period under discussion, local courthouse records, journals of historical societies, unpublished histories, and biographical sketches have been valuable sources of material. Several books written by our brethren on subjects not directly related to the Alabama area, yet touching upon it, and literature by other religious groups have proven helpful. Some historical collections of the brotherhood have rendered valuable aid in this investigation, but the chief source of material has been found in brotherhood journals, beginning with Campbell's first issue of *The Christian Baptist* in 1823, through most major journals until the year 1914. Where occasion has demanded, and opportunity has afforded, different portions of northwest Alabama have been visited, and much valuable information has been gained by diligent research. Such were the sources from whence this history is derived. It is hoped that this uncovering of information will give a better understanding of the Churches of Christ in the two counties under consideration.

The Abner Hill Era

THE FOLLOWING IS the first account by any preacher of any religious group to come into the Colbert-Franklin County area. Abner Hill was possibly the second gospel preacher to enter Alabama—Benjamin Lynn being the first. Hill was born in Rockingham, North Carolina, in 1788 to poor parents. He remembered, "I was raised poor. I am of the opinion that this was a good thing for me as this qualified me to bear adversities of life with patience." As a young man, Hill started preaching among Christian Churches on the frontier.[6] Another young evangelist, B. F. Hall, described him as

> a man of fine memory, quick perception, and ready utterance, somewhat pugnacious, but not very hopeful, and was occasionally seized with fits of hypochondria. He was, nevertheless, a companionable man, and zealous for what he believed to be the truth.[7]

This excerpt was taken from the unpublished journal of Abner Hill. It reads as follows:

I went with Brother Marshal D' Spain [1809] to look at North Alabama and concluded to remove there. I quit riding the circuit, made arrangements, and removed to North Alabama when it was a new unsettled country. South of the Tennessee River, I lost my port hogs as we moved on. After we had built a home, I went back to hunt for them. About 20 miles back, I found some of my hogs one day and lay alone on a Caney branch. I had a good gun and a stout resolute and fierce dog and was not at all afraid. I hobbled my mare and hunted all day on foot but found no more of my hogs. I went upon the point of a knob to listen for turkeys. When I thought of going down where I slept the night before, a sudden and very uncommon chilly feeling struck me. It began at the top of my head and like a wave of water ran slowly down to the end of my fingers and toes. It drew my attention and decidedly I had never felt anything like it before. It is nothing but imagination, I thought, I will not mind it. I got a piece of pine to make a light and started again, and it came on me with double force. It made me shiver all over. Surely, thought I, it is a warning to me not to stay all night where I did last night. I said it is nothing I will not mind it. It seemed to come on me with still greater force. Well, thought I, I will try it and if it leaves me, I will not stay there. I threw down the pine. It entirely left me. I went down and got my mare, went to Big Nance Creek, and stayed all night. I have regarded it as a providential warning from my heavenly father. This, with other circumstances has caused me to look and trust in God for life and breath and all things (Acts 17–25).

After I had procured a good piece of land in Alabama, brother William and I together, I was inclined to follow preaching. I had a good farm, a good house, good water, good health, good neighbors, horses, cattle, and hogs, and a good prospect for living independently. After a while my house will decay, my fence rot down, I grow old and have to die. What shall I do to lay up treasure in heaven? I read (1 Corinthians 3–8) Every man shall receive his own reward according to his own labor. 11th verse. Christ is the only foundation. If any man shall build upon this foundation, men and women [shall be] converted, compared to gold, silver precious stone. Verse 12. He shall receive a reward. (Daniel 1–12–13). They that are wise shall shine as the firmament and they that turn many to righteousness, as the stars forever and ever. I determined to give up my worldly prospects and to do all I could to turn people to righteousness. I gave up the farm and horses to Brother William Hill, who had a sale and sold on a credit my horses, cattle and hogs, reserving two horses for myself and wife to ride.

My wife not having any child, I followed traveling preaching through the prime of my life. I have the comforting recollection that many, through my instrumentality, were turned to righteousness. This to me, now in old age, is a much greater comfort than it had, while in the prime of life, labored for earthly treasure.[8]

We must address the date on which Marshall David DeSpain moved to Alabama. By 1812, he was listed on the Madison County, Mississippi Territory Tax List [in 1818, it became Madison County, Alabama]. He could have moved earlier. This is the first official record in Alabama for him. Obviously, he came in 1809 and spied out the land and moved later. Thus, Hill, who came soon after traveling with D'Spain, entered Alabama to stay in late 1809 or early 1810.

For the next several years, Hill rode circuits and taught school. This would have been between 1810 and 1832. We know this is the time frame for his labors in Alabama due to his work on the railroad from Tuscumbia, Alabama to Decatur,

Alabama. That work began in 1832 and was finished in 1834. He wrote of these years in his journal:

> I continued to ride and preach through the States of Alabama, Tennessee and some in Kentucky, until I had spent nearly all means. I ceased riding and took up a common school in Russells Valley, Alabama. I had two brothers-in-law living there, who both had large families. My object was to teach their families and also to get means to keep house upon. My brother-in-law Gillington Chisholm was raised a Methodist. He had long been convinced that it was right to be governed by the Bible alone—to be called by the name Christian, but he could not see that it was right to be immersed. He and sister Cynthia were at our house one Sunday, as he was fasting. We talked and I tried to persuade him that it was right to be immersed. Robert Bates, my other brother-in-law, had a mill down on the creek, about 150 yards from the house I lived in. On Sunday evening Cynthia, his wife, Katy, my wife, and he and I, went down and sat on some hewn timbers in a cool shade just above the mill. While we were sitting there, he said to me, Abner, you are older than I am and you understand the Bible better than I do and I believe you are honest and upon the whole I would sooner risk your faith than my own; and if you say it will do me any good to baptize me in that creek, I want you to do it. I replied, Gillington, you can read; does it not read that way to you? We read: Jesus went straightway up out of the water. Philip and the eunuch both went down into the water and he baptised him and coming up straightway out of the water. It also says, we are buried with him in baptism. Does it not read that way to you? He replied, these scriptures to me, do not refer to the mode of baptism, but if you think they do and that it will do me any good, I want you to baptize me in that creek. Gillington, said

I, if you yourself have no faith in it, it will not do you any good ....[9]

Gillington Chisholm was not baptized until sometime in the mid-1830s when Dr. W. H. Wharton left the Presbyterians behind and began preaching in our restoration movement. He baptized Gillington. By this time (1836), Abner Hill had moved to Texas. Gillington Chisholm was an early settler near the Big Spring. He was born in Barren County, Kentucky, July 29th, 1796, in 1817, married in White County, Tennessee, and in 1819 moved to North Alabama near Tuscumbia, in which section he lived till October 15th, 1870, when he moved to the place of his decease to live with his son, Dr. L. C. Chisholm. He died near Franklin College, Davidson County, Tennessee, on March 31st, 1872, at the residence of his son at the age of seventy-six years one month and nine days.[10]

It was during these years that Hill helped organize some camp meetings near the Big Spring at Tuscumbia. Mansell W. Matthews wrote of one of these meetings from Thornton, Ala., August 13, '88:

> I confessed my Savior and was buried with him in baptism by Bro. John Mulkey in Spring Creek, Franklin county, Ala., in 1823. Commenced publicly proclaiming his cause in 1825, having brother B. F. Hall for my co-laborer, often associated with B. W. Stone, Scott, Johnston, Smith, Palmer, the Mulkeys, Moore, Hill, Griffin and a host of other pioneer preachers of the restoration. We went and labored without the hope of earthly reward. Our lives were freely spent expecting our reward beyond the cold river ...[11]

Matthews would some years later become Hill's brother-in-law. From this report, we get a list of preachers, many of whom preached in these camp meetings. We know that the Mulkeys, James E. Matthews, Ephraim D. Moore, Abner Hill, Thacker V. Griffin, and many others worked in the upper part of Franklin County, especially around Tuscumbia, where Spring Creek originates at the Big Spring.

For a short period of time, Hill's circuit took him to Tennessee, where he remained for several months. He was listed among the Tennessee preachers in 1831.[12] His funds were almost depleted, so he returned to Franklin County, Alabama, to regroup in early 1832.

Hill now relates in his journal about his contracting to build one-quarter of the Tuscumbia and Decatur Railroad:

> In swapping my interest in the land I owned in Alabama for a piece of land in Tennessee I got in debt and had to go and work upon the railroad as a contractor to raise the money to pay the debt. I worked there three years and graded within a fraction of one fourth of track from Tuscumbia to Decatur, some 40 miles, in North Alabama. If I would have kept whiskey and tobacco I could have speculated greatly on my hired hands. I could not conscientiously do it. Tobacco, I believe, generally is injurious to the users of it. Whiskey, I prohibited from being brought to the shanty where we lodged. Drinking spirituous liquors is one of the great evils indulged in by unthoughted mortals.[13]

By May 1832, Hill had bid on the contract and won the bid. The graduation as far as Leighton, 10 1/3 miles, was begun in July.[14]

Next, Hill related what led up to a baptism in Spring Creek:

> When I first commenced riding and preaching, I got acquainted with Bro. Joseph Matthews in Madison Co., Ala., an industrious, friendly, and liberal man. I also became attached to his wife, Peninah, a mild friendly liberal woman. Their children then were nearly all small. I considered their family of children a very interesting family. Their third daughter, Nancy, was then a small girl, very mild and handsome. She grew up. She professed faith. I baptized her in Spring Creek in Franklin County, Ala. when she was first married to her husband Amos C. C. Bailey. I performed their marriage ceremony.[15]

Nancy was nineteen years of age at the time of her baptism and marriage. She married Amos Christopher Columbus Bailey in 1823.[16] Nancy Evans Matthews was a small child when her family left Kentucky for the frontier of northern Alabama. She grew to maturity in Madison and Lawrence Counties, Alabama. Nancy Matthews married Amos Christopher Columbus Bailey, and the young couple followed the Matthews clan to Tennessee by 1830 and then on to Texas with the 1835 Matthews-DeSpain party. Bailey died about 1846 after the family had settled near White Oak in Hopkins County, Texas.[17] These events happened between 1823 and 1832. That was from the baptism of Nancy Matthews Bailey in 1823 until Hill's Railroad contract in 1832.[18]

During this time, nothing is recorded about a congregation having been established near Tuscumbia. However, due to the fact that Hill was a gospel preacher living in that vicinity and also teaching school there, it only seems logical to think that a congregation was there. Why else would there be a camp meeting on Spring Creek in 1823? Mansell W. Matthews wrote to David Lipscomb at the *Gospel Advocate* in 1888, saying that he was baptized by John Mulkey in Spring Creek in

Franklin County, Alabama, in the year 1823.[19] Also that same year, Hill had baptized Nancy Bailey in the same vicinity. Hill said he baptized her shortly after performing her wedding to Amos C. C. Bailey. She was married in 1823.[20]

Earl Kimbrough, a native of Franklin County and a dear friend of this writer, wrote a history of the Russell Valley area concerning the restoration movement.[21] In his research and writing, he found no churches in Franklin earlier than the establishment of the Russellville congregation by Tolbert Fanning in 1842. Even though we cannot find records supporting a church of Christ before 1842, we have to conclude that there was at least one, and that would be Abner Hill's work. While Hill was living and working near Tuscumbia, he wrote a lengthy article on church government in Barton Warren Stone's journal—*The Christian Messenger*.[22] It is hard to believe that he would be so concerned about church government and not have a church in his community. He wrote this essay on March 21, 1828.

While living here and preaching on a circuit Hill wrote the following to Barton W. Stone:

> Some of the brethren believe and preach that for a soul to believe and repent and be baptized for the forgiveness of sins, is the gospel plan for entering into the kingdom of Christ; others oppose this idea. This is a subject of great importance. I wish you would embrace the subject in a plain, forcible manner. This, no doubt, would have weight with the readers of the *Christian Messenger*.[23]

Hill attended many camp meetings and Christian Conferences, as shown in the *Christian Messenger*.[24] He traveled as far west in Tennessee as Hardeman County and as far east as White County, Tennessee. He traveled as far north as Central

Kentucky and as far south as Blount County, Alabama. All of this was his circuit while he lived near Tuscumbia. He decided to move to Texas in 1835. He even went on an exploratory trip to locate a good place to build a house. Hill had already moved to Tennessee after finishing the railroad work. That was early in 1835. After returning to Tennessee, he came and bid his Alabama and Tennessee brethren goodbye and left with the Matthews-DeSpain party from Waterloo, Lauderdale County, Alabama. Mansell W. Matthews referred to this removal as "the church on wheels."[25]

He and his family arrived in Texas in February 1836, as war was brewing with Mexico. He settled near members of the Matthews-DeSpain party on the plains of North Texas. Hill wrote of this:

> There were quite a number of the Christian brethren moved to Texas and settled not very far apart. We got together and formed a church.[26]

Hill relates this interesting experience during these early days on the prairie, which gives credence to the foregoing supposition: The actions of Hill in helping organize a church immediately after arriving in Texas are more evidence that that is what he did on Spring Creek near Tuscumbia, Alabama, while living there.

This brings to a close the Abner Hill work in early Franklin County, Alabama. He did write a letter years later to Tolbert Fanning, expressing his desire to visit old friends in Alabama and Tennessee. We give an excerpt that reads as follows:

> ... My humble prayer to God is that his blessing may be on the work, and that it may be the means of doing much good. I was engaged in the good cause of the Redeemer, before you came

into the field, and with others came the burden and the heat of the day, before you came on the arena. I am old and poor and have but little means of making money, though I am desirous of reading the Review as well as of being heard through its pages. I am identified with the Disciples in name, though I differ from some of them, at least on some points. Many of your readers will be my old friends, to whom I used to preach, when I itinerated in this country. My old friends, I think, would be glad to hear from me occasionally. I am on my way to North Alabama, and from there on through the North part of Mississippi and on to Texas. I expect to see James E. Matthews, E. D. Moore, Mansel W. Matthews, and many other of the Christian friends. My object in this communication is to make to you this proposition. If you will bestow on me the reading of the Christian Review, I will do what I can in this tour to procure subscribers.

I shall travel through Arkansas, Texas, Mississippi and Illinois, between now and midsummer. I think I can do something in this way. Now if you will do this, you will send me on the three first Nos. of the *Christian Review* to Russellville, Franklin County, Alabama, so soon as it can be done by mail ...[27]

From this letter, it seems as though Hill is on a trip to say final goodbyes to his old friends, including his old Alabama friends in the Franklin-Colbert County area.

The early struggles of the church in Tuscumbia were partly due to the fact that Hill had to be gone on so many preaching tours. That made it difficult for him to attend to matters with his people at home in Tuscumbia. He also would live in Tennessee at intermittent intervals. This contributed greatly to the weakness of the work and seemingly set a pattern for future work in Tuscumbia, as can be seen in the work that followed.

The W. H. Wharton Work

AFTER THE COUNTY was re-established as Colbert County in 1869, Tuscumbia was chosen as the county seat. Tuscumbia is one of the oldest towns in the Tennessee Valley. It grew up around a large spring of freestone water that gushes from under a plateau upon which the city sits. Tuscumbia lies only a few miles across the Tennessee River from Florence.

It was in the year of Alabama statehood, 1819, that a young doctor, only a year out of the University of Pennsylvania School of Medicine,[28] came to set up his practice at the "Big Spring," as Tuscumbia was then called. The young man was William Henry Wharton.[29] He had just moved from Huntsville, where he had set up his first practice. On July 3, 1823, he married Priscilla Dickson, whose parents were reputedly the first white settlers at Tuscumbia.[30] Wharton, at the time, was Presbyterian and, by the early 1830s, had become an elder in the Presbyterian Church.[31] Sometime before 1834, he had been driven out of the Presbyterian Church. He writes concerning the episode:

> I was formerly an elder in the Presbyterian Church and for obeying Peter, into whose hands the keys of the kingdom were given, I have been discarded, called a Campbellite, opposed, calumniated, misrepresented, abused, denied entrance into houses consecrated to the worship of the only living and true God as an authorized teacher of the living Oracles; but although I have been cast down, I am not destroyed; though opposed, not overcome ...[32]

It seems that Dr. Wharton was cast out because he had been immersed. In the same letter, he leads us to believe that Walter Scott had been instrumental in his conversion. He states:

> I did desire greatly to see your face (Scott's face) and shake your hands in gratitude to God our Heavenly Father who through the instrumentality of your labors has imparted to me so much favor and mercy, joy and peace in believing the Gospel concerning his Son.[33]

After his immersion and rejection by the Presbyterians, he aligned himself with the Baptists. By June 1834, Wharton and eleven others were excluded from the Baptists in an unceremonious manner. He writes:

> Sometime in June last, a few names in this place, together with myself, were judged unworthy of longer fellowship, and accordingly been cut off from all connexion (sic) with the Baptist Church, and subsequently with the Association. This pharaical act, though not unprecedented in our days, was quite an unceremonious one - having been accomplished without entering into a formal trial, or preferring a single charge, save a suspicion that we were C----ites, resting upon a

desire on our part to take the Christian Scriptures, as all sufficient rule of faith and practice.[34]

Wharton goes on to say that twelve of them had organized themselves into "the Church of Christ at Tuscumbia." He had been exposed to the writings of Walter Scott's *Evangelist* in the early 1830s. Scott was a close friend and ally of Alexander Campbell. Just to what extent the views of Campbell had been spread throughout northwest Alabama is reflected in a resolution adopted by the Muscle Shoals Association in 1830. The resolution read as follows:

> Through Campbellism we see the divine operation of the Holy Spirit either disavowed or so obscurely avowed, as to amount to disavowal. We see experimental religion ridiculed and reprobated. We see the apostolic mode of ordaining ministers, by the laying of hands of the presbytery, ridiculed and condemned. We therein see baptism presented as producing a change of heart and pardon of sins, when the Holy Spirit can alone produce and bring about a change, while baptism shows our faith, satisfies our conscience, adopts us into His church and makes us one with Him, by thus fulfilling all righteousness, a change of hearts being previously affected by the Holy Spirit. We therein see, as we awfully fear, an effort by man to pull down the old order of faith and practice taught by our Lord and His apostles and establish on their ruins a new order and a new name styled Campbellism.[35]

From this time forward, the brethren of the Muscle Shoals area faced stiff opposition from the Baptists. It seems Wharton and friends had fallen victim to this resolution.

After their expulsion, Wharton wrote to three brotherhood

journals – *The Millennial Harbinger*,[36] *The Evangelist*,[37] and *The Christian Messenger*.[38] This indicates his wide range of reading from the brotherhood writings, even previous to his being "discarded" by the Presbyterians. Wharton was not the only one to read brotherhood publications. He had begun reading Campbell's *Millennial Harbinger* by June there were six other Tuscumbians who read Campbell's *Millennial Harbinger*: John Hogan, William B. Hooper, William Hudson, Willis H. Patterson, Milo Gist (who had come from Lexington, Kentucky) and A. R. Sevier reading the *Harbinger* before June 1834.[39] From these facts, one can see the potential influence the journals had upon the thinking of these people, causing them to search the scriptures for favor and mercy, joy, and peace in believing the gospel concerning the Son. These brethren, in contrast to the Lauderdale brethren, under Wharton's leadership, were starting out with the strong influence of Alexander Campbell and Walter Scott. The original beginning, through Abner Hill, had been the influence of Benjamin Lynn.

From Wharton's renewed beginning of the Tuscumbia church until September, they grew from twelve to thirty members.[40] The little band was growing, but not without opposition. Early in 1835, Wharton had a debate with "a disciple of the Oxford apostle," upon the subject of "baptism for the remission of sins."[41] The Methodist preacher in Tuscumbia at this time was Barton Brown.[42] Wharton said he (Brown) grew "testy" and would have no further discussion with him after this debate. Shortly after this little skirmish, Brothers John Foster from Nashville, E. A. Smith, and W. H. Wharton held a meeting at Tuscumbia.[43] In this group of visitors was a very popular South Alabama preacher—James A. Butler. He reported this preaching tour in late June of that year. Butler wrote:

> Bragg's Store, Lownds Co., Ala., June 27th, 1835. ...I have recently made a tour to north Alabama, in company with brethren E. A. Smith, A. Graham, and Wm. W. Williams—spent five weeks.
>
> For such men as Dr. Wharton, Dr. Favours, McDonald, Carroll Kendrick, Matthews &c. I desire ever to thank God. A few hours after our arrival at Tuscumbia, we had the high pleasure of seeing bro. John Foster, of Nashville, Tenn. who was brought thither in a Locomotive Car. The old brother held forth the word of life, day and night, whilst he remained there, aided by brother Wharton, and Smith. He has found the pearl of great price, the joy inspired by it is sufficient to flush his face with heavenly transport, in the hour of death. The truth will do this ... James A. Butler.[44]

This tells us that strong efforts were being made to strengthen the church at Tuscumbia. The church grew slowly due to the fact that many of the faithful were claimed by death. By October 1836, the number was at twenty-seven.[45] Dr. Wharton blamed the slow increase on death and members having moved away.

Late in the year of 1836, the brethren began to think about building a meeting house of their own. They had been repeatedly refused the use of the local houses of worship; Wharton wrote that the situation was being remedied.[46] Later the Baptists claimed rights to the building,[47] but Wharton said:

> The house was built for me especially, because I was refused the use, upon one occasion of the Presbyterian church to preach the funeral of an estimable young man.[48]

The building was completed sometime in early 1837. It was a brick building and contained a basement. The brickwork was done by the Ragland brothers, whose mother was a member of the Tuscumbia church, and the woodwork was done by Willis H. Patterson, who was an elder in the church.[49] For some time before the Civil War, our brethren shared the building with the Baptists and Episcopalians when they desired it.

In spite of having a building in which to meet, the congregation was still to face many obstacles. From October 1836 until February 1837, only five more souls were added at Tuscumbia, bringing the total to thirty-two members.[50] The work had grown to nearly one hundred members by 1842.[51] Most of this number moved away. This is evidenced by some of their names later appearing in other congregations.

Before this exodus from Tuscumbia, many preachers came and helped in the work at different times. In September of 1839, Carroll Kendrick came and held a meeting.[52] In the spring of 1842, Tolbert Fanning stopped here and visited with Dr. W. H. Wharton and other friends. While there, he baptized six persons.[53] Later that year, after Fanning's visit, Dr. Wharton moved to Nashville, Tennessee.[54] After the removal of Wharton, the work began to decline rapidly.

In December, Alexander Hall's *Christian Register* listed the churches in Alabama and made no mention of any work in Tuscumbia at this time.[55] It seems that the work was dispersed completely. By October 1860, John Taylor had been working in Franklin (containing modern-day Franklin and Colbert counties). He made no mention of any work at Tuscumbia at all during the North Alabama Cooperation Meeting held at Berea Meeting House, Fayette County, Alabama, on October 27, 1860.[56] The only works mentioned in Franklin County at that time were found in the southern end of the county, which is modern-day Franklin County. They were Russellville, Spout Spring, and Frankfort. This indicated a complete absence of any work in the area known today as Colbert County. The work in Colbert County went into the Civil War in shambles. It seems that the work in Tuscumbia had been built around the man who had resurrected it from Hill's work—Dr. William Henry Wharton. For a time, it seemed that the church did not meet for worship, even though there were members who claimed loyalty to the Lord.

Nina Leftwich, a local historian from Tuscumbia, wrote a book entitled *Two Hundred Years At Muscle Shoals*. She wrote of the scattered remains of the church of Christ:

> Tradition has it that Alexander Campbell visited Tuscumbia during the year 1846 and established a congregation of religious people who called themselves Campbellites, later Christians.[57] Among the people whose names are prominently connected with the early efforts of this church are those of Dr. W. H. Wharton, who married Priscilla Dickson, one of the first white settlers of Tuscumbia; and Dr. Ed. Chisholm and family. The efforts of this congregation failed for some years, and many of them attended the Episcopal Church whereupon their children became communicants of this church or of others.[58]

Leftwich was in error concerning Alexander Campbell establishing the church in Tuscumbia. According to Campbell's own day-by-day account on his three trips to Alabama, he never came further north than Tuscaloosa, Alabama. He never came to North Alabama. Leftwich was probably correct in what happened to some of the members of the church in Tuscumbia. There would be an effort by James Madison (J. M.) Pickens to reconvene the work at Tuscumbia after the Civil War.

There were, however, other persons of note in the church at

Tuscumbia before the disastrous demise of the original beginnings. Dr. Lewis C. Chisholm, who had been a prominent member of the church, was son-in-law to Dr. Samuel Sevier of Russellville. Chisholm had married Jane Sevier,[59] the fourth daughter of Dr. Sevier. He moved away from Tuscumbia. Chisholm's father, Gillington Chisholm, was baptized by Dr. Wharton in the early 1830s.[60] He also moved away with his son. Abraham Ricks, who once owned three hundred slaves and 1,000 acres of land, [61] was a member of the church.[62] His wife taught the children of the slaves about the Bible.[63] It was on Ricks's plantation that probably the oldest congregation of our black brethren was founded in Alabama. Ricks built a little log house for them to use to worship, and it was called the "Mother Church."[64] He let the black brethren hold their services to suit themselves. They were allowed to preach, shout, and sing as much as they wished, so long as they conducted themselves with decorum. No one was allowed to molest them or to go there in derision.[65] This was the true Christian character of a servant of God manifested.

Abraham Ricks's son T. L. Ricks, also from this area, graduated from Bethany College on July 4, 1848, with a Bachelor of Arts degree. Young Ricks delivered an oration, "The True Path of Honor," during the commencement exercise.[66] Ricks had enjoyed the company of classmates such as J. W. McGarvey, Moses E. Lard, Thomas Munnell, T. J. Gore, and J. H. Armstrong.[67] There were others of lesser fame in the community, such as Phebee Ricks, who was baptized by Dr. W. H. Wharton and was a member at Tuscumbia. There are countless others whose names are only known to God the Father. Even though the work of these first saints was not permanent, it made a permanent impact on the Tuscumbia and Colbert County communities.

After the Civil War J. M. Pickens came to Tuscumbia and

observed the deplorable condition of the once numerically and spiritually strong church. It was in shambles and had been neglecting the assembling together, on the Lord's Day, for some time. Pickens discovered that the church building had been taken by the Baptists and our brethren had ceased meeting. The following is the account given in Pickens's own words:

> More than thirty years ago, our aged and highly esteemed brother, Dr. Wm. H. Wharton, now of Nashville, Tenn., began preaching at Tuscumbia, Ala., the gospel of Christ, a doctrine better known to certain Baptist preachers and writers of that section, as "Campbellism."
>
> Soon the denominations with one accord denied Brother Wharton the privilege of preaching in any meeting house in the town. On one occasion, Brother W. having been requested to preach the funeral of a most estimable young man, was not allowed the privilege of a house even for that purpose. This excited the indignation of a number of citizens belonging to no church, who declared that Dr. Wharton, whom they esteemed most highly, should have a house in which to preach. The donation of these gentlemen, united with the contribution and labor of the brethren, was the means of erecting quite a respectable little brick house. The brethren (as is the case everywhere), ever ready to extend the use of their house to any denomination which did not own one in the town, permitted the Episcopalians, the U. Presbyterians and the Baptists to use the house as often as desired. In the course of human events Brother Wharton removed to Nashville, the church ceased to increase, the members moved away to other parts and died, till finally, not one was left to tell the tale. Meantime the Baptists continued to use the house, and after a while assumed entire control of it, and finally, it was called "the Baptist Church."

After some years, other brethren moved to Tuscumbia but were led to believe that the house had been sold to the Baptists. In the beginning of the year 1866, we were called by a few brethren to hold a protracted meeting in Tuscumbia and concluded to spend much of the year in North Alabama.

On our arrival in Tuscumbia, we were informed that we could occupy "the Baptist Church," that our brethren had built it and it was understood that we could use it whenever the Baptists did not need it, that such was the understanding when the Baptists "bought it."

As the Baptists were then without a preacher, we were permitted to use the house as often as desired; but this state of affairs did not continue long. Fearing "their craft was in danger," the Baptists soon called G. A. Coulson to be their pastor. During Mr. Coulson's term of service, we were still permitted to use the house occasionally at night; but soon he was superseded by Joseph Shackelford, the present incumbent. The latter began immediately to occupy the house both day and night, and so we were crowded out. About this time, several remarks from citizens of the town led us to believe that the Baptists had no right to the house, and their pretended purchase was a sham.

The records were examined to find if the Baptists had a title, but none could be found. Having been told that they had bought the house from Dr. Wharton, we wrote to him making inquiry and received an answer stating that he had not sold it and that he had no knowledge that anyone else had. We were also told by citizens of the town who were conversant with the whole affair, and who had contributed to build the house, that the Baptists had never bought it and that they had no right to it. While these investigations were going on, Brother C. R. Darnell, of Tennessee, wrote us that he would be in Tuscumbia on a certain Lord's Day, and requested that an appointment be made for him to preach. Mr. Shackelford said if Brother Darnell occupied the house, it must be at an hour that would not conflict with his (Shackelford's) appointment.

It was insisted, however, that Brother Darnell should have the popular hour, and intimated that the Baptists were the party occupying the house by permission. At this they became indignant, and sent for Elder Elliott, who, they said, had bought the house.

After having learned that Brother Wharton denied having any knowledge that the house had ever been sold, Elder Elliott claimed that he had bought it from a citizen who had died many years before, who was neither a member of the Christian Church nor even a friend to it. When asked for his title the Elder said he supposed that it was in the office where recorded. He was then informed that he had no title on record. He then said that a certain lawyer had been employed to draw up the papers, the said lawyer had gone to Texas and died, and he (the Elder) supposed that his lawyer "had taken the deed to Texas and filed it there." He was told that such was a strange disposition to make of a title. And finally, the Baptists were unable to show that they had bought the house, or that they had ever paid one dollar to our brethren who built the house and who owned it; but said since we "had demanded as a right what had been granted as a favor, they withdrew the privilege they had granted us of using the house henceforth, and added an amount of very mean abuse, and heralded their version of the affair through the Baptist paper published at Tuscumbia. Several prominent lawyers were consulted in reference to the matter, who, after an investigation, answered in substance as follows:

"The house justly belongs to you, the Baptists have no right to it, but your brethren committed a blunder in letting the Baptists have the key, and by asking permission of them to use your own house, you have for a number of years recognized and acknowledged the right of the Baptists, and the limitation of the law will give it to them now, if they are a mind to hold it under such circumstances."

Since that time, the Baptists have enjoyed undisputed possession of the house, and oft its walls have been made to ring with an exposition of the errors of "Campbellism."

After almost four years, we have concluded that such a breach of trust and abuse of favor deserves to be held up to public gaze. We have a far better opinion of the Baptists generally than to believe that they would even countenance such flagrant injustice, but we think it is right to brand the Baptists of Tuscumbia with the injustice of which they are guilty, till they shall repair the wrong they have done, which we by no means expect them to do. J. M. Pickens.[68]

When he tried to re-gather the church, he could not get a gathering and one great obstacle was he could not secure a meeting place. That is when he began to investigate the building problem. When he published the above article in his *Christian Monthly*, calling out the Baptist claim to the building in Tuscumbia, he was immediately challenged by Josephus Shackelford. Shackelford was the new minister for the Tuscumbia Baptist Church. After this challenge, Pickens wrote to Dr. William Henry (W. H.) Wharton, who was the very reason the church building was constructed. Wharton wrote a letter back to Pickens which he published in his *Christian Monthly* as follows:

Brother J. M. Pickens: Nashville, March 6, 1867: I have received your letter making inquiries about the meeting house in Tuscumbia. The transaction referred to, occurred over thirty years ago, and I am not able to recall many of the circumstances— only that the house was built for me especially, because I was refused the use, upon one occasion of the Presbyterian church to preach the funeral of an estimable young man. The brick work was done by the Messrs. Ragland, whose good old mother was a zealous member of our communion. The wood work was also done by Bro. Patterson, an elder of the church, and both the brick and wood work were more a labor of love than of profit. I do not think any member of another church subscribed one dollar toward the construction of it. One individual, a Mr. Cooper, contributed $50. The title to the lot was given by a Mr. Bell, I believe who was I believe a member also. I do not recollect how much I gave; I know it was as much as I was able at the time. My impression has always been that it was paid. We agreed to have a basement after the plan was adopted for a school house, I think for $200 more, and this may not have been paid. I know of no difficulty about debt, while I lived there, or in the neighborhood, a year afterwards, before I removed to this city. I do not recollect who was to pay the additional $200 for the school house; it was for the benefit of the town. I learned after I came here that the Episcopalians used the house. Some debts may have accumulated for repairs or for the school basement. I never have any title that I remember member, for in fact I had none individually. I never opposed the Baptists or any other religious party using the house, however, at any time. We once had a church of nearly one hundred members. Most of them moved away or died. I do not recollect the amount of the subscription or what became of it. The builders seemed always thought were satisfied to take it and build the house. Bro. Towns, a popular leader of the Baptists there, was greatly opposed to us. Adieu, W. H. Wharton.[69]

Wharton gave the facts concerning the original intent for the building then in question. To this day (2025), the Baptists still occupy the property without an original deed. Unfortunately, the church lay dormant for over forty years before being re-convened.

Things turned around for the church after James Harvey Morris moved to Tuscumbia in 1908. Basil Overton wrote:

> Soon after John and Mattie moved to Tuscumbia, they were part of group of about twenty-five Christians who began to meet for worship in the Court Room of the Colbert County Court House in Tuscumbia continued to meet there until they erected a meetinghouse on Fourth Street in 1911. This building burned in 1924 and the congregation met in Deshler School building until another Church building was completed in 1925 ...[70]

Thus, the Tuscumbia-Spring Creek work had a rugged hundred-year path to an established permanent work. From Abner Hill's work through Wharton's work, opposition from the denominations was overpowering to our brethren until Morris came and gave it a permanent status.

Southward in Franklin County to Russellville

ALTHOUGH THE MOVEMENT TO restore New Testament Christianity came to modern-day Franklin County, the southern half of old Franklin County, by the 1830s, was in a dormant state. Dr. Samuel Sevier, son of the late Governor John Sevier of Tennessee, had moved into Russellville, Alabama, from Overton County, Tennessee, where he had obeyed the gospel in 1825.[71] Sevier had studied at Martin Academy and Washington College in East Tennessee.[72] He became a prominent physician in Russellville. In spite of these achievements, he and four ladies were the only members of the church found by Tolbert Fanning in February of 1842 when he arrived in Russellville.[73] Fanning takes credit for congregating these souls into a church.[74]

It was on February 14, 1842, when Tolbert Fanning and his wife, Charlotte, rode into Russellville. Fanning preached that evening on "The Importance of Searching the Scriptures." [75] So few came to hear Fanning that the next day, he attempted to travel further south. About a mile south of town, a spring on his carriage gave way, and he and Charlotte had to walk through the mud back into town. He began preaching while waiting for his carriage to be repaired, and began to baptize people. After a week, he sent back to Tuscumbia and requested for Dr. W. H. Wharton to come to Russellville and help. Wharton came, and between the two of them, they had baptized 74 by March 8, 1842.[76] Fanning reported that doctors, merchants, public officials, a lawyer, the jailor, and his household, the wife and daughter of the county sheriff, and people from all walks of life obeyed the gospel.[77] We allow him to tell his own story:

> Russellville, Ala., March 5, 1842: Believing it will not be displeasing to you to hear of the triumphs of the gospel, I have concluded to report some incidents which came under my own observation during a few of the past weeks. Fanning wrote as follows: I left Nashville about the 20th of January, with my family, on a preaching and visiting tour, through the states of Alabama, Mississippi, and several portions of Tennessee. We visited the churches at Franklin and Columbia, Tennessee; but owing to the fact that the disciples fail to keep the ordinances with the zeal and knowledge they should, it was very difficult to interest the world. The brethren, however, seemed willing to "go forward," and I have reason to believe the visit was not in vain.
>
> Before reaching this place (Russellville), I called at Florence, in Lauderdale county, Ala., and addressed a large assembly in the Methodist meetinghouse twice. Next, I spent a few days in Tuscumbia very pleasantly, where I met our esteemed brother Dr. W. H. Wharton and other so four old friends. The church was in a languishing condition owing to the causes before assigned. There were six added, and I have heard from the brethren since, and they all manifest a disposition to meet and keep the ordinances in

future. By this course, the churches will prosper, but without it they will die. On reaching this town, it being the county seat of Franklin, I understood that Doctor Sevier, son of the late governor Sevier, of Tennessee, was the only brother in the place: also, found three or four excellent sisters. Circumstances would not permit me to pursue my journey, and I commenced declaring the words of life to the citizens; and to my astonishment the people generally seemed deeply interested, and the second evening two excellent ladies made the good confession, I continued to labor about a week, during which time nearly twenty were immersed. Being very fatigued, I sent thirty miles for brother Wharton to come to my assistance, who arrived two days after, and labored assiduously one week, and only left on yesterday.

There have been added in all, sixty-two; fifty-two of whom have been immersed in to Christ, and the balance are from the Baptists. There are many others standing near the kingdom, and I trust they will soon sufficiently understand the truth to become obedient. To the astonishment of everybody, people from all walks in life have united to keep the ordinances of Jesus Christ.

It may not be uninteresting to learn that some eight Methodists have been immersed for remission; and some Presbyterians who have been pillars in the church at least 40 years have become disciples of the Saviour. The families of two Doctors and two Merchants have obeyed; we have one Lawyer, the Clerks of the county, Circuit and Chancery Courts, with their families, are rejoicing in the liberties of the gospel. Also, the households at two taverns, the Jailor and all his household, the wife of the Post-Master, the wife and daughter of the Sheriff of the county, one shoe-maker, one carpenter, one hatter, one grocer, several farmers, and several of the gayest young people of the place, have taken upon themselves the solemn profession of Christianity.

The best part of the whole matter is the "eloquence of facts" has done it all; and I am more fully convinced than ever that the truth needs no embellishment to render it victorious. T. Fanning.[78]

Fanning sent another report dated March 8, 1842, which reads as follows:

> Russellville, Ala, March 8, 1842: By last mail I informed you that 62 had been added in this place; but since that time, I have immersed 12 more. Amongst the last are seven young men, and some of them possess the first order of talents.
>
> It is strange to see Presbyterians, Methodists, Baptists, and the world uniting upon the Bible to keep the holy ordinances, and all rejoicing in the one hope. A happier congregation you have never seen than this is at present, and the members pledge themselves to meet weekly to observe the institutions of the Lord's house. Owing to bad health I shall be compelled to leave soon. T. Fanning.[79]

When Fanning left town on March 15, over one hundred persons had been baptized. Only God knows the exact number of souls converted that month. The figure has been given from 105 by Fanning,[80] to 200 by Dr. L. C. Chisholm,[81] who was baptized during that meeting. We can only say that many souls were saved at the beginning of the church in Russellville.

George W. Dehoff gives the following as some of the charter members of the congregation:

> Mrs. Anderson, Mrs. Lucy Maude, Mrs. Rufus Nance, Mrs. Louisa Nance, Dr. and Mrs. D. V. Sevier, D. V. Sevier, Jr.,

probably Samuel Sevier, Jr., Mr. and Mrs. W. A. Orman, and Mrs. Jessie Keelon.[82]

Other members not listed by Dehoff included Dr. and Mrs. Samuel Sevier, Robert P. Bates,[83] N. R. Ladd,[84] and James H. Trimble, Esquire.[85] This newly formed congregation had many intelligent men and women in its number. From this explosive beginning, the church began to go forward. It prospered and remained faithful, with preaching brethren stopping in to keep their spirits refreshed. In February 1843, Brother John Henry (J. H.) Dunn and W. H. Wharton came to Russellville and held a meeting. On February 16, 1843, Dunn wrote of this meeting. He gave the following details:

> I arrived here a few days since and met our worthy Bro. Dr. Wharton of Nashville, Tennessee, who had delivered several discourses previous to my arrival. We are holding forth every evening; and have succeeded enlisting two aged persons for the service of our King—one of them 66 years old. Notwithstanding, the weather is extremely cold and unfavorable, we have good congregations, which are orderly and well behaved, and seem to be interested upon the subject of Christian religion. I expect to remain until Monday or Tuesday next—Bro. Wharton will remain, perhaps several days. We anticipate more additions before our meeting closes. Your Bro. in the hope of eternal life. J. H. Dunn.[86]

In the spring of 1844, Dunn moved from Paris, Tennessee, to Russellville.[87] He spent nearly the next four years preaching in the town and countryside, from one to three times every week. Here, he purchased a house and became the resident minister for nearly four years. It was during 1844 that another evangelist passed through Russellville. Brother Abner

Hill came through on his way to Texas.[88] In November of that year, Fanning returned and spent one day with the Russellville brethren. There were one hundred and sixty members at that time. He wrote of this visit:

> Tuesday, Oct. 29th, 1844, I left Nashville, in company with Mrs. F., Bros. S. E. Jones, P. R. Runnels and John Eichbaum, with a view of preaching the Gospel in the States of Alabama and Mississippi a few weeks, and the first day we reached Franklin, in Williamson county ... Tuesday, the 5th, we travelled twenty-four miles to Russellville in Franklin county and spent one day with the beloved disciples. At this point we left Bros. Jones and Dunn to labour a few days. There are about 160 disciples at Russellville and taking all the difficulties into consideration with which they have had to contend, we have confidence to believe they are doing well. A few, however, have joined the company of Bacchus and are dead to all godly influences. Still there are many truly pious brothers and sisters in Russellville, whom we hope to meet in better climes, when the ills of life shall have ceased. Thursday, the 7th, we set out in the stage for Columbus, Miss ....[89]

Russellville had suffered some difficulties before Brother Dunn came, but by that November, they were doing well. Just how well the band was now doing is shown by their having appointed elders, deacons, and evangelists by January 1845. Dunn states:

> The congregation here is organized; having her Bishop, Deacons, and Evangelist. Thus, we are prepared to practice what we acknowledge in theory, but how long it will be before we carry out practically, what we have theoretically received, I cannot say ....[90]

Dunn expressed his hopes that things would get even better now. Things did seem to get better that year. Nine of the Christians began taking the *Millennial Harbinger*,[91] and others were exposed to Fanning's *Christian Review*. Their expressed interest in reading now indicated a certain willingness to mature as Christians.

By January 1846, things seemed to slow down again. N. R. Ladd writes:

> We are moving on here slowly. Many of our brethren are moving without the limits of the congregation, and no new additions have been made recently to the good cause.[92]

The problem of members moving "without the limits of the congregation" became so disturbing that Brother Dunn wrote Fanning asking if members in distant communities who did not have elders or preachers could meet and take the Lord's supper.[93] Needless to say, Brother Fanning gave a sermon on this problem.[94] Brother Dunn helped get things back on track once more, and things rolled on smoothly. He labored throughout the next year until December and then moved to Moulton. Even though Dunn had relocated to Moulton, he still came and preached for the church monthly at Russellville. In 1848, Alexander Hall's *Christian Register* listed Russellville as having 75 members, having their own house of worship, and Dunn was still listed as their preacher.[95] His labors in Russellville had helped the church grow from an infant into an adult congregation.

Like most congregations of this section of the South, however, it had good times and bad times. After Dunn's departure, the work went into a decline. It really received a bad shock when one of its most respected members, Dr. Samuel Sevier, died on September 25, 1849.[96] He had served as one of the elders in the Russellville church until his death. The congregation remained in a stunned condition for nearly two years, producing very little work. In 1850, L. C. Chisholm obeyed the gospel under the preaching of Tolbert Fanning. Fanning was passing through Russellville on a preaching tour at the time.[97] In the fall of 1851, things began to pick up once more. That fall, eleven were baptized under W. T. Crenshaw's preaching.[98] Three more were baptized that winter under the preaching of J. J. Trott and J. H. Dunn.[99] Trott writes: "... the church at this place is reviving and bids fair to do well ..."[100] Brother Dunn expressed his joy at seeing the church, where he bestowed so much labor and experienced the dawning of a better day.

This better day did not last long. One man, whom Fanning never named, took it upon himself to do all the work, thus causing the church to grow weak.[101] By 1857, in the month of November, the church at Russellville was only meeting when preachers came to them. By this time, other healthy congregations had sprung from the Russellville congregation.

In 1848, Russellville was reported as having its own meetinghouse and having 75 members.[102] By the winter of 1859, the church in Russellville had ceased meeting. John Taylor reorganized the church during that winter and baptized four new persons.[103] By the end of 1860, it had thirty members and was described as "doing tolerably well." In October of 1860, they contributed $100.00 to the Evangelistic Committee of the cooperation meeting in Fayette County. Tolbert Fanning wrote that there were some brethren who were still faithful at Russellville in May 1861, but he did not seem too optimistic about their future.[104]

The brethren at Russellville went into the Civil War in a bad condition and came out worse. The rest of Franklin County fared no better. In spite of the work conducted by so many good men, the candlestick was removed from its place in the Franklin County churches.

There were other works that received only minor attention from our brotherhood journals, which we shall now investigate.

In 1856, John Taylor had gathered the brethren in Frankfort into a church. Upon his coming to Frankfort, a town northwest of Russellville, five or six miles, he found thirteen disciples in "a disorganized condition."[105] During the month of February 1858, Taylor had two debates with two Baptist preachers, Mr. Rahauf and Mr. William Alexander.[106] Each preacher finally refused to continue with Taylor. After this, Taylor had little or no resistance from the Baptists of his community. By 1859, they had grown to sixty-three members. Sad to say, this congregation was scattered during the Civil War.

Another effort put forth at this time by Taylor was the congregation at Spout Spring.[107] This work came across the pages of the *Gospel Advocate* and then vanished forever. We only know that a John A. Taylor and a James Taylor were members there. They attended the cooperation meeting of 1860 in Fayette County, Alabama. The congregation had seventeen members at this time. It also donated $40.00 toward evangelizing for the next year. George L. Brown preached there on occasions during 1861.[108]

Another work was mentioned, possibly twice, in John R. Howard's *Bible Advocate*. The report was sent to the *Bible Advocate* by a brother in Mississippi. It was concerning the western part of Franklin County. He stated the following:

> ... Bro. Dunn was at Liberty Spring meeting house, on Big Bear Creek, last week, and delivered a series of discourses to a very attentive audience. There were nine additions, one from the Methodists, one from the Cumberland Presbyterians, one

from the schismatics, two from the Baptists, and four who were not professors. Prospects are good for more. Your bro. in the Lord, J. M. Downs.[109]

Dunn also reports of a location eighteen miles west of Russellville. That would be the right distance west of Russellville to be on Big Bear Creek. The report is as follows:

Russellville, Ala: September 8, 1845. Beloved Bro. Hamby! While engaged in writing to you, I will say to you that last Thursday, I preached 18 miles west of this place, where four noble souls confessed the Saviour and were baptized. Prospects are good for more, at this point. Your affectionate Bro. in Christ. J. H. Dunn.[110]

The above two articles were reported in the same journal and on the same date. This sounds like the same location with two different persons reporting on the same work. The writer is persuaded that they are the same work. This is all of the information on the above works that has come forth in our research. Maybe someone in the future will discover more information on Spout Spring and the Big Bear Creek work. The church would be scattered at Frankfort, but some of its members would retain their faith and survive the horrible conditions of the Civil War.

In spite of a frail beginning, opposition from the denominations, and an unfavorable religious climate dominated largely by sectarianism and strong Calvinistic influence, the Church of Christ in early Franklin County managed to grow large and was a powerful religious influence in this area for a period. Reflecting upon the church's history, one wonders how such a small, frail infant church could have grown to adulthood at that time. Needless to say, it took many tears, prayers, and much diligent work of godly men and women to nurse the church back to its present state. Unfortunately, the troubles that came prior to and during the Civil War left the early Franklin County work in a wrecked condition. Our brethren ceased meeting in Russellville and Tuscumbia, which had temporarily put the churches in that area out of business. This left some faithful Christians in a state of shock from which it took several decades for them to recover. There is evidence, however, that some Christians in this area tried to remain faithful even though the large congregations became dormant. We shall discuss them later in this work.

There are many questions one could ask concerning this growing period, such as: What would the church be like today if the Civil War had not occurred? What would the church be like had Campbell's people come first instead of Stone's followers? We may never know the answers concerning these questions, but we can learn a few facts about this early work.

A gentle reminder—remember that Franklin and Colbert Counties were one county during the pre-Civil War period. We therefore conclude this section on the early Franklin County work.

Post-Civil War Franklin County

OUR NEXT PERIOD of this history is of Franklin County after the Civil War. We begin with the conditions of the church in Russellville. To highlight the disorganized conditions, the lack of any information demonstrates the sad state of the work at Russellville. The first mention of the work was in Fanning's obituary. This mention was in passing. The next mention was by Dr. L. C. Chisholm, who was formerly of Tuscumbia and now of Nashville, Tennessee, and attended most of Fanning's 1842 meetings at Russellville.[111] [112] Chisholm gave the following report upon meeting an old Alabama co-laborer:

> We left Goliad April 16. Hacked and staged it to Harwood, thence to San Antonio by rail, where we took the train for home. By a failure in connection, we were delayed one day at Palestine, Texas, and a more agreeable day we ever spent. Here we met Bro. J. L. McMeans, formerly of North Alabama, with whose memory is associated the most interesting incidents of our early Christian life. We labored together in the same congregation over thirty years ago, and

though it was with trembling hands and faltering voices that we both tried to lead in the worship of that early day, we do not now regret the circumstances (want of a preacher) that drove us to it. We spent the whole afternoon with this dearly beloved brother in calling up old recollections of the congregation, built up under the preaching of our late Bro. Fanning at Russellville, Alabama. And while it is true that this congregation never did much at Russellville, owing to some factional spirit among its members, we will challenge the world to show a work of a more widespread influence than this. Its members and their influence may be found in almost every neighborhood in the vast territory of Texas, not to speak of other States, scattered though they were. They went everywhere preaching the word ...[113]

Chisholm was well qualified to say such things of the condition of the Russellville church since he had been associated with its work for several years, and what he was referring to with J. L. McMeans.

Ausbun Cicero (A. C.) Henry came into the area and preached at Russellville. He gave a report on his efforts on that trip. He reported nine additions, two near Landersville, four at Russellville, and three at Mt. Hope, Ala.[114] Henry later reported on another visit:

I go to Pleasant Grove, Lawrence county next Saturday, and Saturday week from there to Russellville, Franklin county. A. C. Henry, Hartselle, Ala., August 20th, 1883.[115]

Henry reported on the Russellville work again:

We had a good meeting at Russellville; organized the scattered material into working order; had six new accessions, one restored, and left two who could not be baptized until the next visit. The brethren at Russellville have bought a house which, with a little work, will be a very good house, and say that they are going to work right for the Lord. We left them on Friday morning, after preaching eleven discourses. A. C. Henry, Hartselle, Ala., September 9, 1883.[116]

Henry continued to give an insight into the Russellville Church:

I have just returned from a preaching tour, at Town Creek Ala.; Landersville, Ala.; Bel Green, Ala.; Russellville, Ala. Had sixteen additions in all was from home two weeks and a half. A. C. Henry, Hartselle, Ala., October 17, 1883.[117]

W. H. Nance wrote in October of 1886, concerning Russellville:

Russellville has secured Bro. Larimore to preach for 1st part of the year. Russellville is in a fine valley. About three hundred inhabitants and it is increasing rapidly. The railroad running from Sheffield is now being built through it. It is surrounded by quite a number of rich iron ore banks. Russellville is likely to be a city someday and is a very desirable place to live. Brethren who wish to live in a town like Russellville would do well to go there, and I will promise you a hearty welcome from the brethren and sisters. They need some good preaching brother to make Russellville headquarters and labor in and around Russellville. If some good worker wishes to go there, he can get any information by writing Bro. W. H. Nance.[118]

Larimore's coming to Russellville for part of the year was a boost to the work there. His popularity always aided the cause of the Lord Jesus. Russellville had high hopes for growth.

A. C. Henry writes from Hartselle, October 7th and reported on a mission sponsored by the church in Russellville:

> I write to report a meeting of seven days in which have been, and from which I have just returned. The meeting was in the interest of the congregation at Russellville, Ala. The immediate fruits, or results of the work were ten added to the body, seven from the Baptists, one from the Methodists and two from "the other part of the world." The meeting was held six miles from Russellville in the hills northwest. Considering the opposition, and prejudice with which we had to contend, and the very busy season with the farmers, the meeting was a grand success, the brethren think. There are many disciples who live as these do, remote from their place of membership, who do not break bread once a year, but these agreed together to meet weekly and show themselves "workmen that needeth not be ashamed.[119]

This mission point must have been Frankfort, as Frankfort was only six miles northwest of Russellville.

One of "Larimore's Boys" came and preached at Russellville and gained one soul for the Lord.[120] Holbrook had just moved from the Tennessee Valley. He had worked in and around Rock Creek after he graduated from Mars Hill. Another "Larimore Boy" from Mississippi was hired by the church at Russellville. He was Lee Jackson. A potential problem was in the making, and the elders were trying to get ahead of the situation. They asked Jackson to inquire concerning a certain man in question. Jackson's inquiry went thus:

Lee Jackson, writes from Landersville, Ala., Jan. 22, '89: "As I am preaching for the church at Russellville, Ala., the elders of that church have requested me to write to you in reference to one J. C. Clegg. Is he a Christian preacher, or a Seventh Day Adventist? He has written us to make preparations for him to hold a meeting at Russellville, and we do not wish to give him further encouragement if he is an Adventist preacher."[121]

The *Gospel Advocate* responded to Jackson with a short, to-the-point answer. "We published a short time ago that he was an Adventist, and not a member of the Christian church. We publish this letter of inquiry and our answer again that all may know."[122]

In the early fall of 1889, R. W. Norwood made a preaching tour through North Alabama. He described the state of the church at Russellville:

> ...On the 5th Lord's day, I preached twice in Moulton. Cannot tell how the cause is there, as I was not there only the one day. On the 1st Lord's day in July, I preached in Russellville, Sunday night and Monday night, and aimed to have preached Tuesday night, but it rained so that we had no meeting. I found a warm-hearted, faithful, God-loving, and God-fearing little band of brethren there. They seemed to be knit together in the unity of the Spirit, and the bond of peace... Duck River, Tenn. R W. Norwood.[123]

W. D. Harris, a preacher and member of the church at Russellville, wrote a very dismal letter concerning his personal health, but also he gave a view into the church at that place. He also mentioned two other works out in the county, Mt. Mills and Rock Creek. The letter gave the following:

> I am now living, or rather suffering, at Russellville, Ala., where I and family can have church and Sunday-school privileges once more, provided we can all get well again. We have all been sick with measles and flux for the last six weeks. I went out last night to hear Bro. L. R. Sewell preach, who preaches for us monthly, but am not able to go out today. Preaching and singing do not have the effect on me that they used to have. I do wish that I could become enthused and have zeal, and enjoy religion, like I did when you (F. D. Srygley) used to preach for us at old Mt. Mills and Rock Creek. It seems that all of my enjoyment in all things is gone forever. I would be glad judgment day would come tomorrow, provided we were all prepared to meet it, and I find some there in the same condition. W. D. Harris. Russellville, Ala., May 18, '90. [124]

From the above letter, we learn that Russellville seemingly did not have a regular preacher at that time. Even though L. R. Sewell was preaching for them once a month; it appears that they no longer had a full-time minister laboring with them.

In August, the matter of John Taylor's grave having no headstone came to light. Taylor died on February 19, 1885. This saga began in the spring of 1890 when J.H. Holbrook visited one of the most remote areas of Franklin County, Alabama. He had come near Frankfort to hold a gospel meeting. While in this region, he travels a few miles to a lonely hilltop to visit the grave of his old friend, John Taylor. His soul was stirred with remorse to find the grave still unmarked after more than five years. This prompted Holbrook to write an article to the *Gospel Advocate* in which he said of Taylor:

> He labored longer and harder, and endured more persecution and hardship, and received less in the way of remuneration

than almost any man I ever knew. After having preached for about a half century, he sleeps in an unmarked grave with not even a slab to mark the spot where his ashes now repose.[125]

Someone had informed F. D. Srygley of the situation. Srygley, who had known Taylor all of his life, described it as follows:

... his grave is in the woods, near a humble country church in the mountains of North Alabama, and that it is not marked at all (F.D. Srygley, Ibid). Srygley continued: "in a few years it will be impossible to identify it if it is not marked.[126]

Holbrook decided to raise money and place a tombstone at Taylor's grave. He began by writing the following appeal:

Now I wish to make this one appeal to all who have been blessed by his labors and to all who have read of him and loved him, to contribute something to help put a respectable little stone at this head.[127]

Bro. W. D. Harris, of Russellville, Ala., wrote to Holbrook to inform him that the church at Russellville would contribute liberally to the fund. He volunteered to transport the tombstone to the cemetery where Taylor was buried and erect it when it arrived at Russellville. The cemetery was about ten miles west of Russellville, near Frankfort.[128]

Holbrook informed Srygley that he was receiving money to aid in placing a monument at Taylor's grave. He wrote:

Dear Brother Srygley: After love to you, please allow me space in the Advocate to acknowledge the receipt of eleven dollars from the brethren at Russellville, for the Taylor monument Ten dollars was from the church at Russellville, fifty cents from James Kennedy and fifty cents from Robert Blankenship. J. H. Halbrook. New River, August 28th.[129]

The monument was purchased and placed at the head of Taylor's grave. It is noted that the church at Russellville played an important part in securing Taylor's monument.

Even though the Russellville congregation had gained the W. D. Harris and family, they lost the Walter C. Craig family by removal to another community. The church gave them a letter of recommendation to take with them to any place they chose to move. The letter read as follows:

Christian Church,
    Russellville, Ala.,
    October 21st, 1890
    To the Church of Christ Greetings,

This is to certify that Bro. Walter C. Craig and wife are members in good standing with the Church of Christ at Russellville, and we cordially commend them to any congregation wherever they may go.

    Done by the order of the church at Russellville.

                              W. H. Nance
              Elders   James C. Allen
                              R. M. Clark[130]

For many years, our brethren practiced "Letters of Recommendation," but at some point in time, this practice fell by the wayside. This writer has seen dozens of these letters in various congregational records.

The next we hear from Russellville is from L. R. Sewell. He reported a meeting by F. W. Smith from Franklin, Tennessee:

The meeting at Russellville, Ala., began on the third Lord's day in June and closed Tuesday after the first Lord's day in July. The preaching was done by Bro. F. W. Smith, of Franklin, Tenn. Audience good from the beginning. Result, six were added, three by obedience and three restored; much prejudice removed, the church much strengthened and money raised to build a house of worship. Bro. Smith did a grand work for the Master and endeared himself forever to the hearts of the people or Russellville ...[131]

Brown Godwin, a former "Larimore Boy," who graduated from Mars Hill in 1885,[132] sent the next report on Russellville. He only preached once on his tour, but gave a good review of his experiences there:

Russellville, Ala., I preached once. Here is where I did my first work after leaving college. Although I met many of the faithful workers, who worked with me, when I lived there, many voices have been hushed on earth, others are looking older, while many others are scattered over the United States. Sweet is the remembrance of my work with this congregation. In my rambles, none have been of more assistance to me than it. Previous engagements forbade that I should remain with them longer. Bro. L. R. Sewell preaches for them monthly and is held in very high esteem. They are building a nice house of worship. Many changes there since I made my home with them—town several times larger. I had the pleasure of being with R. M. Clark, who lives here, and who preaches as often as his health will permit. He says he is serving the poor man's God. " Bob" was at Mars' Hill when I was there, and was then, as he is now, a zealous worker for the salvation of souls.[133]

In August of 1892, O. P. Barry came and held a meeting of ten days. He had just ended a week-long meeting at Isbell. His original intentions were to preach on Sunday morning and evening and return to his home. Those intentions were changed by the responses that happened on that Sunday. He gave a good description of what transpired at Russellville:

> ... I stopped to preach Sunday and Sunday night for them, but the interest that was manifested during these two services justified us to make a protracted effort, which lasted ten days, resulting in forty being added to the church. The brethren at Russellville are doing a grand work. During my stay in Alabama I preached fifty-three discourses, resulting in seventy being added to the local churches. O. P. Barry.[134]

In a report to the *Gospel Advocate* from Russellville in 1894, John Hayes of Mooresville, Alabama, wrote:

> I have just closed a meeting fourteen miles from here, at Mount Zion Church. Results: Four by obedience and one from the Baptists. I preached twice for the brethren here [Russellville]. I leave today for my home, Mooresville, Ala., to get everything ready to return to the [Nashville] Bible School:[135]

In 1895, a short note appeared in the *Gospel Advocate* about a meeting being conducted by Paul Hayes. It simply read: "Brother Paul Hayes is holding forth with good interest at Russellville."[136] By 1896, I. B. Bradley had located at Russellville and was preaching a circuit of churches in the Russellville area. The *Gospel Advocate* contained the following report:

Brother I. B. Bradley is located at Russellville, Ala. He is preaching for this church, at Bear Creek, and Isbell. The church at Russellville has a membership of about one hundred and forty, worshiping after the primitive order. This is a fine field for Brother Bradley, and we believe he will cultivate it well, and be instrumental in adding many to the Lord. He will hold protracted meetings in North Alabama through the summer. Any church desiring his services in a meeting should write him at Russellville.[137]

Bradley sends in the next report:

Russellville, Sept. 14. Our meeting at Russellville began on the third Lord's day in August, and continued until the first Saturday night in September, with two services each day. There was a fine attendance at the night services, the house being full every night; day services were well attended also. The interest increased from the beginning, and the brethren say there has never been such an interest manifested in this place before. Interest was fine, attendance large, preaching poorly done, results excellent. The accessions from all sources were twenty-four. Of this number seven were Baptists, who decided to take their stand with us upon the Bible; four were Methodists, and two were reclaimed. Sixteen were baptized ... I. B. Bradley.[138]

From this report, it is evident that Russellville was back on a strong spiritual track. Things were looking up; Bradley had proven valuable to the work in Russellville as well as to the entire area. Bradley was always busy for the Lord, as the following account demonstrates. The report is given below in full:

Dear Brother McQuiddy: Please send the Gospel Advocate, beginning with the next issue, to Miss Rosa Hammel, Kimbell, S. D. [South Dakota], and I will pay the subscription when I come to Nashville in December, on my way to Dixon Springs, Miss Hammel was a German Lutheran, and was convinced of her error while here on a visit to her brother, and I baptized her the first Lord's day in September. She left this week for her home at Kimball, S. D., and has no brethren in that country as far as she knows. She wanted some good church paper, and I spoke for the Gospel Advocate and took her subscription. She is very earnest in her 'new religion,' and needs encouragement. I gave her all the advice I could about the life required to be lived, and, like Paul to the church at Ephesus, commended her 'to God and the word of his grace.' (Acts 20: 32.) She said she never heard the Bible preached until she heard me preach here the last week in August. She said that there were no disciples in South Dakota of whom she had ever heard. She says that 'South Dakota is one of the ripest mission fields in the world,' to use her own language. She says that the people are dissatisfied with the teachings of the Methodists, Presbyterians, and Lutherans, and want to hear the Bible. What a grand opportunity for some of our brethren who have means to do a great and good work for the Master! Who will heed the 'Macedonian cry?' I would be glad for you to speak of this field in your columns, and call attention to the cry of the lost who desire the "bread of life." I. B. Bradley, Russellville, Ala.[139]

His dedication is shown very clearly in the above report. Two weeks later, Bradley sends his final report for that year:

Russellville, Dec. 14.—Yesterday closed a very pleasant year's work with the church of Christ at this place. One united with us from the Baptists, at our evening service. He said that he had "obeyed from the heart that form of doctrine," and just wished to be a Christian, and nothing else. I. B. Bradley.[140]

He was also preaching for some other congregations in the surrounding areas. He had been hired by the church in Russellville to help establish new congregations and to encourage the ones that were in need of strengthening. That is true evangelism. While working with Russellville, Bradley was married. The announcement was printed in the *Gospel Advocate*:

> "Mr. and Mrs. Robert M. Young request your presence at the marriage ceremony of their daughter, Minnie Julia, to Mr. Isham Beasley Bradley, at their residence, Mount Hope, Ala., 9 A.M., December 1, 1897." Brother Bradley has been preaching for the past year or longer at Russellville, Ala. He is a young preacher of much prominence, and we would think he had made a wise selection, judging of the choice from what we know of the man. The Advocate offers congratulations.[141]

An unusual report came from Russellville in the form of an advertisement. It was concerning a plow invented by W. D. Harris, a member and part-time preacher there. The *Gospel Advocate* spoke highly of this invention:

> W. D. Harris, of Russellville, Ala., has patented a combination double plow and cultivator which is highly commended by many intelligent farmers and business men who have seen it operated. From the number and character of testimonials, it seems that this new invention promises to revolutionize the methods of tilling the soil.[142]

Bradley would later speak highly of Harris's invention, as Bradley had grown up on a farm. He felt qualified to commend the plow. He wrote the following:

> I have examined and plowed with Mr. Harris' improved plow, and, in my honest judgment, it is the best plow I have ever seen. I was raised on a farm, and think I know a good plow when I test it. I heartily recommend this plow to all farmers. —I. B. Bradley, Preacher in Charge Christian Church, Russellville, Ala.[143]

R. N. Moody of Albertville gave the next report on the work at Russellville. The note was encouraging and spoke well of Bradley and the work at that place:

> I preached twice for the brethren in Russellville. They seem to be doing well. Brother I. B. Bradley lives there and preaches for them. It was my good fortune to take supper one evening with him and his new wife. If I am not mistaken in him, he is a man of sterling worth, besides being a Christian of the Bible order. It is encouraging to meet strong young men in, these days who, are true to the Lord's way.[144]

In July, Bradley reported the sad news concerning one of the brightest young men in the congregation at that place. Archie Trimble Jones, together with his father, Dr. T. S. Jones, obeyed the gospel under the preaching of Brother Larimore in August 1894. He had been in the State Normal College at Florence for about seven months and had won the love and highest esteem of both teachers and pupils. His young, promising life had been taken away.[145]

Happier news was to come later that year. M. H. Northcross came to Russellville and held a meeting in

September of that year. His report was very short, but encouraging:

> I have just closed a meeting at Russellville, Ala., with sixteen additions—fourteen confessions and baptisms, one reclaimed, and one from the Baptists.[146]

Northcross returned for a lengthy meeting the following year. Bradley reported it in an extended report:

> Russellville, Sept. 1: A splendid meeting was held at this place, embracing the second and third Lord's days in August, continuing twelve days. There were sixteen accessions to the church as the visible results. The church could not help being strengthened and confirmed by the preaching, such as it was—as good as the best. Brother M. H. Northcross, of Franklin, Tenn., did the preaching, and to those who know him I need not say it was "well done." Brother Northcross endeared himself very much to every disciple here and made friends of many of the sectarians. The Baptist minister was in attendance almost, if not quite, half the time, and has since expressed himself as pleased with the sermons. Someone suggested to me that he came to watch his flock, lest some escaped into the "Campbellite" fold. Possibly so. Well, one did get out of the Baptist fold and come into the church, after all his watching them. The subjects Brother Northcross discussed were all familiar to the disciples here; but his way of treating a subject is peculiarly his own, and thus they were full of interest to everyone. Brother Northcross "shuns not to declare the whole counsel of God," yet he does it in such a way that not even the sectarians can take offense. His sermon on "The Divinity of Jesus Christ" is unanswerable. All of his subjects were strongly put and

amply proven. Of the sixteen who united with the church, fourteen were students in the Sunday school, having been taught in the word almost from babyhood. One was restored to the fold upon a confession of his wrongs, and one came over from the "Johnnies."[37] The meeting was one of pleasure and profit to the disciples, and Brother Northcross will long be remembered by all of us. Brother R. N. Moody, of Albertville, Ala., and Brother J. K. Hill, of Tucker's Cross Roads, Tenn., were with us for a day or two during the meeting and aided in song and prayer. For a year or more I have been, by force of circumstances, keeping books for a mercantile firm here, but on October 1, I am to turn this work over to another and go to preaching the word and dispensing "the bread of life" again. Any church wanting a meeting can communicate with me, and I will try to come and preach for them. Brethren, pray for us and for me. I. B. Bradley.[148]

From the above report, one can see that things had much improved in the congregation at Russellville. Meetings such as this would continue to aid in its growth. We also learn that Bradley supported himself partly by working in secular work. Earl Kimbrough wrote of Bradley's secular work:

> He lived in Russellville ten years, 1896–1905 and supported himself as a bookkeeper for Wilson Mercantile Company and as a carpenter. He was one of the most successful evangelists that ever preached in the county.[149]

It was about four years before we heard anything further about the church in Russellville. That report would come from the pen of one of the Rock Creek Srygley boys. The brief report reads:

Under date of May 24, Brother F. B. Srygley writes from Russellville, Ala.: "I am here in a meeting which began on last Sunday. Two Baptists and one Methodist agreed to take the Bible only, and there has been one confession to date. I will continue the meeting into next week."[150]

Srygley's meeting resulted in ten additions. The meeting was proclaimed a good one.[151] While in Russellville, Srygley rekindled an old friendship with William S. McNatt. McNatt had apparently been a friend of the Srygley family since their Lawrence County, Alabama, days. Both families had moved from Lawrence County in the early days of the settlement of Franklin County. McNatt passed to his eternal reward in a day or two after Srygley had returned home in Nashville, Tennessee. Srygley wrote the following obituary notice in the *Gospel Advocate*:

William S. McNatt was born in Lawrence County, Ala., on December 22, 1820, but came to Franklin County, Ala., in early life. His long and useful life was spent near Russellville, Ala. In 1841 or 1842, under the preaching of Tolbert Fanning, he obeyed the gospel. The bitter persecutions of those early times never weakened his faith nor cooled his zeal. While there were but few brethren and sisters with whom he could associate in his early Christian life and but few preachers and little preaching, his faith grew; and he contended earnestly for the faith till he was called up higher. He died at the home of his daughter, Sister Rebecca James, eight miles west of Russellville, on September 13, 1901. For about sixty years he was in the service of Christ. He had seen many of his comrades fall with their faces toward Zion, and many others turn back to the enemy's camp, but he fell in the triumph of a living faith. He left a blessed heritage to his family and friends, an upright life, a godly walk. In my boyhood days it was my privilege to know Brother McNatt. I hope to meet him in that glad city. F. B. Srygley.[152]

It would be two more years before news comes from the church in Russellville. It would come from P. H. Hooten of Lewisburg, Tennessee. He states:

> I have just closed a good meeting of twelve days' duration at Russellville, as a result of which six souls were born into God's family. The church there has been carrying a debt of three hundred dollars on the house for several years, but the members say they will lift that by the first of next year. So, all in all, I think we had a good meeting. P. H. Hooten.[153]

He gives us information, not only on the spiritual growth but on the financial problem concerning an owed sum of money on their building. That was not the only problem at Russellville. I. B. Bradley was preparing to move to Nashville, Tennessee. Bradley gave his final report from Russellville:

> Brother I. B. Bradley writes us as follows: "Please say through the Gospel Advocate that my address is changed from Russellville, Ala., to No. 613 North Third street, Nashville, Tenn. I desire to correspond with churches wanting meetings during May and June and also during September and October, as I have some time to engage during these months."[154]

After Bradley's removal to Nashville, F. W. Smith came and held a meeting at Russellville. Smith's resulted in nine additions, and then he went to Sheffield and preached for five days, resulting in five additions.[155]

Brother L. R. Sewell began a series of meetings at Russellville, Ala., in January 1907.[156] He returned in June and began a series of meetings on June 9th and concluded on June 21st with fifteen additions.[157] Sewell gave the following account:

> ... Everything was in readiness for the meeting, and much interest was aroused. Brother Logue did most of the preaching. Brother Sewell was in to see us last week, and we were sorry to learn that he is again in very poor health.[158]

It must be noted that Sewell's health was failing him. That explains why Logue did most of the preaching. It seems that Sewell was working in some capacity with the church at Russellville, because when Logue returned to hold a meeting later that year, Sewell assisted Logue in the meeting. Logue reported:

> My first meeting was with the church at Russellville, Ala. The meeting continued for two weeks. The body was edified and strengthened, six persons were baptized, four were restored, and two took membership. Brother L. R. Sewell was my efficient co-laborer in this meeting. S. R. Logue.[159]

By October, the congregation at Russellville was supporting a student at Potter Bible College, Bowling Green, Ky. He was F. E. Peden. Russellville was aiding him so he could work with the smaller congregations and edify them. T. H. Roberson of Russellville sent the report:

> Russellville, September 15.—Brother F. E. Peden, a student of the Potter Bible College, Bowling Green, Ky., held meetings at the following places during July, August, and September: Weatherford Schoolhouse, Isbell, Landersville,

Mount Hope, and Spruce Pine. In all these meetings twenty-nine persons were baptized. While in this work Brother Peden made Russellville his headquarters and was partially supported by the congregation there. T. H. Roberson.[160]

Our next report on the church at Russellville came two years later. G. Dallas Smith came in the first week of October 1909 and began a meeting at Russellville. He closed the meeting after two weeks with two baptisms.[161] Smith returned for another meeting in June of 1910. At the end of that meeting of two weeks, he had baptized twenty-seven souls and had two restorations. Through Smith, we learn that Russellville was looking for a new preacher to work with them at that time.[162]

A new minister was hired soon after Smith's report. He was L. S. Lancaster of Campbell, Missouri. He spoke of his intentions to move to Russellville, which appeared in the *Gospel Advocate* as follows:

> Brother L. S. Lancaster writes: "I preached at Greenway, Ark., on Sunday, October 16, and baptized one person. I am to preach at Cardwell, Mo., on Sunday, October 23, and at Campbell, Mo., on the following Sunday, after which time I go to Russellville, Ala., to begin work with the congregation at that place, where all mail matter should be addressed to me after November 1."[163]

Lancaster would work at Russellville for four years. He would also preach in the small, struggling congregations nearby, which Russellville had helped to establish. For some reason, he did not send any reports to the *Gospel Advocate* for his first two years. The next report came from G. A. Dunn. He wrote under date of June 11, 1911:

I began a meeting here last Sunday. The house is full at night. We have had five baptisms so far. We expect to close next Sunday. I am booked to begin a meeting at Haleyville, Ala., the first Sunday in July.[164]

His meeting closed with ten additions—nine baptized.[165] The following year, G. Dallas Smith returned for another meeting. This was reported by Lancaster. That was his first report to the *Gospel Advocate* after two years of silence from him. The report read:

Brother G. Dallas Smith held a two-weeks meeting at Russellville, Ala., with fine results. Four were baptized and four reclaimed. Brother L. S. Lancaster says: "There were some splendid lessons on Christian living."[166]

A year later, Lancaster writes:

Russellville, Ala., October 23 ... On September 23 a young man of Russellville informed me that he had learned from a study of the Bible that it was his duty to be baptized and asked me to assist him. We quit our business and went to the water, and I baptized him. This was somewhat on the order of the eunuch's obedience (Acts 8:36), except that the Holy Spirit performed his part through the medium of the written word. L. S. Lancaster.[167]

His next report is concerning his removal to Henderson, Tennessee. It simply read: "Change of address: L. S. Lancaster from Russellville, Ala., to Henderson, Tenn."[168] We do not mean to be too critical of Lancaster, but it seems he was more interested in the mission works around Russellville than he was of the work at the congregation that had hired him. The congregation, however, must have liked his work; they kept him for four years.

This brings us to a close to the study of the church in Russellville, Alabama—this being the date (1914) we selected to terminate our studies on Franklin and Colbert Counties.

Churches in Rural Franklin County—Frankfort

FRANKFORT WAS the first rural work in the Franklin-Colbert County period. The exact year it was established cannot be ascertained. We do know that it was there in 1855. The following excerpt will verify this date:

> In 1855 Bro. J. B. Hamilton was baptized by Bro. John Taylor and "lived a consistent member," meeting regularly with the disciples at Frankfort, until their dispersion caused by the war. Like many others he strayed from the fold but returned a few years before his death lamenting the lost years.[169]

In 1859, B. F. Manire of Pontotoc, Mississippi, came and held a meeting at Frankfort and baptized three into Christ. In 1860, John Taylor, who was still living at Frankfort, gave a report to the *Gospel Advocate* on a cooperation meeting at Berea in Fayette County, Alabama. He listed Frankfort as having Thomas B. Trotter as the evangelist and Obediah Chisholm as one of the leaders at that place. During the Civil

War, the young church suffered tremendously. To get a proper picture of this tragedy, we insert a letter to the *Gospel Advocate* from J. B. Hamilton, a deacon at Frankfort. It was printed in the *Gospel Advocate* under the heading—

"Destitution:"

Bros. Fanning & Lipscomb— I write this by request of many of our brethren, and will say there are a number of them in a starving condition, and they will have to quit their crops unless they can get some relief, and are willing to pay for it this fall, and are willing to secure the payment by giving a deed of trust to each, and if it is possible for you to have corn sent to Tuscumbia, I will take it in charge and have the trust deeds, and they are willing to pledge everything they possess for corn. Say five hundred bushels, and if we cannot get that amount, say less. Yours in Christ J. B. Hamilton, Deacon of Frankfort Church.[170]

In spite of these horrific conditions, the church stayed the course and continued to be evangelistic. To help prove our point, we give the following example. Isabella Chisholm, wife of Dr. L. C. Chisholm, was baptized by John Taylor. The baptism occurred during the Civil War at Frankfort, Alabama. This reveals that even though the church there was scattered, to a degree, it was still evangelistically engaged.[171] In August 1866, J. M. Pickens came to Frankfort and held a two-week meeting in which over one hundred persons submitted to Christ during this protracted meeting.[172] Three of these baptized persons established the church at Rock Creek later that year. They were J. H. Srygley, his wife Sarah J. Srygley, and F. G. W. Flake, all of whom began the Rock Creek congregation within just a few weeks.[173] Immediately after the war, this evangelistic fervor was demonstrated again in spite of the ravages of the war. A portion of the obituary of Sarah Jane Srygley, the mother of F. D. and F. B. Srygley, bears testimony to this fact. It reads as follows:

> She was married to James H. Srygley on October 28, 1844... She was baptized by our talented and long-lamented brother, J. M. Pickens, in August 1866. Immediately after her baptism she and her husband and four others established, at her home, Rock Creek, Ala., the church of Christ of which she was an active and faithful member till she moved to Coal Hill, Ark., in October 1887 ....[174]

The brethren at Frankfort were trying to find an evangelist for the Black brethren. David Lipscomb published the following note concerning this matter:

> Brethren from North Alabama, In the neighborhood of Frankfort, inquire for a colored preaching brother, who will labor among the freedmen. There are great numbers of this class of our fellow beings in that county, who are open to receive instruction. Evil influences have closed the ears of this people to the gospel preached by the white. It is the duty of the whites notwithstanding this, to encourage and to aid, in every way in their power, those of our colored brethren who are worthy ln laboring among the freedmen for their spiritual and temporal good. If any of our colored brethren will go to that field of labor, they will meet with the hearty cooperation and aid of the white brethren, and large and inviting field for labor among the colored population. David Lipscomb.[175]

This request shows the concern for the Black people in

their community. Frankfort was trying to recover from the horrible period known as the Civil War.

Our next report on the Frankfort work was reported many years later by F. B. Srygley, who was looking back through the years with fond memories of his boyhood when he first saw T. B. Larimore. Larimore came to Frankfort in 1868, trying to recruit students for Mountain Home School, conducted by James Madison (J. M.) Pickens. F. B. Srygley wrote of Larimore's visit to Frankfort:

> I suspect I knew Brother Larimore longer than any one who will write for this issue of the Gospel Advocate. The first time I ever saw him was the second Sunday in July 1867. I was then eight years old and he was twenty-four. Brother Larimore came to old Frankfort, Ala., to get students to attend a school which had been founded by J. M. Pickens at Mountain Home, Ala. He was to be associated with Pickens in that school, and he was out to get students for it. He first came to old Frankfort; but there were only a few members of the church there, and they were not very aggressive, and so he was invited by my father to Rock Creek, where a church had been started by old Brother John Taylor with seven members, my grandmother, my father and mother, Uncle Jim Quillen and Aunt Martha, and Brother Silas Flake and wife. [176]

F. B. Srygley was wrong on the date of July 1867. According to his brother F. D. Srygley's book—*Larimore and His Boys*—Larimore went directly to the newly established Hopewell congregation in Lauderdale County and preached one time, and then was taken to the Middle Cypress community to preach.[177] The church organized by Larimore on this visit is now the Bethel Berry Church of Christ. That was the year 1868, according to the Bethel Berry Church book.[178] T. B. Larimore returned in August of that year. Srygley said that he preached at Frankfort, and "four others obeyed the gospel and united with our congregation.[179] It was during this visit that Larimore was challenged to his one and only debate. The details of this debate were given by F. B. Srygley, who attended the debate while a young boy. He wrote:

> He held his only debate with William Blackburn in the hills of North Alabama, only about two miles from where we first met. He preached five sermons at Rock Creek on that trip, and I think that I have never heard such preaching in all my life. Someone in the darkness in the churchyard handed him a list of forty questions to which he demanded an answer, but there was no name signed to them. When we reached home that night, Brother Larimore took my father into the room and showed him the questions and asked his advice. My father said, "Mr. Blackburn, the Methodist preacher of the neighborhood, is the author of these questions;" and he advised Brother Larimore to publicly state that he had received some questions which demanded an answer, but there was no name signed to them, and before he could afford to publicly read the questions and answer them, he should have the name of the querist. This was the last meeting of the series, and the incident was closed then. But after Brother Larimore left the neighborhood Mr. Blackburn came to my father and admitted that he was the author of the forty questions. Arrangements were then made for Brother Larimore to return in 1868 and for Mr. Blackburn to answer his own questions and give Brother Larimore an opportunity to reply to him. A large crowd heard that discussion, which lasted all day. While Brother Larimore was not of an aggressive disposition, he

answered Mr. Blackburn according to the teaching of the word of God, and more was done that day to plant the principles of primitive Christianity in the hearts of those mountain people than could have been done in any other way. While Brother Larimore never sought a discussion, and so far, as I know, never had another, yet he had one debate that I have never forgotten.[180]

This debate, according to Srygley, was held two miles from where Srygley first heard Larimore.[181] That was at Frankfort when Larimore was on a recruiting trip for Mountain Home School near Moulton.

Four years after the war, J. H. Srygley, who still retained membership at Frankfort, ordered seven hymn books.[182] This showed the congregation at that place loved singing. From this region came the Greenhills and the Sparks, who produced great song leaders for generations. This also showed that the brethren around Frankfort were trying to get back to a state of normalcy.

F. B. Srygley wrote the following bit of trivia inserted here concerning the area around Frankfort. It is humorous yet underscores the large population of Black people living in the Frankfort area.

Dr. W. H. Wharton was a practicing physician as well as a preacher, living then near Frankfort, Ala. All who were familiar with him well remember two leading characteristics of the man. One was his tender and gentle, yet earnest sympathy for all, but especially for the poor and unfortunate. The other was the facility with which, on all occasions he would introduce the subject of religion into conversation, and in a meek and inoffensive manner, urge its claims. On this occasion a [Black] boy had been sent for him to attend a case of sickness. On the way to see his patient he improved the opportunity to introduce the subject of religion to his pilot, the [Black boy], and preached to him Jesus. They came to a certain water, the [Black boy] desired baptism, they both went down into the water, and he baptized him. His wet clothes told on him. If we could generally be as instant in season and out of season, to warn our fellowmen of the Savior's love and their obligations, our service as Christians would be greatly more blessed.[183]

This incident had to have occurred between 1834, the date of Wharton's conversion to our restoration movement, and late 1842, when Wharton moved to Nashville. Srygley was in error about Wharton living near Frankfort. In the Dixon letters, it is stated that Wharton came to Tuscumbia and set up his medical practice.[184] Sadie Dickson Shrader was Wharton's great-niece. There is not even the slightest bit of evidence that Wharton ever lived near Frankfort. Srygley was trying to relate an event that had happened years before he was born (F. B. Srygley was born in 1859). In all probability, Srygley never personally knew Wharton, as Wharton had moved to Nashville in 1842, long before Srygley was born. He simply had his facts wrong. This shows that historians are fallible; we can and do make mistakes when we do not get all of the facts and just speculate about someone or something. Even knowing Taylor so well did not keep Srygley from recording some errors in his sketches of Taylor.

John Taylor was most important to the church at Frankfort in his latter days. He lived with his daughter's family only two miles west of Frankfort. His last days were spent just up the road in sight of a new congregation he had established—Shady Grove.

F. B. Srygley often wrote about John Taylor. Was Taylor

ever involved in controversy? A correspondent said John Taylor was a gentle person and never involved in controversy. Srygley, who had known Taylor all of his life, was setting the record straight about Taylor. He wrote that Taylor would stand his ground in defending the truth. Srygley's answer is recorded here below:

> I want to bear record to the fact that he (John Taylor) pointed out the errors of others. He had two debates in the town of Frankfort, Ala., before I can remember—one with a Baptist brother named "Rawhoof (Ruhoff)," and the other with another Baptist preacher named "Alexander." My father was the president moderator in the first debate, and Brother Taylor was so logical and severe on Rawhoof (Ruhoff) that the debate closed at the end of the first day. The Baptists felt their defeat so much that they secured the services of Brother Alexander for another debate. My father was so impressed with the truth on the design of baptism by these debates that in a few years he became obedient to the gospel. One of the judges of that district heard those debates, and he never entirely got away from the truth as it was so ably defended by Brother Taylor, and in the evening of his life he became a humble Christian and lived up to it till the day of his death... F. B. Srygley.[185]

Just when these debates took place, Srygley did not tell us. We do know that they occurred before the Civil War because, after the war, Taylor was getting old and much less active than he had been prior to the War. J. H. Srygley wrote of Taylor's age:

> Brother Taylor is a faithful soldier, but age has bleached his locks, dimmed his eye, made pale the cheek that once with

health and vigor glowed, bowed down his manly form and tells us that ere long we must give him up. While these reflections trouble us, we rejoice to know that as he approaches the grave, he approaches the land of the blessed ....[186]

This sketch proves our point—Taylor was more than likely so overcome with age problems that he would not have debated anyone after the Civil War.

With Taylor's advanced age came the eventual demise of the Church of Christ at Frankfort. This became evident when A. C. Henry came to this area and preached at a point six miles northeast of Russellville, which was obviously Frankfort since it was located six miles northeast of Russellville.[187] In 1898, Brother R. N. Moody labored in Franklin and Colbert Counties from the first Lord's Day in August until the third week in October—nearly three months. He preached at most of the county congregations but never mentions Frankfort, the home of W. A. Womble, who traveled with Moody his entire preaching tour.[188]

Our next view into the work at Frankfort comes in 1902. W. A. Womble reported on a meeting held at Frankfort by S. P. Copeland of Altitude, Mississippi. The report stated that Copeland began his meeting on Thursday night, October 16th. It ended on the following Tuesday night. The results were as follows:

> ... six persons coming forward and making the good confession and being baptized—two from the Methodists and four from the world. Brother Copeland is a model man and is strong in the faith. W. A. Womble.[189]

Womble reported another meeting in September 1907. The preacher, this time, was locally grown. John T. Underwood had grown to manhood in the Franklin-Colbert area. The report read:

> Frankfort, August 21. Our meeting at this place was begun on the second Lord's day in this month by Brother John T. Underwood, of Marietta, Miss. We had good audiences and excellent attention. There were two discourses each day, with dinner on the ground. Three young men, three young ladies, and an old gentleman and wife made the good confession and were baptized. We have about forty members at this place. We are keeping house for the Lord under the apostolic order. W. A. Womble.[190]

Underwood returned the following year and conducted another meeting at Frankfort. He had held a meeting near Nettle, Mississippi. From that point, he came to Frankfort. He thus wrote concerning Frankfort:

> ... I went from there to old Frankfort, Ala., where I began a meeting on the second Lord's day in August and preached six days, with eleven baptisms ... John T. Underwood.[191]

In 1909, another North Alabama preacher came to Frankfort. He was William M. Behel (better known as "Uncle Will Behel") of Lauderdale County, Alabama. He reported:

> Thinking it might be of interest to many, I here give a report of my work in North Alabama, especially in Lauderdale County, and call the attention of the churches to this field. From July 17 to July 23, I was in a meeting at Frankfort, which resulted in five persons becoming obedient to the faith. [192]

The following year, 1910, Behel came back to Frankfort and preached.[193] We do not have any results.

Two years later, Behel returned to conduct another meeting. He had five additions.[194] He came back for another meeting in August 1913. He reported the results as: "Frankfort, Ala., six baptized, one restored."[195] Again, he returned in October and held a third meeting, resulting in seven additions.[196]

With this next report, we go beyond our projected cutoff date of 1914. We do this because we have such a small amount on the Frankfort work, and so we desire to take within our range of study the last two known reports mentioning the church at Frankfort.

Behel returned for a protracted meeting in September 1917 and baptized six souls into Christ.[197] The last report does not speak directly to the Frankfort work but gives us a clue as to what became of the church at that place. It did not just die, and the members stopped worshipping, but they merged with a new congregation two miles to the west of them. William M. Behel gave the clue:

> William Behel, Russellville, Ala., Route 4, July 20: "I closed a six-days' meeting at the water, yesterday, with five baptisms. A new meeting house has recently been built between Rock Creek and Frankfort, Alabama, called 'Shady Grove,' about six miles from F. B. Srygley's boyhood home. Some of the best people I ever saw live in this section. I go to Mississippi for a meeting. Brethren, I need your prayers."[198]

The county seat had been relocated to Belgreen, which was 7 miles due south of Frankfort. The town became a forgotten site as all legal transactions had gone to Belgreen. The membership had grown so small, and the old log meeting house was so old and in need of repairs—it was easier to travel the two miles and worship with Shady Grove than to spend money on a building that was very old and perhaps not worth repairing. This concludes our study of the Frankfort Church of Christ, which had contributed so much to the Restoration Movement in Franklin County.

Pleasant Site

The church at Pleasant Site was established by F. B. Srygley in the summer of 1882. He held a meeting in that community, which began on the 2nd Lord's Day of that year. Srygley preached six sermons and baptized two young men. This was the first time the gospel had ever been preached in that community.[199]

John Taylor preached there several times before his death in 1885. The Srygley boys preached there a few times as Pleasant Site was about 10.5 miles from their old homeplace at Rock Creek. Other men came and preached, but no one bothered reporting on their work at Pleasant Site. The congregation struggled for several years and barely survived.

The next report came seventeen years later and was written by W. A. Kimbrough, who lived at Frankfort. He wrote about R. N. Moody's visit:

> Leaving this place, he went to a schoolhouse about three miles from Pleasant Site, in Franklin County. This meeting

began on the second Lord's day in September and continued over the third Lord's day, resulting in several baptisms and setting the congregation, which was considerably scattered, in order. Remaining over here, the third Lord's day, he failed to meet with the Weatherford Schoolhouse congregation, according to appointment, which was filled by myself. However, he arrived at night and began the work, which resulted in twenty additions to the congregation.[200]

Moody had come to the Franklin-Colbert Counties area in the summer of 1898 and preached for nearly three months in that region. He had begun his work in this area of Northwest Alabama on the first Lord's Day in August; he closed his labors there the third week in October.[201]

The congregation had become scattered through the last several years, as was noted by Kimbrough. He had stated that Moody had set the congregation, "which was considerably scattered, in order."[202]

Our next report came from R. N. Moody in August of 1902. From Mount Pleasant, in Franklin County, he went to Pleasant Site and preached. He wrote:

... From there (Mount Pleasant), I went to Pleasant Site and held a meeting near there, beginning on the third Lord's day and closing, with three additions, on the following Wednesday. R. N. Moody.[203]

The denominational churches in the area of Pleasant Site refused our brethren the use of their buildings; therefore, they had to travel far and wide to worship in a building during inclement weather. That is the reason some of these meetings were two or three miles away from the location of Pleasant Site.

Pleasant Site

In 1904, A. H. Taylor of Rock Creek, Alabama, wrote:

> Brother W. M. Oldfield will begin a meeting at Rock Creek on the fourth Lord's day in July; he will begin a meeting at Pleasant Site on the fifth Lord's day in July.[204]

The meeting must not have been considered a success by Oldfield. He never reported on the meeting. Pleasant Site had a reputation concerning the people who lived in the community. He tried again to hold a successful meeting, beginning on the third Sunday in July, and closed it on the following Friday night, with two baptisms.[205]

The following year, things had deteriorated to a sad state. I. B. Bradley came and found the congregation had shrunk considerably. He wrote the following concerning the state of things at Pleasant Site:

> On the first Lord's day in this month, I began a five-days' meeting at Pleasant Site, Ala. We have no house there and only about half a dozen brethren, perhaps a few more. I preached in a grove, morning and night, until Thursday night. The crowds were small at first but increased till the close. Large crowd at the last service there were no additions, but I never saw better interest. The people listened as if it were all new to them, and I am sure good was done. This is the first time we have ever had a hearing there. I promised to return next year and hold another meeting for them. I will be at Lancaster (Tenn.) on the second Lord's day in October. I. B. Bradley.[206]

Apparently, Bradley had never seen F. B. Srygley's report where he made the claim that he had preached the first gospel sermons there at Pleasant Site.[207] Or could Bradley have simply meant that that was the first time that he had preached there? In 1908, I. B. Bradley had this to say about the people near Pleasant Site:

> ... I closed a fine meeting at Rock Creek last week, with eleven additions by primary obedience. Four of these were Missionary Baptists. I also held a twelve-day meeting at Pleasant Site, with no additions. This is a hard place. The people seem determined not to see the truth. We had a very small hearing, except on the two Lord's days we were there. I held a three-days' meeting at Mynot, with none added, beginning on July 23 ... I. B. Bradley.[208]

To further illustrate how tough preaching in the Pleasant Site community really was, we give a report on John T. Underwood's effort at Pleasant Site. The report read as follows:

> That the way of the true gospel preacher is not always smooth: and delightful, but is often really exciting, is indicated by some of Brother John T. Underwood's experiences as detailed in the following report, sent under date of September 16: "I began a meeting at old Rock Creek, the Srygleys' old home, on the first Lord's day in August and closed it on the second Lord's day, with ten added to the one body and the church much edified. I began at Pleasant Site on the third Lord's day in August with my tent, and preached five days, with thirteen added to the one body. This meeting deserves more than a passing notice. On the fourth night of the meeting some fellows who believe in Holy Ghost religion cut every rope around my tent and cut my rubber blackboard into strings. The next night, which was the last night of the meeting, we had nine confessions. The sister of the Methodist

preacher who lives there came to the water's edge next morning to make the confession and be baptized. She came close to where I stopped to make a talk before baptizing. Her mother took her stand on one side of her, and her brother, a brother to the Methodist preacher, took his stand on the other side of her, with a large knife open in his hand, to keep his sister from confessing her Savior. Seeing this, she backed off a few steps and commenced to cry. A pretty good sample of Holy Ghost religion ...."[209]

This report speaks for itself about how tough the community of Pleasant Site really was. A debate occurred at that place in 1914. It was between O. C. Dobbs and William Lindley. One of the attendees, R. L. Shook, gave the following report in the *Gospel Advocate*.

This discussion took place at Pleasant Sight [sic], Ala., between O. C. Dobbs (Christian), of Berry, Ala., and William Lindley (Missionary Baptist), of Red Bay, Ala., beginning on February 18 and continuing three days. The first two days they discussed the establishment of the church. On the third day they discussed the design of baptism in the forenoon and apostasy in the afternoon, with Brother Dobbs in the lead on both propositions. The disputants verified the fact that men can meet together and in a friendly way discuss God's word. They held the debate on a high plane, and the best of feeling was maintained between themselves and among the people. Everyone seemed to enjoy themselves and I feel sure the truth was advanced. Brother Dobbs did a good work for the truth. The brethren were pleased with his work in the debate and asked him to return and hold a meeting for them in the summer, which he agreed to do. Mr. Gregory moderated for Mr. Lindley; Brother John T. Underwood moderated for

Brother Dobbs the first two days. and the writer the last day. R. L. Shook.[210]

This was the final report set in our parameters of time, 1914. Pleasant Site struggled on into the twenty-first century and finally gave up the ghost. It closed its doors for good sometime during the year 2013.

Belgreen

THE ESTABLISHMENT of the congregation at Belgreen, Franklin County, Alabama, is not clear due to the fact that John Taylor, Lee Jackson of Mississippi, A. C. Henry of Athens, and R. N. Moody of Albertville, Alabama, were all preaching at this place as a mission-stop, for a few years before the congregation was finally established. The first mention of Belgreen in the *Gospel Advocate* was by A. C. Henry on November 21, 1883. It is given in full here:

> We went on Monday, the 2nd, to Belgreen and preached at night, and twice, each on Tuesday and Wednesday. On Wednesday, the brethren of the surrounding neighborhood, with the friends, brought their baskets of provisions for the physical man, and prepared a sumptuous dinner at a large spring near the house of worship. A very pleasant episode in the work of the day was the union in matrimony of Bro. John T. Underwood and Miss Arsie E. Grissom at the conclusion of the morning service. Bro. Underwood is a young preacher of much promise, a pupil of Bro. T. B. Larimore. We also met

the venerable John Taylor, a pioneer in the cause, worthy of double honor, "for his work's sake." He informed me that he had baptized; with his own hands, over forty-five hundred. He is quite old and feeble, (about seventy-six,) but oh, how he loves the cause of the Master. We met also, a Bro. (Lee) Jackson, a young preacher, able to do good work, and many others whose hearts are in the work of the Lord. Among them the father, mother and sisters, (with their husbands,) etc., of the Srygley brethren. It is no wonder that they are preachers and love the work, with such a mother as they have. God bless her and would to God that our Israel was full of such women. There was only one addition to the cause at Belgreen, but the brethren are very anxious for us to return and say that good will result if we can make only one more visit. We expect to do so in October, if not before. A. C. Henry, Hartsville, Ala., July 10, 1883.[211]

From this letter, we learn quite a number of historical facts. People brought basket dinners for the gathering at Belgreen. John T. Underwood and Miss Arsie E. Grissom were married at this gathering. The parents and other Srygley family members were present at this gathering. This was a good beginning for a congregation to be established at Belgreen. At this point in history, Belgreen was the county seat of Franklin County. The town was large enough for the planting of a church there, but the people of the area were very much like the society around Pleasant Site. They were very intolerant toward our brethren at this time. Even after it was established, it had very many struggles. Some of these struggles are made clear by what is revealed in this next note:

Bro. A. C. Henry, in a private note, says, "Look out for news of a debate at Belgreen, Ala.; between T. W. Caskey and J. M. Wells, a Methodist."[212]

In 1885, Brown Godwin came to Belgreen and held a meeting in the courthouse. It was during this meeting that John J. Underwood was baptized. He will be discussed later.[213] Godwin would play an important part in the development of the church at Belgreen.

The Methodists and Baptists were the antagonizers at Belgreen. Three years later, the battle was still ongoing. A Brother John A. Benson of Belgreen sent an inquiry to the *Gospel Advocate* concerning a denominational publication that had some strange logic contained within its pages. It was as follows:

> On page 90 in Cates' "Voice of Truth" Mr. Cates says, "It is very evident that no overt act intervened between the looking of the bitten Israelite and his being healed. He was not required to look, and then go to a stream, or fountain of water, and be washed or wash himself before he could be cured. God gave no such directions." On same page, he says, "With the Jew it was look and live; with the repenting sinner it is believe and live." Please give a few thoughts on the above for the benefit of some who think it an unanswerable argument. Belgreen, Ala. John A. Benson.[214]

This infant body of believers was constantly searching for the truth. By this time, it had help from the person of Brown Godwin. He was from Linden, Perry County, Tennessee, and would later become an osteopathic doctor and would continue to preach until he died in 1903.[215] He preached for nine months for the Belgreen church.[216] Nothing, up to this time, had been said as to whether or not Belgreen church had a building of their own.

John T. Underwood was living at Belgreen at that time and poised to be a great asset to the small band there.[217] In 1888,

W. T. Kidwill of Smithville, Tennessee, came to Belgreen and held a meeting.[218] Nothing was ever reported in the *Gospel Advocate* concerning this meeting. Consequently, we know nothing of whether there were any results from Kidwill's efforts.

The next effort at Belgreen came in 1892. Brown Godwin returned to Belgreen and held an eight-day meeting. We insert Godwin's report in full:

> Belgreen, Ala., eight days; thirteen accessions. The brethren have no house of their own but agree to commence and continue to meet on the first day of the week. With plenty of good, pure water to drink, and with the privilege of breathing pure mountain air, and among good brethren and sisters like we have here, one is loath to leave, but life's duties calls on ... Brown Godwin.[219]

From Godwin's report, it seems that the brethren at Belgreen had not been meeting regularly. He stated that they agreed to "commence and continue to meet on the first day of the week." This sounds like they had not been meeting on a regular basis. He also revealed that no building had been constructed by the brethren at that time.

Our next report came from F. D. Srygley, who gave a combined report on Belgreen and Bankston. He reported:

> Brother F. D. Srygley, our first page editor, is away in Alabama, preaching the word. He has held a meeting at Bankston and is now at Belgreen. Up to October 4 he had baptized eleven; and taught two Baptists the way of the Lord more perfectly since he went to Alabama.[220]

From this report, we do not know if the eleven baptized

were all at Bankston or if all were baptized at Belgreen. All we know for sure is that Srygley preached at Belgreen while on this tour.

Three years passed before another report came from Belgreen. That would be from R. N. Moody's preaching throughout Franklin and Colbert Counties in 1899. Moody had come to the Franklin-Colbert Counties area in the summer of 1898 and preached for nearly three months in that region. The report was written by W. A. Kimbrough, who lived at Frankfort. His report stated that Moody had held a meeting at Rock Creek and went from there to Belgreen. He wrote the following of Moody:

> ... His next meeting—at Rock Creek Church, the old home of Brothers F. D. and F. B. Srygley—resulted in one addition. From there he went to Belgreen—no congregation—and preached six days, baptizing three: ...[221]

From this, we learn that Kimbrough did not find a congregation upon this visit. It seems as though there was no permanency to the work of the church at Belgreen. Brown Godwin had found the brethren lacking in commitment as far as meeting on a regular basis. Our preaching brethren, however, did not give up on the Belgreen work. In August of that year, Moody returned to the Franklin and Colbert Counties area, and he preached at Belgreen again. This time was a little more promising. He began there the last week in August and ended the meeting on the last day of the month with six baptisms. He wrote:

> I closed a meeting at Belgreen last night, which resulted in six baptisms. The Interest was good throughout the meeting, closing with a full house. R. N. Moody.[222]

The full house was a borrowed house. There was still no building owned by our brethren at Belgreen. Things were no better when I. B. Bradley came to Belgreen. It was reported:

> Brother I. B. Bradley, of Dickson, Tenn., began a meeting at Belgreen, Ala., on Sunday, September 2. This is a mission meeting, and Brother Bradley is holding it at his own charges ....[223]

Bradley went to Pinkney, Tennessee, which was near Westpoint, Tennessee, and held a tent meeting. He returned to the Belgreen area, but this time, he preached four miles away from Belgreen and with very good results. The report reads:

> Brother I. B. Bradley's meeting at a place four miles from Belgreen, Ala., continued six days and closed with thirty-one baptisms and one added from the Missionary Baptists. Some of those baptized were men who have spent long years in sin, while others are boys and girls of tender years. Brother Bradley held a meeting at this place two years ago and baptized twenty-eight persons. They kept up the worship for some time, but in the course of time they ceased to keep up the regular meetings. Since having been stirred up by this meeting, they have promised to meet regularly in a schoolhouse to break bread and to build a meetinghouse in the near future. Brother Bradley is now in a meeting at Pinkney, Tenn. [224]

Did Bradley give up on the brethren in Belgreen? Is this a separate work that would later become Bradley's Chapel? It was located near Belgreen.[225] It seems to be Bradley's Chapel. Somehow, the two works were tied together in their beginnings.

The latter congregation will be discussed in another section of this work.

Our next bit of information from Belgreen comes from a sweet young lady just ten years old. She wrote to Emma Page's "Children's Corner" in the *Gospel Advocate*. She discussed things relating to her family and how she loved to read the "Children's Corner." She was Lizzie Rickard.[226] In December, her brother James Henry Rickard wrote "Children's Corner" and also talked about his family." He wrote:

> Dear Miss Emma: Papa takes the Gospel Advocate, and I like to read the children's letters. Papa, mamma, two of my sisters, and one of my brothers are members of the church of Christ. I am not a member but expect to be some day. If I see this in print, I will write again, but I will ring off for this time. Yours truly, James Henry Rickard.[227]

The Rickards have been strong members of the Lord's church throughout the years. Several of them have been strong in the church in Franklin and Colbert Counties to the present day. As a matter of fact, this writer has a good friend from this family of Rickards—Bart Rickard. There was hope for the Belgreen church through the young folk, such as the two children listed above.

In 1910, William Behel from Greenhill, Alabama, came and held a meeting with the brethren at Belgreen. Behel wrote: "I am now at Belgreen, to begin today a series of meetings. From here I go to Frankfort. William Behel."[228] A few days later, he spoke of the meeting once again: "My meeting at, Belgreen, Ala., closed with one baptism and one from the Baptists."[229]

Our next correspondence comes from two young people

who addressed their letters to Miss Emma Page (who later became Mrs. T. B. Larimore).

The first letter was from Earl Rickard, the brother of Lizzie and James Henry Rickard. We include Earl's letter here:

> Belgreen, Ala.—Dear Miss Emma: I will write you, as I saw your picture in Brother Larimore's book, and think you are such a sweet-looking woman. I wish I could see you. I love you now; but if I could see you, I know I would love you better. I am just five years old. I go to Sunday school nearly every Sunday. I do not go to school, because I am not old enough, and school is so far from home. I can spell, but I cannot write; and sister is writing for me. Your little friend, Earl Rickard.[230]

Even though his sister wrote this for Earl when he was only five years old, it illustrates how these young people loved Emma Page's column in the *Gospel Advocate*. A little more than four months later, another letter came from the Belgreen area. This one was from Dona Dempsey, who was ten years old. Her letter was full of interesting information about her family. It is included here:

> Belgreen, Ala., Route No. 1.—Dear Miss Emma: I am a little girl, ten years old. I go to school and like it. I am in the third grade. I like my teacher. Her name is Miss Alice Ezell. I go to Sunday school every Sunday. I have four sisters living. My oldest sister was killed by lightning July 11, 1900. We miss her so much. She was a Christian. Papa, mamma, and my oldest two sisters are Christians, too. Two of my sisters are married. One of them has the sweetest little baby I have ever seen. Her name is "Eunice Loyd." My baby sister is fifteen months old. Her name is "Willie Ruth." I will close this letter,

lest you kindle the fire with it some cold morning. Your little friend, Dona Dempsey.[231]

One is led to believe that the baby was named after R. N. Moody's character in his book—"Eunice Loyd,"[232] as his book was published in 1909. Moody came to that community and preached in gospel meetings during this time period.

Young people were the hope of the congregations. They were and are the future of the congregations, and the training and encouragement they received while still young help them to be prepared for the future.

Brother John A. Benson was a good spokesman for the *Gospel Advocate* around Belgreen. He helped get enough subscriptions that he received a fountain pen from the Gospel Advocate in appreciation for his work. He sent a letter to the *Gospel Advocate* along with three subscriptions for friends he had encouraged to subscribe to the *Gospel Advocate*.[233]

We give the obituary of a man who grew to manhood at Belgreen. He was John J. Underwood. The obituary is given as it was published in the *Gospel Advocate*:

> John J. Underwood, son of A. J. and Rebecca Underwood, was born in Green County, Ala., on December 7, 1847. His father moved to Franklin County in 1857 and settled on Little Bear Creek. John J. Underwood was married to Julia Key on October 4, 1866. His wife came of a good Southern family. To them were born ten children— five boys and five girls, seven of whom are living. This was a very interesting family to the writer when visiting this hospitable home, which he did many times, and he always regretted to leave. The deceased enjoyed, or rather suffered, the distinction of being one of the largest men, perhaps the largest man, Alabama ever produced. In the fall of 1885. In the court-

house at Belgreen, he listened to a gospel message delivered by Brown Godwin. The message convinced Brother Underwood. Owing to his weight, Brother Godwin called an assistant when he baptized him. Brother Underwood ever afterwards vigorously contended for "the faith which was once delivered unto the saints" and condemned the wrong. He was a kind and patient father, ever governing his children with firmness and tenderness. His family was very much devoted to him and he was a true and devoted husband. He died on August 25, 1912. Bereaved ones, weep not as those who have no hope and are without God. "I commend you to God and to the word of his grace, which is able to build you up, and to give you an inheritance among all them which are sanctified." A Friend.[234]

The north Alabama area had lost one of its faithful Christian men. We have no information on whether or not John J. Underwood was related to our John T. Underwood. We do know, however, that John T. Underwood—the preacher—was married at Belgreen in 1883, during A. C. Henry's meeting for that year. It is possible that these two men were closely related.

In August 1913, G. A. Dunn came and held a meeting at Belgreen. Dunn reported twenty-nine baptisms. Dunn said that the meeting ended too soon. The message was very succinct.[235] Four days later, Bradley wrote his report, and L. N. Sparks preached at Belgreen. The report below confirms this fact:

> On the first Sunday in August, at 11 A.M., I will preach at Belgreen from the text: 'Now if any man have not the Spirit of Christ, he is none of his.' (J. E. Hester.) If it is not asking too much, I would like for you to write an article in the Gospel Advocate from the same text, and I will send it to him.

By so doing you will oblige a brother in Christ. L. N. Sparks. [236]

This report is rather confusing and leaves us wondering— why was J. E. Hester's name inserted into this report? There is no explanation for that name placed there. Who is Sparks intending to send the article to if it is written and published in the *Gospel Advocate*? The fact that is relevant to Belgreen is that Sparks preached there on the first Sunday, August 4, 1913. That was the first Sunday in August 1913.[237]

I. B. Bradley came back to Belgreen in August 1914 and held another meeting. He wrote that that was his tenth consecutive meeting at that place.[238] The last report in 1914 relating to Belgreen was an obituary written by I. B. Bradley. We give the obituary in full.

> The joy and pride of a father's heart and the idol and hope of a mother's heart is gone from the once happy home of Brother and Sister John A. Benson, of Belgreen, Ala. There is a vacant chair, a footfall silenced, a voice of mirth stilled, an aching void in the hearts of the family, and a broken circle; for one of the jewels has gone to take its place in the Master's casket of gems in the jasper-walled city and add to its beauty. Sad indeed is the once happy and unbroken family circle on account of the tragedy of the taking away. It is hard to give up a young and tender child when it can die in the home surrounded by those who love it more than life, but harder still when the taking is sudden and by violent means. Such was the taking of little Sidney M. Benson. On Saturday, November 7, 1914, he went to the home of his uncle, and he and a cousin were allowed to ride a pair of mules to water. The one Sidney rode became frightened and threw him. While falling, the rein of the bridle caught round his neck

and he was dragged to death. The poor little fellow was dead when found. He was born on June 7, 1903, being eleven years and five months old. Dear brother and sister, grieve not for Sidney. He has only gone over to be with Him who loved little children, and who said: "Suffer little children to come unto me and forbid them not; for of such is the kingdom of heaven." He is safe with Christ and is waiting on the other side to welcome you. Only be constant and faithful a few short years, and Jesus will take you to be with him forever. God has only transplanted the tender bud to bloom and flourish in his garden in the "land that is fairer than day," and "where no evil thing cometh to despoil what is fair." I. B. Bradley.[239]

This obituary closes our information about Belgreen that is reported in the brotherhood papers. Belgreen continues until this day (2025) as a functioning congregation of the Lord's servants.

Forgotten Churches of Franklin County

We now turn to churches that most people of our time have never heard. Earl Kimbrough gave us an insight concerning these elusive churches. In his book on the restoration movement in Russell's Valley, he wrote the following:

> If Franklin County has no "ghost town," it does have a number of communities that became a fraction of their former size. There were also viable congregations in earlier times that eventually ceased to exist. Population shifts and improved transportation made it possible for those who before were confined to a struggling little group of Christians near home to reach another place with better spiritual amenities for their families. Preachers' reports of their work mention churches in Russell's Valley that no longer exist. Among these are Mount Mill, Mount Pleasant, Mount Zion, Frankfort, Lost Creek, Bunker Hill, and Kimbrough's Chapel (Antioch).
>
> The county paper refers to "Kimbrough's Chapel (Christian Church) on the Waterloo Road" in an obituary of James

M. Kimbrough in 1902. Chester Stout said the Antioch church was between Crooked Oak and Piney Grove. J. D. Patton taught singing schools at the Antioch meetinghouse. Mount Mills, or Mount Mills Factory, was near Barton Station on the Memphis-Charleston Railroad over in Colbert County. Mount Pleasant was about three miles north of Belgreen toward Rock Creek. John Hayes held a meeting at Mount Zion in 1894, saying it was fourteen miles from Russellville. R. N. Moody preached there in the early part of the century. In 1932, a homecoming was held at Belgreen "for the old Mt. Pleasant congregation." After the Mount Pleasant church ceased to function, most of its members united with the church at Belgreen.[240]

This gives us a quick overview of the forgotten congregations that appeared for a time and then slipped into the faded memories of long ago.

Mount Pleasant

LET us now look at the old congregation known as Mount Pleasant. The congregation was located about three miles north of Belgreen on the road going toward Rock Creek. Our earliest report came from the pen of R. N. Moody. Moody was from the Albertville area of northeast Alabama.

He first made an announcement in the *Gospel Advocate* of his intentions to go and hold a meeting at Mount Pleasant.[241] Two weeks later, he was published as saying the following:

> I began a meeting at Mount Pleasant, in Franklin County, on the second Lord's day in this month and closed it with eleven additions on the following Friday night. From there I went to Pleasant Site and held a meeting near there, beginning on the third Lord's day and closing, with three additions, on the following Wednesday ... R. N. Moody.[242]

Isham B. Bradley came in 1906 and held the gospel meeting at Mount Pleasant. He reported this in the *Gospel Advocate* in a short statement that said:

> I began a meeting with the church of Christ at Mount Pleasant, Franklin County, Ala., and continued it till the following Friday, with two baptisms and one reclaimed. The church, too, was awakened, and the members proclaimed their determination to do more than they have ever done. Several brethren declared the church was in better shape at the close of the meeting than it had ever been. I. B. Bradley.[243]

Moody returned in 1908 and preached in another gospel meeting at Mount Pleasant. Moody wrote:

> My next meeting was at Mount Pleasant, in Franklin County, beginning on the second Sunday in July and continuing over the third Sunday, resulting in one baptism. R. N. Moody....[244]

Moody noticeably reported one baptism during this meeting. He wrote another report on this meeting in November and gave information that may explain the reason for only the one baptism. He stated:

> My next meeting was at Mount Pleasant, Franklin County, beginning the second Lord's day in July. There was but little available material at this place, so there was but one addition. This is a live congregation and has a strong hold on the community.[245]

He returned again in 1911. On this visit, he preached for two weeks with only two baptisms. This demonstrates the dwindling importance of religious interest in the Mount Pleasant community. The statement "There was but little available material at this place" illustrates this very fact. He made another preaching visit to Mount Pleasant in 1911. He gave a report that stated:

> On the fourth Sunday in July, I began a meeting with the congregation at Mount Pleasant, Franklin County, Ala. We continued the meeting two weeks and baptized two persons. This congregation is composed of the best people of the community and sectarianism is about out of business there. R. N. Moody.[246]

Three years later (1914), his son, B. F. Moody, came and held a meeting in his father's place. This report showed a very dismal picture of the diminished fervor for religion at Mount Pleasant. The report was a concise statement:

> Our last meeting was at Mount Pleasant, in Franklin County, Ala., which was closed early on account of the very busy season. No visible results. B. F. Moody.[247]

Here, we extend our normal timeframe by a few years to show how this congregation ended. It was 1917 when R. N. Moody returned. After three years, the religious mood was still dismal. The report speaks to this situation:

> From R. N. Moody, Albertville, Ala., July 28: "I began a meeting at Mount Pleasant, in Franklin County, last Sunday, which closed last night. We were hindered by rain, but the attendance was fairly good and there was a good interest among the members, but no additions. I go from here to Hall Town for a meeting. This a new place for us. We are hoping for a good meeting."[248]

For the next three years, J. Petty Ezell came and preached

in gospel meetings. His only report in the *Gospel Advocate* summed up a short report on his work at Mount Pleasant:

> I am now in my third consecutive meeting at Mount Pleasant, Franklin County, Ala. J. Pettey Ezell.[249]

Ezell never gave a follow-up report on these three visits. We do not know anything about his results or if he even had any kind of response for his meetings.

Our last report on Mount Pleasant is that they had disbanded, and many of the members were attending the church in Belgreen. It was reported in the *Franklin County Times* that R. N. Moody returned for a kind of homecoming for the now-defunct congregation at Mount Pleasant. The odd thing about this was that the homecoming was held in Belgreen, not at Mount Pleasant. This report is the last mention of Mount Pleasant to be found in any source. Earl Kimbrough wrote:

> There was once a church at Mount Pleasant three miles north of Belgreen and described as being near Frankfort. I. B. Bradley, R. N. Moody, L. S. Lancaster, and others held meetings there in the early years of the twentieth century. In 1932 there was a homecoming held at the Belgreen church. The county paper reported a homecoming for the old Mount Pleasant congregation. R. N. Moody was present and described as "one of the old pioneer preachers in this section of the country in long gone-by days:" After Mount Pleasant ceased to meet, most of the members apparently worshiped at Belgreen or Shady Grove.[250]

In the local press, Moody was described as

one of the old pioneer preachers, having labored in this section of the country in long gone-by days .... Elder Moody did evangelistic work in this section of the country more than a quarter of a century ago and is pleasantly remembered by a large number of friends.[251]

In this closing material, Earl Kimbrough offered a solution as to why Mount Pleasant disappeared. His seems to be the most plausible explanation. Kimbrough was a generation ahead of this writer, and he had access to many of the people who had firsthand knowledge of these things. Therefore, he was more qualified to write some of the things he wrote. With this summation, we close our study of the Mount Pleasant congregation. Maybe, in the future, someone else will find new information on this church.

Mount Zion

EARL KIMBROUGH GREW to manhood around Russellville and knew several of John Taylor's grandchildren. He interviewed many of them concerning their grandfather, Taylor. In June 1965, one of his granddaughters, Paralee Annie Gassaway, related to Kimbrough the following event about her grandfather, John Taylor. Kimbrough wrote of that story:

> Paralee Annie Gassaway, the granddaughter of John Taylor to whom reference has been previously made, told the writer that she remembered her grandfather taking her with him to Mount Zion church several miles below Frankfort when she was quite young. He rode his mare and he put her on a pillow in front of him so she could hold on to the saddle horn. At the meeting house, he would set her on a bench behind the pulpit where she quietly sat while the old man preached. She recalled that her grandfather wanted John T. Underwood to keep Mount Zion church going after his death. But a Brother [J. B.] Billingsley, a one-legged man from Mississippi; was secured to preach there monthly. He came by train to Russell-

ville. However, due to his frequent absences, Mrs. Gassaway believed, the church went down and died out.[252]

This interview gave more information than what has been gleaned from any other source concerning Mount Zion. From the Taylor family, he learned that John Taylor had established Mount Zion after the Civil War.[253]

Just what year this congregation was established is not known, but we have the first news about the church at that place published in the *Gospel Advocate*. It states:

> John T. Underwood writes from Belgreen, Ala., Sept. 1, '88: I am preaching regularly at various points. I commenced a meeting at Mt. Zion, Saturday before the third Lord's day in Aug., preached five discourses. Result: Ten made the good confession. Had to close too soon on account of sickness in my family ....[254]

From this report, we know that the congregation was established before Underwood's meeting in October of 1888. The following year, J. B. Billingsley came and held a meeting. He spoke of Underwood aiding in this meeting:

> I assisted the brethren in a meeting at Mt. Zion, Franklin County, Ala., including 3rd Lord's day in July, immediate results, twenty additions by baptism, four reclaimed. Had good crowds and interest to conclusion. We continued the meeting over the 4th Lord's day. The brethren number about eighty. Bro. J. T. Underwood did valuable service through the meeting. J. B. Billingsley, Mt. Zion, Franklin County.[255]

Earl Kimbrough wrote that Bro. J. B. Billingsley began a meeting at Mt. Zion on the first Lord's Day in September 1891 and continued for six days.[256] It would be three more years before we hear through the pages of the *Gospel Advocate* any news concerning Mount Zion. In a report to the *Gospel Advocate* from Russellville in 1894, John Hayes from Mooresville, near Athens, reported on a meeting he held in 1894. The *Gospel Advocate* published Hayes's letter:

> Hayes said, "I have just closed a meeting fourteen miles from here, at Mount Zion Church. Results: Four by obedience and one from the Baptists."[257]

Four years later, R. N. Moody came and held a gospel meeting. His report read:

> Since writing my last notes I have traveled nearly across North Alabama in a buggy! I have in two trips covered the ground from Fort Payne, in DeKalb County, to Belgreen, in Franklin County; so, these notes will cover a good deal of North Alabama. In December last I made a trip into Franklin. County, and held a meeting for Mount Zion church, which resulted in two baptisms. From Mount Zion I went to Belgreen and preached four times in the Methodist meeting house. R. N. Moody.[258]

Later that year, Moody returned to Franklin County and held another meeting at Mount Zion. His report read as follows:

> I closed a meeting at Mount Zion, Franklin County, the 12th inst., with nine additions, and am, at this writing, in a meeting at Rock Creek, in Colbert County. R. N. Moody. Albertville. Ala.[259]

W. A. Kimbrough of Frankfort, Ala., who traveled with R. N. Moody, gave a different number than did Moody. Kimbrough wrote:

> There were eight additions to the Mount Zion congregation in the six-days' meeting there. His next meeting—at Rock Creek Church, the old home of Brothers F. D. and F. B. Srygley, resulted in one addition. W. A. Kimbrough, Frankfort, Ala.[260]

Just why Kimbrough's report had the number of eight converted rather than the nine reported by Moody is a mystery. Was another person baptized immediately after the meeting ended, and Moody had already headed to Rock Creek, or did Kimbrough have a lapse of memory concerning the number? Moody, like most preachers of the day, kept a journal in which he wrote the results of his meetings for future reference. This writer has copied several of these journals in his research. That would explain the difference in the numbered results.

The following year, Moody returned for a six-day meeting in which he baptized seven. His report on the Mount Zion results read:

> The first Lord's day in August I began a meeting at Mount Zion, Franklin County, where I preached six days and baptized seven. R. N. Moody.[261]

Van Bradley, who, along with his brother I. B. Bradley, had preached many times at Mount Zion, came into the Belgreen area in 1923[262] and held meetings at nearly all of the small congregations there, yet he never mentions Mount Zion, which normally would have been included in his meetings. This suggests that Mount Zion had already ceased meeting as a congregation.

There were active congregations in earlier times that eventually ceased to exist. People moved from one community to another as interests shifted and roads and transportation improved. This made it possible for those who had been tied to a struggling little congregation near their homes to attend further away. That enabled the population to shift to other places with better spiritual conditions for their families. Preachers' reports of their work mention churches in Russell's Valley that no longer exist, among which is the Mount Zion church.[263] Mount Zion is unknown to the people of Franklin County today. It is only known through historical sketches, such as books and journals. This closes our study of the Mount Zion Church of Christ.

Spout Spring–Lost Creek

ACCORDING to John Taylor's granddaughter, Paralee Taylor Gassaway, John Taylor built a log cabin in Franklin County near Lost Creek. It was about two miles west of what became the town of Frankfort in the north-central part of the original Franklin County and about eight miles northwest of Russellville. This was in the portion of the county that was formerly in the Chickasaw Indian Nation.[264] It was on Lost Creek that John Taylor established the congregation that was eventually called Lost Creek. Earl Kimbrough believed that Spout Spring and Lost Creek were the same congregation. In 1860, it was called Spout Spring in the report published in the *Gospel Advocate*.

This was the first and only mention in the *Gospel Advocate* of Spout Spring and was given by John Taylor. John had taken the minutes of a cooperation meeting inscribed by Thomas B. Trotter and had forwarded them to the *Gospel Advocate*. Trotter, the secretary for the cooperation meeting held in 1860 at Berea, Fayette County, Alabama, gave scant information on Spout Spring. Trotter wrote that John Taylor was the preacher and that two of his sons, John A. Taylor and James Taylor, were representing that congregation.[265] In this report, we learn that Spout Spring had 17 members and that they donated $40 to the evangelistic fund, which would support John Taylor and George L. Brown as the evangelists for the year 1861. Let us look at the latter part of the report published in the *Gospel Advocate*:

> Brethren John Taylor and George L. Brown agreeing thereto were chosen to labor as evangelists, during the year 1861, within the bounds represented at this meeting, as follows, namely: Brother Taylor, at Union, Miss., Gum Fork, Berea, Liberty, North River. and Wolf Creek, and Brother Brown, at Russellville, Stony Point, Frankfort, Spout Spring, and Union, Ala.
>
> Adjourned to meet at Gum Fork, 10 miles east of Fulton, Miss., on Friday before the 3rd Lord's day in Sept. 1861. G. L. Brown, Chairman, Thomas B. Trotter, Scribe.[266]

The distress of the churches before the war may have been the reason for a cooperation meeting held at Berea church in Fayette County in the fall of 1860. Kimbrough observed:

> ... the secession of Alabama from the Union on January 11, 1861, the state's preparation for war, and the actual beginning of armed conflict apparently prevented the cooperation from ever meeting again.[267]

Let us reflect upon the information in the foregoing report. John Taylor was the preacher at Spout Spring. Two sons of John Taylor, John A. Taylor and James Taylor, were representing the Spout Spring congregation. After the Civil War, no mention of Spout Spring can be found, but the Taylor family was associated with the Lost Creek congregation. As has already been stated, Earl Kimbrough believed that Spout Spring and Lost Creek were the same congregation. This does sound logical since both congregational names were associated with the same neighborhood where the Taylor families lived. This happened in Jackson County, Alabama, with the Rocky Spring congregation (formerly known as Antioch).[268] The two congregational locations were less than one-half mile apart. In Lauderdale County, Alabama, the Stony Point congregation had been formerly known as Republican, Old Cypress, and Liberty. All of the locations for Stony Point were within a mile of separation from each other. With John Taylor, this congregation had to have a positive influence on the Lost Creek Community.

We realize that this study is rather short, but with such little information, we are forced to end our study on Spout Spring and Lost Creek. We do not manufacture new information. Maybe some future day, someone will find an amazing source from which a complete history can be written of this work that appeared so suddenly in 1860 and disappeared just as rapidly. We feel we would do an injustice to the reader if we neglected to give what information we have found on these forgotten churches, no matter how scanty that may be.

Kimbrough's Chapel–Christian Chapel–Antioch

WE RESTATE what Earl Kimbrough said about the forgotten churches in Franklin County:

> Preachers' reports of their work mention churches in Russell's Valley that no longer exist. Among these are Mount Mill, Mount Pleasant, Mount Zion, Frankfort, Lost Creek, Bunker Hill, and Kimbrough's Chapel (Antioch).[269]

Our study concerns the Kimbrough's Chapel work. There seems to be confusion as to what part of the county the congregation was located. Robert Leslie James indicates that Kimbrough's Chapel was on a mountain south of Newburg. He tied this church to William Kimbrough, who settled there. Keep in mind that James wrote his book in 1927. That was about 25 years after James Kimbrough's obituary was written, in which James Kimbrough was associated with Kimbrough's Chapel/Antioch congregation. The problem is that the obituary was written in 1902, during the time the Kimbrough's Chapel was still a viable church, and the writer, Chester Stout,

Kimbrough's Chapel–Christian Chapel–Antioch

said that Antioch (formerly called Kimbrough's Chapel) was located between Crooked Oak and Piney Grove. This congregation was on Waterloo Road, which ran northwest of Russellville. That was on the opposite side of Russellville than Newburg Mountain. The obituary should be an accurate source since it was written during the existence of Kimbrough's Chapel/Antioch Church of Christ.[270]

The congregation was established sometime in 1885. Brown Godwin apparently was the preacher who established it. His first report appeared in the *Gospel Advocate* in September 1885. He wrote:

> Including the first Sunday in August, at a school house near Kimbrough's Chapel. At the Chapel nine were added, four from the Baptists and five from the world ... Brown Godwin, Russellville, Alabama.[271]

He began that meeting on August 2nd. He wrote an interesting follow-up about a month later:

> Bro. Godwin, writing from Russellville, Ala., under date of September 2d, says: I went last Friday night to Kimbrough's Chapel, (the same place I visited the first Sunday in last month and had nine additions). On entering I was handed a note from a Methodist preacher, which was a warning to me to get out of their house, as they unjustly called it. Of course I got out without a word. A Bro. Baptist led me to his house which was close by, and I stayed there until the morning. Spoke nine times, immersed two; three Baptists, two Methodists and one Cumberland Presbyterian united with us. There are now seventeen members at that place. They, the Methodists, Baptists and the world, are to build a good large meeting house in a short distance from the one we were

driven from. They aim to commence next Monday and build it this month. I think we will soon have a large congregation there.[272]

In this report, one can easily see that this was a new work still in its formative stage. We see, as is true of most communities in western Franklin County, that the denominations were very prejudiced against our brethren. Godwin knew how to deal with this kind of situation. He had to deal with many similar situations in his early preaching career.

We found one more report in the *Gospel Advocate* concerning Kimbrough's Chapel. It was written by W. O. Srygley. It was a report about J. B. Billingsley of Mississippi and a meeting he held in 1891. Srygley wrote:

> Frankfort, Sept. 23, '91. —Bro. Billingsly began a meeting at Mt. Zion the first Lord's day in this month and continued six days, visible results, two from the world, three from the Baptists and three reclaimed. I began the second Lord's day at Kimbrough's Chapel, results, two from the Baptists, one from the Methodists, one from the Presbyterians, three from the world and one by recommendation. Interest good. Bro. B. is an able teacher. W. O. Srygley.[273]

This would be the last reference to Kimbrough's Chapel to be published in the *Gospel Advocate*.

Isbell

In 1890, the courthouse was moved from Belgreen. At this time both Russellville and Isbell were large enough to challenge to be the county seat. Russellville won out in the contest. Isbell, however, was still one of the largest communities in Franklin County. A church was finally established there, but it had serious problems from its beginning. We questioned whether or not we should put Isbell on that forgotten list of churches for Franklin County. It was established in the 1880s and then disappeared before 1930. It would be around twenty years or more before another effort at re-establishing a congregation at Isbell was attempted. Our first knowledge of the gospel being preached at Isbell comes to us from the pages of the *Gospel Advocate*. The report was made by one of "Larimore's Boys," C. F. Russell, of Apple Grove, Alabama. But just who was C. F. Russell? F. D. Srygley gave us a snapshot of Russell in his book, *Larimore And His Boys*:

> C. F. Russell, of Apple Grove, Ala., was one of Mars' Hill's brilliant young preachers: but unfortunately, his labors were

cut short by failing health soon after he left school. While yet a student, he held several very successful protracted meetings, and but for the failure in health he would unquestionably have taken high rank in our Southern pulpit. He was modest, quiet and unassuming; original, earnest and untiring. Professor Larimore once had an appointment he could not meet, and asked brother Russell if he could fill it for him. With characteristic modesty and willingness to do his best, he said: "I don't think I could fill it for you, professor; but if it will accommodate you and do any good, I am willing to go and wriggle about in it." His labors were principally confined to Alabama and Mississippi with an occasional tour into Tennessee.[274]

Russell's report told us of the first recorded attempt to start a work at Isbell:

Friday night before the fifth Lord's day in September I began a meeting near Isbell, four miles south of Russellville, Franklin County, Ala., and continued until Monday night, the immediate result was five added to the army of the Lord, four by confession and baptism and one from another congregation. We have several scattered brethren at that place, and I hope they will soon organize and build up a good church. Traveling preachers should give them a call. Brethren who want me to preach for them should write to me at Apple Grove, Ala. C. F. Russell, Apple Grove, Ala.[275]

It should be noticed here that there were Christians living in the vicinity of Isbell, but they had not been organized into a functioning congregation. The next meeting was held by L. R. Sewell, with some help from John Hayes from Mooresville, Alabama. Sewell reported:

... I preached at Moulton the first Lord's day in July; two were added. Began a meeting at Isbell schoolhouse the second Lord's day in July. Bro. John Hayes, of the Bible School, joined me on Monday and we continued the meeting till Friday; seven were added ... L. R. Sewell.[276]

Still, there was no organizing of a congregation at that place. That would come to pass when O. B. Barry came and held a meeting at Isbell in 1892. R. K. Terry of Isbell wrote in an obituary reporting that John Burfield was baptized by L. R. Sewell in July 1892. This was incorrect as the following portion of the obituary reveals:

John F. Burfield was killed last Tuesday by the bursting of a boiler, which also killed two others. John joined the church of Christ July 14, 1890, under the preaching of E. G. Sewell at this place...[277]

In the August 11th issue above, L. R. Sewell reported that he held the meeting at Isbell, with aid from John Hayes. In the fall, O. P. Barry came and held a meeting that changed everything for the better. He reported:

Alexandria, (Tenn.) August 17.—I have just returned from North Alabama where I have been for about a month, trying to preach the unsearchable riches of Christ. My first meeting was at Bear Creek, which resulted in six being added to the local congregation. From there I went to Hackleburg where I preached for a few days, resulting in seven being added to the "one body." My next meeting was at Isbell, where I preached to a crowded house for a week, during which seventeen were brought to the Lord. At the close of the meeting, we organized a congregation or church of fifty members. During our meeting here we were visited by a number of the good brethren at Russellville. I stopped to preach Sunday and Sunday night for them, but the interest that was manifested during these two services justified us to make a protracted effort, which lasted ten days, resulting in forty being added to the church. The brethren at Russellville are doing a grand work. During my stay in Alabama I preached fifty-three discourses, resulting in seventy being added to the local churches. O. P. Barry.[278]

In the November and December issues of the *Gospel Advocate*, O. P. Barry established the church at Isbell, Alabama.[279] As was true of many congregations, they did not report regularly on the work in their churches. This was true at Isbell.

The next report of a meeting did not come until Isham B. Bradley moved into the Russellville area. He was located with the Russellville church, and they partially supported him in evangelizing the surrounding area. It was reported by the *Gospel Advocate* that Bradley was preaching for Isbell and Bear Creek. Bradley's intentions were to preach in some meetings for other churches that summer. The *Gospel Advocate* stated:

Brother I. B. Bradley is located at Russellville, Ala. He is preaching for this church, at Bear Creek, and Isbell, The church at Russellville has a membership of about one hundred and forty, worshiping after the primitive order. This is a fine field for Brother Bradley, and we believe he will cultivate it well, and be instrumental in adding many to the Lord. He will hold protracted meetings in North Alabama through the summer. Any church desiring his services in a meeting should write him at Russellville.[280]

In August, Bradley announced his intentions to hold an extended meeting at Isbell. The report simply read:

> I will begin today with a ten-day meeting at Isbell. Pray for us. I. B. Bradley.[281]

The next meeting held at Isbell, according to the *Gospel Advocate*, came seven years later. In 1903, I. B. Bradley held a meeting that he reported to the *Gospel Advocate* in which he said:

> Beginning on the first Lord's day in October, I held an eight-day meeting at Isbell, four and one-half miles from Russell—ville, preaching only at night during the week. There were ten additions by confession and baptism. The brethren agreed to go to work and meet regularly to break bread and study the word of the Lord. They have not been meeting regularly for several years. I trust that great good will result from the meeting there ... I. B. Bradley. Russellville, Ala.[282]

The congregation was on the verge of extinction when Bradley came and put lifeblood back into a dying congregation. He reminded the reader that they apparently had ceased partaking of the Lord's Supper, except maybe sporadically. He said that they had ceased meeting on a regular basis. These were the signs of a dead church. It would, however, struggle on for a few more years. Bradley returned the following year to give more lifeblood in the form of a week-long meeting. The report simply read:

> ... I shall then preach for one week at Isbell. Ala.: beginning on the third Lord's day. I. B. Bradley, Russellville, Alabama. [283]

This would be Bradley's last visit to Isbell. He moved away to Nashville, Tennessee, in early 1905.[284] Nearly three years later, a young student from Potter Bible College in Bowling Green, Kentucky, came to Isbell and held a meeting. His name was F. E. Peden. That is all we could report since Isbell was included in a report on Peden's work for the months of July, August, and September of 1907. This was reported by T. H. Roberson of the Russellville congregation.[285] For some reason, the *Gospel Advocate* published the same report by Roberson on Peden's labors one week later.[286]

The next report was made thirteen years after Peden's effort at Isbell. This was reported about D. C. Williams's labor at Isbell. It was reported that the crowds and interest increased each night. No responses of any nature were reported. The signs of a near-death congregation. We realize that we have gone beyond our time boundary. But we do this to show the slow death of a congregation that gave up years before. The last mention of this congregation was when J. H. Morris came and preached one sermon there. T. H. Roberson wrote:

> T. H. Roberson, Russellville, Ala., April 21: "J. H. Morris, of Tuscumbia, preached a splendid sermon at the Isbell Schoolhouse last Lord's day. He walked a distance of about four and one-half miles in company with five others to Russellville, where he delivered another excellent discourse to the Russellville congregation. He is doing a good work at several mission points. He goes, pay or no pay."[287]

After this visit by Morris and friends, Isbell is found no more through the *Gospel Advocate* or any other brotherhood paper. It is so sad that so much time and energy were expended in a community, and the work seemed doomed from the start.

Sometime in the late forties or early fifties, another congregation was established at Isbell.

Later Franklin County Churches

Bradley's Chapel

A young I. B. Bradley moved to Russellville to work with the church at Russellville in 1896. He preached in most of the struggling rural churches while working with the congregation at Russellville. He moved to Nashville, Tennessee, in 1905. He penned a short report that was published in the *Gospel Advocate*:

> Brother I. B. Bradley writes us as follows: Please say through the Gospel Advocate that my address is changed from Russellville, Ala., to No. 613 North Third street, Nashville, Tenn. [288]

Even though he moved to Tennessee, he never neglected to return to Franklin and Colbert counties and hold meetings. Earl Kimbrough wrote in his book on Russell's Valley:

> Bradley's interest in Franklin County continued for many years after he left Russellville. He frequently returned for

funerals and gospel meetings. Bradley's Chapel, a building near Belgreen, was named in his honor. He started the church that met there while living in Russellville and held meetings there nearly every year for at least twenty-eight years through 1924.[289]

John A. Benson wrote a lengthy letter to the *Gospel Advocate* in 1919 concerning Bradley's work, especially around the Belgreen area and Bradley's Chapel. Even though some of the events in this letter occurred beyond our time limit, they are relevant to this study. At this point in our study, we feel compelled to give Benson's letter in full:

> Belgreen, August 30. Brother I. B. Bradley, of Dickson, Tenn., began a meeting at Bradley's Chapel on the fourth Lord's day in August and closed it on Friday following, with the house full of anxious hearers, many of whom wished that he might stay longer, but Brother Bradley had to go to begin another meeting, and the meeting here had to close too soon. He baptized nine persons. Five of whom are heads of families; and he did some of the best preaching that I have ever heard him do, and I have been hearing him for a long time. His first preaching was done here in the year 1896. He baptized thirty-six that year. In 1906 he baptized twenty-eight, and in 1907 he baptized thirty-four, preaching about one week each time. He has preached for us every year, except three or four, since his first work here in 1896, and he has baptized about two hundred during these meetings. Some of his converts here have removed to other places, and I can now think of three congregations doing regular work, meeting on the first day of the week, which are principally fruit of his labors. The opposition was strong against him when he began

work here twenty-three years ago, but by his faithful and kindly presentation of the word of truth he has won the good will and respect of all who know him. He promised to come back to hold us another meeting next summer, the Lord willing. Brother Bradley is fifty-one years old and in good health, able to do lots of hard work in the vineyard of the Lord. John A. Benson.[290]

We now look at the development of Bradley's Chapel in a chronological context. The first report in the *Gospel Advocate* relating to Bradley's Chapel was published in 1906. It read as follows:

Brother I. B. Bradley's meeting at a place four miles from Belgreen, Ala., continued six days and closed with thirty-one baptisms and one added from the Missionary Baptists. Some of those baptized were men who have spent long years in sin, while others are boys and girls of tender years. Brother Bradley held a meeting at this place two years ago and baptized twenty-eight persons. They kept up the worship for some time, but in the course of time they ceased to keep up the regular meetings. Since having been stirred up by this meeting, they have promised to meet regularly in a schoolhouse to break bread and to build a meetinghouse in the near future. Brother Bradley is now in a meeting at Pinkney, Tenn. [291]

Benson must have been writing from memory because the actual report gave the total converts as thirty-one, and Benson gave the number as twenty-eight. In reality, the twenty-eight were baptized two years earlier, in 1904. Bradley reported that the church had ceased meeting regularly, but Bradley stirred up them to keep the ordinances as they should do. Two years later, Bradley reports on his intentions to hold another meeting at that place. It stated:

> I will be at Mount Hope for two weeks, beginning on August 9; at Bradley's Chapel, one week, beginning on August 23; Hamilton, ten days, beginning on the first Lord's day in September. Then I will return to Tennessee for several meetings. I. B. Bradley.[292]

We do not know the final results of Bradley's meeting at Bradley's Chapel, but he gave a total on his entire trip to Northwest Alabama and Dennis, Mississippi.

> Brother I. B. Bradley writes from Dickson, Tenn., under date of September 23: "On September 19 I returned from a ten-weeks' trip through Alabama and Mississippi. I held meetings at the following places: Pleasant Site, Mynot, Rock Creek, Mount Pleasant, Mount Hope, Bradley's Chapel, and Hamilton, Ala., and Dennis, Miss. From all sources twenty-two persons were induced to lead a better life. Twelve of these were baptized and ten from the Baptists. My work this year was more difficult than ever, on account of some church troubles. But I am glad to report that all were practically settled and peace again reigns among the children of God. I have yet about eight weeks' more protracted-meeting work."[293]

The following year, Bradley sent another report on his work, including Bradley's Chapel. By September 1909, Bradley could declare that Bradley's Chapel was "in good condition." The congregation had improved so that concerns for its future were removed. Bradley writes from Decatur, Alabama, under date of September 4:

I am here on my way home to rest and get well. I have been sick with fever ten days. I closed a good meeting at Bradley's Chapel on Thursday, with three baptized and good interest. The church there is in a good condition and prospering in the work of the Lord. I closed a meeting at Mount Pleasant Church on August 28, with two baptized.[294]

Bradley had the *Gospel Advocate* publish the obituary of a close friend from Bradley's Chapel in 1910. Within that obituary is useful information that provides us a small window through which we see into the congregation at Bradley's Chapel.

Miss Nannie E. Dempsey was born on July 21, 1885 and was the oldest daughter of Brother and Sister W. H. Dempsey, of Belgreen, Ala .... The writer held a meeting near her home in September 1906, and she was one among the first to confess her faith in Christ during that meeting. On the morning of September 4, 1906, with fifteen others. I baptized her in the clear waters of Bear Creek, near Belgreen, Ala. She met with the church at Bradley's Chapel where the church met for worship, every Lord's day, except two, until she died, barring a few times when she attended services elsewhere. She always took her place in the Bible class and delighted in the service. She was killed by a stroke of lightning on July 11, 1910, about sunset, and passed from the scenes of earth to the quiet country of departed ones, to await the summons of the Lord. She was laid to rest in Friendship graveyard to quietly sleep till Jesus comes. Nannie was a good girl—a dutiful and faithful daughter, an affectionate sister, a true friend, and, above all, a devoted and earnest Christian. Mourn not for her as lost, for she is not lost only gone before. "Blessed are the dead which die in the Lord ..." I. B. Bradley.[295]

In 1912, Bradley reported that he was planning to hold another meeting at Bradley's Chapel.[296] The next year, he returned and held another meeting. It was published in the October 9th issue of the *Gospel Advocate*:

> I will be in a meeting with the Bradley's Chapel congregation near Belgreen, Ala., beginning on the third Lord's day in this month, and at Mount Pleasant, also near Belgreen, following the Bradley's Chapel meeting.[297]

Bradley returned in 1913 and held another meeting at Bradley's Chapel and baptized. The meeting lasted eight days, and he also promised to return in 1914 for another meeting.[298]

In 1913, L. S. Lancaster was filling a regular appointment at Bradley's Chapel. He wrote:

> Russellville, Ala., October 23.—I filled my regular appointment at Bradley's Chapel on the first Lord's day in this month. We had two good services. One lady made the confession and was baptized ... L. S. Lancaster.[299]

In 1914, as promised, Bradley returned for another meeting. This was Bradley's eleventh meeting at this place. It was reported on September 3, 1914.[300] Two weeks later, the *Gospel Advocate* reported:

> I. B. Bradley, of Dickson, Tenn., ... He also reports one baptism in a six-days' meeting at Bradley's Chapel, near Belgreen, Ala. He will begin at Rome, Tenn., next Sunday. This is his boyhood home.[301]

One could justifiably say that Bradley's Chapel was a "pet project" of I. B. Bradley. He established it, he loved it, and he nourished it until he was too old to come back and hold meetings. This ends our exposé on Bradley's Chapel.

Red Bay

The material available to us concerning Red Bay before 1923 is nearly non-existent. The only *Gospel Advocate* reference is the one that immediately follows:

> Brother John T. Underwood recently baptized one person at Lynn, Ala., and seven at Haleyville, Ala. He is now engaged in a meeting at Red Bay, Ala.[302]

This is the only reference to Red Bay in *Gospel Advocate* before 1923. Was there an established congregation there, or was it just a mission point? If it was already established, why was so little information given? It appears that Underwood's report was in reference to a mission meeting. Just when Red Bay was established is a mystery.

Spruce Pine

SPRUCE PINE, the community, sits atop Spruce Pine Mountain, located on the north side of the mountain. It was to this quiet little community that F. E. Peden came and held the first gospel meeting to be recorded in 1907. T. H. Roberson was the reporter on this meeting. His report was published in the *Gospel Advocate* as follows:

> Russellville, September 15. Brother F. E. Peden, a student of the Potter Bible College, Bowling Green, Ky., held meetings at the following places during July, August, and September: Weatherford Schoolhouse, Isbell, Landersville, Mount Hope, and Spruce Pine. In all these meetings twenty-nine persons were baptized. While in this work Brother Peden made Russellville his headquarters and was partially supported by the congregation there. T. H. Roberson.[303]

Peden returned to Spruce Pine and held another meeting two years later. Five souls were added to the Lord's body during this meeting.[304] The information about this work is almost nonexistent. Therefore, our study on Spruce Pine is very short.

A moral issue developed at Spruce Pine and prompted a letter of inquiry to be sent to E. G. Sewell of the *Gospel Advocate*. Sewell answers rather promptly, and nothing else is mentioned in the *Gospel Advocate* about the problem. The inquiry deserves space in this study. It is here given:

> Brother Sewell: A and B are both members of the church of Christ. A is a dram drinker and also loans his money at ten per cent interest. B refuses to commune with him on Lord's day, claiming him to be an extortioner. The civil law allows eight per cent. Would you consider A, an extortioner? Did B do right in refusing to eat with A? (2) Please explain, also, 1 Cor. 5: 9–12; 11: 27–29. How should we examine ourselves? Please answer through the *Gospel Advocate*, as this has created quite a stir In the church here. Spruce Pine, Ala. A Subscriber.[305]

In 1912, John T. Underwood moved his family near Spruce Pine and lived there the remainder of his life. The same year, he reported a meeting at Spruce Pine:

> Brother John T. Underwood reports a fine meeting at Spruce Pine, Ala. Ten were added to the congregation. He also baptized four persons at Red Bank. He is now preaching to large audiences at Hodges, Ala.[306]

The following year, he made a report on another meeting at Spruce Pine.:

> John: T. Underwood, Spruce Pine, Ala., 5 additions; Tippeca-

noe, Miss., 3 additions; Beech Grove, Ala., 6 additions; Rock Creek, Ala., 8 additions.[307]

Spruce Pine Church of Christ continues into the year 2025. It is almost passed by from highway US 43 as travelers drive up and down the mountain. The church building sits off Highway 43, just far enough to go unnoticed by passersby. The church has a large cemetery that contains the mortal remains of Brother John T. Underwood and his wife, where they await that great day when the Lord returns to claim His own.

Vina

VINA IS LOCATED in the southwestern corner of Franklin County. It is situated about the same distance from the Marion County line as it is from the Mississippi State line. This area is sparsely populated as compared to other communities in the county. It is located where originally four roads came together and was named Jones Crossing. Stores grew up around the crossing. A post office was granted in 1907, and W.H. Weatherford was appointed postmaster. The Illinois Central Railroad (IC) built a route through Alabama in 1908. The town of Vina was incorporated in 1909. This community was known as a difficult community for religious teachers. This proved true with the coming of our brethren, who pioneered the establishment of a Church of Christ in that community.

John T. Underwood was a native of western Franklin County and was well-versed in the temperament of the people in that section of Franklin County. On September 2, 1909, J. F. Pelfrey announced through the pages of the *Gospel Advocate* that Underwood intended to go to Vina and hold a meeting.[308] On the 30th of September, we find Underwood preaching in that meeting at Vina.[309] The following report that Underwood sent to the *Gospel Advocate* gives testimony to the difficulties faced by our brethren. We give Underwood's letter in full:

> Our year's work will soon be a thing of the past. What have we done? I have preached more this year than any year past. The Lord has blessed my labors in every way. I have had over one hundred additions to the one body. I have been supported reasonably well, for which I feel very thankful, and I am determined to try to do more next year. I established one new congregation at Vina, Ala. Vina is said to be one of the hardest places on the Illinois Central Railroad between Corinth, Miss., and Haleyville, Ala. There had been about six meetings there before I went there, without any additions. Two of said meetings were held by our brethren. I preached there two weeks, with ten baptisms, and found about seven others who took membership. They began meeting on the first day of the week to break bread in the public-school building. They were forbidden to do this in that building. They then went to meeting from house to house until they can build; but, brethren, they cannot build without help. Therefore, I appeal to every God-loving and God-serving man and woman that reads this to send these struggling brethren and sisters a freewill offering to assist in building a house in which they can worship God. The sects have tried to build up there and have failed. Vina is a growing town of about three hundred inhabitants, with no church house at all, with two Baptist preachers living in the town. A Baptist gave us an acre of ground to build on. The "creed is in the deed." Let us be first and the town is ours. I have never in life seen a better opportunity to permanently establish the cause of the blessed Master. Please do not turn this appeal down, but help some, whether it be much or little. Send all remittances to W. W.

Reed, Vina, Ala.; and if the house is not built, I will see that the money is returned to the contributors. May the Lord bless all richly that will fellowship us in this work.[310]

The following summer, Underwood gave another report on the church at Vina. He wrote under the heading — "The Church At Vina, Ala.":

I made an appeal last fall for help to build a meetinghouse at Vina. The brethren were slow in getting the building on foot. One acre of land has been secured in a desirable part of the town, with a restrictive clause in the deed. They have gone to work on the house with part of the lumber on the ground. I herein acknowledge receipt of money sent in so far: From V. B. Jones (address unknown). 50 cents; Armstrong & Co., Town Creek, Ala., $5; J. A. Pettus, Antioch, Tenn., $5; H. N. Flash, Linton, Ind., $2.60. church at Lynn, Ala., $5.25: A. E. Jones (address unknown) $2; church at Bradley's Chapel, Ala., $3.10. Total, $23.45. I appeal to the brethren everywhere to help in the building. It will cost about eight hundred dollars or one thousand dollars to build. So, you see what is before us. Brethren. Please do not turn this appeal down. Our work here will soon be over, then we can rest under the shade of the tree of life. John T. Underwood.[311]

Two years later, P. G. Wright, of Rienzi, Mississippi, came and held a meeting at Vina. Nothing further was reported on this meeting.[312]

Here, we must depart from our set boundary of time, 1914. To give a proper picture of the church at Vina, we must go a few years beyond. In June of 1916, A. D. Dies came from Texas and held a meeting at New Castle, Alabama, which lasted until the first of June. After this meeting, he came to

Vina. He referred to Vina as a "mission point."[313] Keep in mind that this was 1916, and the work at Vina is still referred to as a "mission point." From all of the efforts put forth by Underwood and others, Vina is still a mission point. He returned in 1917 and still called Vina a mission point.[314]

To further illustrate the struggles at Vina, we give another appeal for help to build a house of worship. This came from a Brother W. W. Reed, of Vina. Under the heading of "Need Assistance In Building," this appeal was published in the *Gospel Advocate*. It read:

> W. W. Reed, Vina, Ala., March 5, says: "We have been reading the Gospel Advocate since before the Civil War. We were reading the Millennial Harbinger before the Advocate was published. It came to us at Fulton, Miss. I was in the Civil War. My wife and I are seventy-six years old. A few brethren meet at our house on Lord's day, read the Word, pray, and break bread. Our house and about all we had, except a few bedclothes and other things, was burned up last May. Lightening ran in on the switchboard and the fire started. There are four of us in the family: daughter and granddaughter. We keep boarders for a living. We owe two hundred dollars on the house we now live in. The Haleyville brethren sent us a check for nineteen dollars. It might be that the brethren would help us out if they knew our circumstances. Reference: Whitt Sparks, postmaster, Vina., Ala."
> [315]

The struggles never let up for the Christians at Vina. In spite of this, the people there at Vina extended kindness to others in need. Brother Reed wrote another letter about three years later and addressed it to Brother A. M. Burton of Nashville. It was published in the *Gospel Advocate* as follows:

The following letter, addressed to Brother A. M. Burton, of this city, is self-explanatory: Vina, Ala., September 8, 1924. A. M. Burton, Nashville, Tenn.—Dear Brother: Will say that I got your address from Birmingham, Ala. We, a few members of the church of Christ at Vina, Ala., meet each Lord's day to read the Bible and break bread. My wife and I are eighty years old. We have a daughter. I served through the Civil War and get a pension. It helps us to live. We have one boy who works on the railroad. He has a wife and five children. Our oldest boy here is a carpenter. He is taking care of an old preacher, Brother John Dale, who has been preaching for about sixty years. He will be one hundred and two years old on November 13. We have begun to build a house to have worship in. We are building, or trying to build, between our house and our son's, where the old brother stays. We have the foundation of the house, thirty-two by forty feet, and have a few thousand feet of lumber on the ground. But we need help. Send donations to W. W. Reed, Vina, Ala.[316]

Brother A. M. Burton was probably the wealthiest brother we knew. This appeal was to get help in completing the house of worship at that place. The letter also mentions John Dale. Dale was baptized by Barton W. Stone, and he had baptized over 8,000 souls into the body of Christ. Earl Kimbrough wrote that John Dale moved to Vina in 1913 and preached there until 1920.[317] This concludes our study on Vina.

Bunker Hill

Bunker Hill was another church that was mentioned twice by Kimbrough in his book on Russell's Valley that appeared and disappeared forever. The congregation just flashed across the pages of history and disappeared. C. O. Stout was born on November 6, 1891, and grew to manhood in Franklin County. Stout told Earl Kimbrough of a congregation during his childhood called Bunker Hill. He said it met in a community building made of hand-hewn logs.[318] The only reference to Bunker Hill, in any other printed form, was a note by William M. Behel. It simply read:

> On July 25 I began a week's meeting with the congregation at Bunker Hill, Ala., which resulted in six baptisms.[319]

You may note that the date on Behel's report was dated August 19, 1920, even though the church existed years before it was noted in Behel's report. Who established it is unknown, and when it ceased meeting is unknown. Bunker Hill was and still is a mystery.

This is the sum total of what we know of the Bunker Hill church in Franklin County. This brief study of Bunker Hill concludes our study of the post-Civil War and the forgotten churches in Franklin County, Alabama.

Post War Colbert County

Tuscumbia

THE CIVIL WAR ended on April 9, 1865. Less than a year later (February 1866), James Madison Pickens came to Tuscumbia and found the church there in disarray. He observed the deplorable condition of the once numerically and spiritually strong church. It was in shambles and had been neglecting the assembling together, on the Lord's Day, for some time. He soon began preaching and trying to correct this situation. He reported his efforts in the *Gospel Advocate*. We give the report in its entirety:

> Aberdeen, Mississippi, April 16th, 1866, Brothers Fanning & Lipscomb— According to your request published in the Advocate, I give you a report of my labors South of the Tennessee. Seeing that the laborers were few in this section, and that the cause of our Master was sadly neglected, and likely still to be, I left the pleasant associations of our brethren in Tennessee in the month of February. The first point I visited was Tuscumbia, Ala., where I preached for eight days, during which time we succeeded in organizing a small

congregation from the scattered remains of a once large one, that assembled in that place, to which we also had some additions. This congregation contains some good material, and displays commendable zeal, and is under the care of a competent elder, we being judge; but a meetinghouse is yet to be built.[320]

This was the first recorded mention of the Tuscumbia church situation after the Civil War. Pickens took an interest in the Tuscumbia work until his death on February 3, 1881. He worked with them and tried to get them back on solid footing, but the post-war conditions worked against his efforts.

Lewis Clark (L. C.) Chisholm wrote of Pickens and his coming to Tuscumbia:

During last winter our young brother, J. M. Pickens, rather accidentally visited Tuscumbia, where he very soon assembled a little flock that seemed both willing and anxious to keep the ordinances of the Lord, but at that time it seemed next to impossibility to get a hearing, but the scale is now turned. The people begin to see something of the original Gospel and feel the power of its truth. Men of talent and influence are hearing and willing to hear and say that it is the only teaching they ever heard on the subject of Christianity that appeals to the intelligence of a community ... Yours in the hope, L. C. Chisholm.[321]

They steadily gained ground and added to their number, but the labors of Bro. Pickens had not been confined to Tuscumbia alone. He was constantly engaged in attacking sin and sectarianism at other points. Alabama had two years of drought following the war, which enhanced the dire need for help from other brethren. Pickens made the following appeal on behalf of the Tuscumbia brethren and the surrounding communities. This appeal was made through the pages of the *Gospel Advocate*:

> Tuscumbia, Ala., April 2, 1867. To the Christian Brotherhood: The following facts are respectfully submitted to your attention and consideration, and you are most earnestly requested and urged to take timely notice of the same.
>
> There is great destitution and want (need) among many of the people of North Alabama. The very moderate supply of provisions yielded by the crop of last year is continually falling, which renders their wants greater daily; and although there is much actual suffering in the country now, it will soon be greatly increased.
>
> Notwithstanding the brethren have done much to relieve the suffering in many places, it is to be borne in mind that of all they have done, there has not been a single donation of anything whatever made to Franklin and other adjoining counties; but Christianity and humanity demand that something be done.
>
> We have about two hundred brethren in Franklin County, and some in each adjoining county, many of whom are in need. Our appeal is in their behalf particularly; however, we would not ignore the wants of others. A number of the brethren have requested me to present their wants. We therefore ask those who may have a surplus of the good things of this world to send them a donation. Mark as follows: For the Destitute South care of L. C. Chisholm & Bro., Tuscumbia, Alabama. Whence shipments are to come via Nashville, send through Metcalf, Bros. & Co., and rest assured that your donations, whether bread, meat, clothing, or money will be carefully and scrupulously distributed. Shipments will be duly acknowledged when received, and it

would be well to notify us as soon as they are made. It is also to be remembered that some expense will have to be incurred. J. M. Pickens.[322]

In our opening page of this study, we mentioned how, by a legislative act on February 6, 1867, the northern half of Franklin County was organized as Colbert County. Later that year, the county was abolished, but in 1869 it was reestablished with Tuscumbia as the county seat.[323] Thus, we treat the earliest days of the Franklin-Colbert County union as one segment of their history.

With these difficulties, the brethren seemingly had lost their "Polar Star" — "Faith in God." The church was in shambles and had been neglecting the assembling together on the Lord's Day for some time. Pickens discovered that the church building had been taken by the Baptists when our brethren had ceased meeting. The following is the account given in Pickens's own words:

> More than thirty years ago, our aged and highly esteemed brother, Dr. Wm. H. Wharton, now of Nashville, Tenn., began preaching at Tuscumbia, Ala., the gospel of Christ, a doctrine better known to certain Baptist preachers and writers of that section, as "Campbellism."
>
> Soon the denominations with one accord denied Brother Wharton the privilege of preaching in any meeting house in the town. On one occasion, Brother W. having been requested to preach the funeral of a most estimable young man, was not allowed the privilege of a house even for that purpose. This excited the indignation of a number of citizens belonging to no church, who declared that Dr. Wharton, whom they esteemed most highly, should have a house in which to preach. The donation of these gentlemen,

united with the contribution and labor of the brethren, was the means of erecting quite a respectable little brick house. The brethren (as is the case everywhere), ever ready to extend the use of their house to any denomination which did not own one in the town, permitted the Episcopalians, the U. Presbyterians and the Baptists to use the house as often as desired. In the course of human events Brother Wharton removed to Nashville, the church ceased to increase, the members moved away to other parts and died, till finally, not one was left to tell the tale. Meantime the Baptists continued to use the house, and after a while assumed entire control of it, and finally, it was called "the Baptist Church."

After some years, other brethren moved to Tuscumbia but were led to believe that the house had been sold to the Baptists. In the beginning of the year 1866, we were called by a few brethren to hold a protracted meeting in Tuscumbia and concluded to spend much of the year in North Alabama.

On our arrival in Tuscumbia, we were informed that we could occupy "the Baptist Church," that our brethren had built it and it was understood that we could use it whenever the Baptists did not need it, that such was the understanding when the Baptists "bought it."

As the Baptists were then without a preacher, we were permitted to use the house as often as desired; but this state of affairs did not continue long. Fearing "their craft was in danger," the Baptists soon called G. A. Coulson to be their pastor. During Mr. Coulson's term of service, we were still permitted to use the house occasionally at night; but soon he was superseded by Joseph Shackelford, the present incumbent. The latter began immediately to occupy the house both day and night, and so we were crowded out. About this time, several remarks from citizens of the town led us to believe that the Baptists had no right to the house, and their pretended purchase was a sham.

The records were examined to find if the Baptists had a title, but none could be found. Having been told that they had bought the house from Dr. Wharton, we wrote to him making inquiry and received an answer stating that he had not sold it and that he had no knowledge that anyone else had. We were also told by citizens of the town who were conversant with the whole affair, and who had contributed to build the house, that the Baptists had never bought it and that they had no right to it. While these investigations were going on, Brother C. R. Darnell, of Tennessee, wrote us that he would be in Tuscumbia on a certain Lord's Day, and requested that an appointment be made for him to preach. Mr. Shackelford said if Brother Darnell occupied the house, it must be at an hour that would not conflict with his (Shackelford's) appointment.

It was insisted, however, that Brother Darnell should have the popular hour, and intimated that the Baptists were the party occupying the house by permission. At this they became indignant, and sent for Elder Elliott, who, they said, had bought the house.

After having learned that Brother Wharton denied having any knowledge that the house had ever been sold, Elder Elliott claimed that he had bought it from a citizen who had died many years before, who was neither a member of the Christian Church nor even a friend to it. When asked for his title the Elder said he supposed that it was in the office where recorded. He was then informed that he had no title on record. He then said that a certain lawyer had been employed to draw up the papers, the said lawyer had gone to Texas and died, and he (the Elder) supposed that his lawyer "had taken the deed to Texas and filed it there." He was told that such was a strange disposition to make of a title. And finally, the Baptists were unable to show that they had bought the house, or that they had ever paid one dollar to our brethren who built the house and who owned it; but said since we had demanded as a right what had been granted as a favor, they withdrew the privilege they had granted us of using the house henceforth, and added an amount of very mean abuse, and heralded their version of the affair through the Baptist paper published at Tuscumbia. Several prominent lawyers were consulted in reference to the matter, who, after an investigation, answered in substance as follows:

"The house justly belongs to you, the Baptists have no right to it, but your brethren committed a blunder in letting the Baptists have the key, and by asking permission of them to use your own house, you have for a number of years recognized and acknowledged the right of the Baptists, and the limitation of the law will give it to them now, if they are a mind to hold it under such circumstances."

Since that time, the Baptists have enjoyed undisputed possession of the house, and oft its walls have been made to ring with an exposition of the errors of "Campbellism."

After almost four years, we have concluded that such a breach of trust and abuse of favor deserves to be held up to public gaze. We have a far better opinion of the Baptists generally than to believe that they would even countenance such flagrant injustice, but we think it is right to brand the Baptists of Tuscumbia with the injustice of which they are guilty, till they shall repair the wrong they have done, which we by no means expect them to do. J. M. Pickens. [324]

Here we give a sample of how the Baptist rumor was perpetrated among some of Tuscumbia's leading citizens:

The church building was erected by the Campbellites, or Christians, mainly through the personal efforts of Dr. W. H. Wharton, but it was not paid for, and the contractor. W. H. Patterson sold his claim to George W. Carroll, who sold it to Edmund Elliott, a member of the Baptist Church. Through him the title passed to his church.[325]

When Pickens tried to re-gather the church, he could not get a gathering, and one great obstacle was that he could not secure a meeting place. That is when he began to investigate the building problem. When he published the above article in his *Christian Monthly*, calling out the Baptist claim to the building in Tuscumbia, he was immediately challenged by Josephus Shackelford. Shackelford was the new minister for the Tuscumbia Baptist Church. After this challenge, Pickens wrote to Dr. William Henry (W. H.) Wharton was the very reason the church building was constructed. Wharton wrote a letter back to Pickens, which he published in his *Christian Monthly* as follows:

> Brother J. M. Pickens: Nashville, March 6, 1867: I have received your letter making inquiries about the meeting house in Tuscumbia. The transaction referred to, occurred over thirty years ago, and I am not able to recall many of the circumstances— only that the house was built for me especially, because I was refused the use, upon one occasion of the Presbyterian church to preach the funeral of an estimable young man. The brick work was done by the Messrs. Ragland, whose good old mother was a zealous member of our communion. The wood work was also done by Bro. Patterson, an elder of the church, and both the brick and wood work were more a labor of love than of profit. I do not think any member of another church subscribed one dollar toward the

construction of it. One individual, a Mr. Cooper, contributed $50. The title to the lot was given by a Mr. Bell, I believe, who was a member also. I do not recollect how much I gave; I know it was as much as I was able at the time. My impression has always been that it was paid. We agreed to have a basement after the plan was adopted for a school house, I think for $200 more, and this may not have been paid. I know of no difficulty about debt, while I lived there, or in the neighborhood, a year afterwards, before I removed to this city. I do not recollect who was to pay the additional $200 for the school house; it was for the benefit of the town. I learned after I came here that the Episcopalians used the house. Some debts may have accumulated for repairs or for the school basement. I never had any title that I remember member, for in fact I had none individually. I never opposed the Baptists or any other religious party using the house, however, at any time. We once had a church of nearly one hundred members. Most of them moved away or died. I do not recollect the amount of the subscription or what became of it. The builders seemed always thought were satisfied to take it and build the house. Bro. Towns, a popular leader of the Baptists there, was greatly opposed to us. Adieu, W. H. Wharton.[326]

Wharton gave the facts concerning the original intent for the building then in question. With Pickens's attempts to reconvene the church in Tuscumbia dying with him in 1881, the church lay dormant for over thirty years before being gathered into a congregation again. There were a few faithful Christians left in Tuscumbia and the adjoining area.

In 1883, Larimore married a young couple, who made up part of this scattered band. He performed the wedding of Charles E. Cook and Fannie C. Carter, both of Tuscumbia, Ala. This occurred on December 31, 1882.[327]

Another example of the scattered Christians at Tuscumbia was found in an obituary published in the *Gospel Advocate* in November 1883, where we find the baptism of a young lady by Pickens in 1866. We give an excerpt from the obituary:

> Died, in East Nashville, October 28, 1883, Mrs. Fannie Anderson wife of Frank Anderson, in the 37th year of her age. Mrs. Moore, only daughter of John and Ruth Moore, was born in Moulton, Alabama, January 22nd, 1847. She was educated in Salem, North Carolina. She united with the Christian church, in Tuscumbia, Alabama, when she was nineteen (1866) years old. She was married in November, 1868, to Frank Anderson, of Nashville, Tenn., where she lived an exemplary Christian life until she died. She was good and kind to all, graceful in person, educated, and accomplished; all who knew her loved her ....[328]

We find enough proof that even though the church was not convening on the Lord's Day and observing the ordinances, there were some Christians who were trying to keep some semblance of Christianity during this dismal period. There were other attempts to re-establish the work, even after Pickens's work. G. A. Reynolds was coming to Tuscumbia, sporadically, to hold services wherever he could find a few souls to meet with him. In a short note in the *Gospel Advocate*, we find the following:

> Bro. G. A. Reynolds, of Florence, Ala., enlivened us with his presence one day last week ... He thinks now would be an excellent time to make an effort to firmly establish the ancient gospel at Tuscumbia. He had one addition there at his last appointment.[329]

This proves that at least some efforts were being made with the Christians in Tuscumbia at this time. It seems that some brethren bought into Brother Reynolds's suggestion about the work in Tuscumbia. That same year, we found the following report by a Tuscumbia brother:

> From Fayette I came to Tuscumbia, Ala., where I found Bro. Reynolds, of Florence, and Bro. L. R. Sewell, of Nashville, holding forth until I could come and assist them in a meeting. We have been much rejoiced at having these two brethren with us, as well as Bros. Richardson, of Lawrenceburg, Tenn., and Underwood, of Barton, Ala. These are sacrificing preachers of the gospel, and I pray God to bless their labors. Bro. J. D. Patton, of Cherokee, Ala., is leading the singing for us, and he does it well. He seems to be fond of Christian Hymns. We are preaching in the court house with much opposition. We trust that God will yet bless our efforts. We shall continue the meeting as long as it shall appear to be God's will to continue. H. G. Fleming, Tuscumbia, Ala.[330]

The brethren were finally buying into the idea that the Tuscumbia brethren needed an organized work established. The next we hear from Tuscumbia through the *Gospel Advocate* was concerning a meeting by a T. T. Pack. This was seventeen years after the efforts by Reynolds. Pack wrote:

> Sheffield. July 29. Since my school closed at Bowling Green, Ky., I have been laboring with the church at this place. We have a fine congregation here. Our church house is in Sheffield, but we have a great many members in Tuscumbia. The two towns are just two miles apart. I am laboring in both places. We want to have our meeting later on. I have been here six weeks, and three persons have entered the fold by

baptism, and many more are "almost persuaded." I want to hold a meeting in Tuscumbia, but we have no house to hold it in; so, I want to ask if anyone knows where I can get a tent for August and September. I would like to have one for two months, anyway. I think I can do great good here with it. If anyone knows of one that I can get, I would like to hear from him or her at once. We are commanded to carry the gospel to sinners, and that is what I am trying to do. The harvest is ripe, but laborers are few. T. T. Pack.[331]

He at least followed through with his intentions to work with Tuscumbia. His work started off seemingly in a good way but turned very sour at the end of his stay, as we shall soon see. At first, he did what he intended to do. The *Gospel Advocate* gave this report:

Brother T. T. Pack began a meeting at Tuscumbia. Ala., on Wednesday, November 6. There are only a few brethren in Tuscumbia, and it is hoped that much good may be done during this meeting. Brother Pack recently closed a meeting at Furnace Hill, Sheffield, Ala., with four additions.[332]

Here is where things go badly. We shall let the report speak for itself:

There is one T. T. Pack (alias Peck) now traveling Alabama, claiming to be a Christian preacher, who eloped with the wife and child of Brother Dimit Lafoon, of Tuscumbia. Ala., last November. Pack is about six feet two inches high, with dark complexion, dark hair, gray eyes, and is very affable. The woman, whose name is Myrl, is of heavy build, a blonde, with eyes of a yellow shade. She is about twenty years old. The little boy is very fair, with dark eyes; and is about two years old. His name is Enrique Milton. If he comes your way, inform the officers. Signed: S. I. S. Cawthon, Andalusia, Ala.; J. M. Barnes, Montgomery, Ala.; and John E. Dunn, Montgomery, Ala.[333]

Pack's reputation turned bad and reached South Alabama. When J. M. Barnes, S. I. S. Cawthon, and John E. Dunn were speaking out against Pack, that tells us that Pack had already fled to South Alabama. Many times, through these years, fraud artists took advantage of our struggling brethren.

The work began to become more stabilized with the coming of a family who had moved to Tuscumbia in 1908. Things turned around for the church after James Harvey Morris moved to Tuscumbia. Basil Overton wrote:

> Soon after John and Mattie moved to Tuscumbia, they were part of group of about twenty-five Christians who began to meet for worship in the Court Room of the Colbert County Court House in Tuscumbia. They continued to meet there until they erected a meetinghouse on Fourth Street in 1911. This building burned in 1924 and the congregation met in Deshler School building until another Church building was completed in 1925 ....[334]

Overton said twenty-five Christians were meeting in the courthouse when Morris moved to Tuscumbia in 1908. Within two years, the number grew to about fifty, according to J. M. McCaleb.[335] McCaleb wrote:

> Tuscumbia and Sheffield are twin cities, the corporation limit of one being the beginning of the other. I also spoke twice at Tuscumbia. The brethren here number about fifty and meet in the courthouse. They have secured a lot, however, and

have raised part of the money to build a house. At Tuscumbia is one of the largest springs I ever saw. It is just in the edge of town and comes out at the foot of a small hill from beneath a great ledge of rock It is really an underground river that bursts forth to the surface. J. M. Mc Caleb.[336]

G. A. Dunn came to Tuscumbia and held a meeting in 1910[337] and again in 1912. He wrote a short sketch of the Tuscumbia work under the heading—"The Church At Tuscumbia, Ala." It read:

> I am now in a pleasant meeting in Tuscumbia. Ala. This is the first meeting in their new house. Two years ago, I came here and held their first meeting in the courthouse. We gathered strength enough then to buy a lot. Since then, they have built a nice brick house. We are now having the largest audiences ever had here, and one is to be baptized this evening, G. A. Dunn.[338]

The following year, L. S. Lancaster wrote about the churches in Tuscumbia, Sheffield, and Florence. We give the full report.

> Tuscumbia, a town of perhaps more than four thousand inhabitants, located on the Southern Railroad near the halfway point between Chattanooga and Memphis, Tenn., is a railroad town; and having the Southern and Northern Alabama Railroad shops just on the outside and being the terminus of the Northern Alabama, it is, of course, the home of many railroad men.
>
> Tuscumbia is also closely connected with Florence and Sheffield, Ala., by means of an electric railway, with cars running every forty minutes. These three towns are familiarly

known as the "Tri-Cities." I understand that the church in Florence has been well established and doing good work for several years, and we have also had a good little congregation in Sheffield for some time. The loyal brethren in Tuscumbia seem not to have fared so well in the past, yet "we are thankful to Him who doeth all things well" that now the prospects for them in the future are bright.

Many years ago, there was a congregation established at this place which soon became digressive. They went in debt for their meetinghouse, and later on lost it, not being able to meet the payments when they fell due, and they soon disbanded. However, there has been a remnant of loyal members to be found there all along, and some of them met regularly with the church in Sheffield. In the fall of 1910, Brother S. A. Frazier, now of Pulaski, Tenn., and a few loyal and untiring workers began meeting on Lord's days in the courthouse, and in November 1910, had Brother G. A. Dunn, of Memphis, Tenn., with them in a two-weeks' meeting, which strengthened and encouraged them very much. In November 1911, Brother J. Paul Slayden was with them in a two-weeks' meeting, and in June 1912, Brother Dunn was with them another two weeks. Brother Daugherty, of Louisville, Ky., is to begin a meeting with them on July 20. At present Brother Farrar, of Florence, is preaching for the congregation twice a month; Brother Paul Hanlin, occasionally; and the writer, on the fourth Lord's day in each month.

This little band, numbering, perhaps, from six to a dozen three years ago, has been doing a remarkable work, having built for themselves a nice little brick meetinghouse, conveniently located, which will cost them four or five thousand dollars when completed (which will be in the near future). All of this they have raised among themselves, with the exception of about five hundred dollars given by outside friends and congregations. They have never made an appeal for help through any of the papers, but, realizing their needs, they simply went to work with heart and hand both to will and to do, and we now see the fruits of their labors.

In addition to the work done at home, these brethren have been liberal contributors to mission work. The membership is now about sixty, and it is certainly an inspiration to be with them in their meetings. I commend this example to all those Christians who happen to find themselves in towns or communities where they have no church with which to meet. "Go and do thou likewise."[339]

Lancaster sent a second report on his meeting at Tuscumbia:

Russellville, Ala., December 5. I spent eight days, including the fourth and fifth Lord's days in November, with the church at Tuscumbia, Ala. The meeting was well attended, and we trust that good will come of our efforts. The congregation is comparatively new, but in fine working order. L. S. Lancaster.[340]

Even though no responses were recorded, Lancaster's eight days spent in evangelistic work with the small band at Tuscumbia were profitable to the church at that place. It helped to solidify the group into a church family.

Black Brethren's Work in Colbert County

NOTHING HAS BEEN MENTIONED CONCERNING the work amongst our Black brethren up to this point. That is because no reports could be found until Brother J. Hannon entered the church scene at Tuscumbia. He sent the first report on the Black work in Tuscumbia through the pages of the *Gospel Advocate,* and it was one year beyond our cutoff date of 1914, but it was necessary to involve this work at this time. His first report read:

> I am glad to say that work is progressing in Spring Valley, Ala. I have been preaching here for the past two years and they have arranged with me for this year. The brethren in Tuscumbia, Ala., are planning to open a mission work. We are going on with the work of the Lord in Corinth, Miss., by meeting each Lord's day and breaking the loaf. We have a few faithful members in Corinth. I am arranging with them for us to do more this year than in the past. J. Hannon.[341]

His work in Spring Valley was on the Abraham Ricks plantation. That was the home of George Ricks, a very active Black evangelist who had died seven years earlier.

He sent a more extensive report in May 1915. We give the full report:

> I am glad to say the churches in and near Tuscumbia, Ala., are taking on new life. We have a strong body of disciples at this place. We are now arranging a Bible class among the young brethren. We have nineteen young men that belong to the faith going into this Bible class. They will start with Matthew, to read the New Testament through, meeting one night in each week. The sisters and one brother made up a nice box of groceries and sent me, for which I was glad. The box sent me was worth about seven dollars. We have two members in Florence that are arranging to begin a work among our people. The white brethren are so nice and kind to offer their help. We thank them many times for their love toward the work among the [Black] people.
>
> The little band in Corinth are meeting each Lord's day. I am busy every Lord's day trying to take care of my home congregation at Tuscumbia. Being poor in this world's goods, having to work six days and study at night, makes it very hard. I hope to be able to do more in the work of the Lord this year than the past. I have a few calls already. I shall, the Lord willing, meet all of them. J. Hannon.[342]

With Hannon's report, this closes our history of the Black churches in Tuscumbia. We leave the rest of the history of Tuscumbia to some historian in the future to write the next chapter of Tuscumbia's history.

We now take a look at the rural work amongst our Black brethren. The earliest work among the Black brethren, perhaps in the state of Alabama, was begun on Abraham Ricks's plantation—"The Oaks," before the Civil War. Ricks's wife, Charlotte, taught many of the slaves to read, especially the Bible. Many of the slaves were baptized by Abraham Ricks. One such slave was George Ricks. He became a preacher and established a church of Christ on the plantation. It was known and still is as Christian Home. George's grandson Percy Ricks told students at International Bible College in Florence, Alabama, in the Spring of 1972 that he was— "baptized by the man who was baptized by the man who was baptized by Alexander Campbell." That was a true statement because Alexander Campbell had baptized Abraham Ricks back in Virginia.[343] When Abraham Ricks's wife died, the account of her death in the *North Alabamian* stated that she became a member of the Christian (Church of Christ?) Church, under the preaching of Dr. Wharton and Mr. Abe Ricks, said that his grandfather, Abraham Ricks, was a member of the "Christian Church."[344]

The account of her death in the *North Alabamian* stated that she became a member of the Christian (Church of Christ?) Church, under the preaching of Dr. Wharton and Mr. Abe Ricks, said that his grandfather, Abraham Ricks, was a member of the "Christian Church."[345]

The Black brethren had built a meetinghouse on the Ricks's plantation after the Civil War, but they had difficulty paying for it. "Parson George," as he was called, wrote to the editors of the *Gospel Advocate*, asking for financial help. The appeal read:

> Tuscumbia, Ala., December 20, 1867. Bro. Chisholm: After saying howdy to you, I will state that I am doing very well, preaching at my old mistress Ricks', and have about fifty members, and at my last baptizing, which was this day three weeks ago, I baptized three members into the Church of

Christ. So, you see we are well with the exception of need of money. We have not yet paid for our church-house. Supposing that there may be some [Black] brethren in the vicinity in which you live, belonging to the Christian ranks, who are not so poor as we are, and who are willing to devote a small amount, be it ever so little, I write to give you the fact that we are in need of money to pay the amount we are behind on our church-house. Will you please show this also to the white brethren—Brother Fanning and others, and ask their aid in the matter? If you can do anything for us, we will be thankful. Howbeit, let me hear immediately, say by Christmas, what you have done for us. Direct your letter to me in care of your brother, Dr. Ed Chisholm, at Tuscumbia. We are obliged to raise as much as twenty or twenty-five dollars by Christmas, if we possibly can. I hope and trust you will be successful enough to do it. Yours in the hope, George Ricks.[346]

David Lipscomb responded on behalf of the appeal:

We have the assurance from Brother Chisholm and others that Brother Geo. Ricks is a most worthy, unassuming brother, and is doing a good and faithful work for the Lord and his people. We learn the Church at Franklin College has furnished Brother George with the amount he asks for immediately, but other small remittances, as above, to Dr. E. Chisholm would be most worthy appropriated. We are very anxious to aid all efforts to Christianize and elevate the [Black] and prepare him for living usefully here and hereafter. But all these politico-religious organizations to instruct or elevate him, or rather to use him, will do him harm. We have no sympathy with them; and cannot do evil that good may come. The congregation that encourages such, under any influences, we are satisfied, will nurse a viper that will but poison and destroy it. D.L.[347]

T. B. Larimore brought the money to the Ricks Plantation on behalf of the students at Franklin College. He became popular with the white and Black folks on the plantation. He organized a church on the plantation among the Blacks. By this, it is understood that he helped to appoint elders and deacons for the congregation already meeting on the Ricks's Plantation.[348]

George Ricks made a trip to Nashville and visited the office of the *Gospel Advocate*. The editors published this report:

> Elder Joe (George) Ricks, (Colored) of Spring Valley, Ala., gave us a call last week. He has been preaching about seventeen years, during which time he has baptized about 300 persons. His home congregation, Christian Home, Colbert County, Ala., numbers 96 members, and besides himself, there are six preachers. There is also a church at Fayetteville, Talladega County, with 49 members that Bro. Ricks has been mainly instrumental in building up.[349]

According to this article, George Ricks had been preaching since 1868. George Ricks died in 1908. His death was described in the *Leighton News* as follows:

> Rev. George Ricks, [Black], seventy-three years of age, died December 25, 1908. As the angels of God sang out on the Christmas air, "Glory to God in the highest, and on earth peace, good-will toward men," the summons came to him— "Come unto me, all ye who are weary and heavy laden, and I will give you rest." He laid down his cross and took up his crown. Parson George, as he was familiarly known, like

Joshua, was a good fighter for the right. His characteristics were honesty, truthfulness, generosity, freedom of religious thought, and faith in the eternal God. Early in life, he began working in his Master's vineyard. He was never happier than on the Sabbath days when he could gather his people together to sing the songs of Zion and tell of Jesus and His love. He has sung his last doxology, but to his flock and large family of sons and daughters, weep not, but walk in his footsteps, so on the other shore you may clasp hands and sing hallelujah. R. I. Tuscumbia.[350]

Thus, North Alabama lost its most prominent Black minister. It was a loss to all the churches of Christ—both Black and white.

Rock Creek

THE ROCK CREEK community was named for Rock Creek, a small stream located nearby. Rock Creek's community name first appeared on maps as "Big Rock Creek" by General John Coffee's survey in 1834 and Michael Toumey's 1849 map. There was a small spring branch, at the time, also known as "Rock Creek," that was the reason for Coffee's "Big Rock Creek" on his map. It last appeared on maps in 1915.[351] Rock Creek's location was 6 ½ miles west of Crooked Oak and 1 ½ miles north of the Franklin County line.[352]

The church at Rock Creek unofficially began in 1866 after J. M. Pickens came and preached at the Frankfort congregation. In August 1866, J. M. Pickens came to Frankfort, held a short meeting, and baptized three persons who, later in that year, established the church at Rock Creek. They were J. H. Srygley, his wife Sarah J. Srygley, and F. G. W. Flake. These three, along with four others, began the Rock Creek congregation within a short time.[353]

The following excerpt from the obituary of F. D. and F. B.'s mother, written by T. B. Larimore, bears out this fact:

Rock Creek 159

Sarah Jane Coats was born on November 7, 1831. Her father, Benjamin Coats, was a Cumberland Presbyterian preacher. She, being perfectly satisfied with the word, the will, and the way of the Lord, content to "walk in the light" and believing "the church of God" to be not a human, but a divine, institution, never belonged to any denomination. She was simply a pure, prayerful, pious, devout, consecrated Christian—"only this, and nothing more" believing God, had he willed us to be something else or something more, would certainly have told us so, and told us what and how—if not, indeed, why, and when. She was married to James H. Srygley on October 28, 1844 ... She was baptized by our talented and long-lamented brother, J. M. Pickens, in August 1866. Immediately after her baptism she and her husband and four others established, at her home, Rock Creek, Ala., the church of Christ of which she was an active and faithful member till she moved to Coal Hill, Ark., in October 1887. Immediately after she reached Coal Hill, she encouraged and constrained the few Christians there to begin to work and worship publicly in the name of Christ and to build "a meetinghouse" all of which they did. T. B. Larrimore.[354]

The Rock Creek Church was the first congregation of the Church of Christ to be established in Colbert County after the Civil War. T. B. Larimore gave a good description of the Rock Creek church from his first visit to that community. His first sermon was given on June 14, 1868. On this visit, he made lifelong friends with the Srygley family and many other precious souls on that visit. He wrote:

More than thirty years ago I went from Nashville, Tenn., my native State—to Rock Creek, Alabama, to the new historic Rock Creek Meetinghouse. My mission was to "preach the word." The church there then numbered seven souls. As, the first time, I approached the door of that old log cabin "meetinghouse," a penniless stranger in a strange land, I saw, standing about thirty feet away, to the right and in front of me, twenty feet from the path I was travelling and thirty feet from the door I was approaching, a bright, little black-eyed, bareheaded, barefooted boy; a picture of health, happiness, peace, and contentment; perfectly beautiful to me—then as, on memory's page, now. His cheeks were rosy; his eyes were black. Faultless in form and feature, he stood silent, motionless, and erect. The body of that faithful friend, than whom no was born into the church, the family of God, "the human friend was ever truer, lies, in the silence and stillness of death, before us."[355]

Larimore wrote this on the occasion of the death of his dear friend, F. D. Srygley. On this visit, he helped set in order the "soon-to-be" strongest church in the Lord's body in western Colbert County. According to F. D. Srygley's letter below, Larimore returned in August of that year. Srygley wrote:

We came together for the first time, at this place, to worship the Lord in a congregational capacity, on the second Lord's day in June 1868. We then numbered seven. In August 1868, Bro. T. B. Larimore visited us, delivered five discourses, which resulted in the accession of about a dozen faithful souls to our little, despised band.[356]

The church at Rock Creek was an infant in the Lord's body at this time. A record book was begun upon Larimore's first visit. The first entry in the book read as thus:

Rock Creek

A congregation organized at Rock Creek Colbert Co Alabama, June 14th, 1868. We the Disciples of our Lord and Savior Jesus Christ, whose names are here in subscribed do agree to come together in Gospel Order taking the word of God for the Man of our council in all things and the Rule of our faith and practice.[357]

Following the first entry was a list of the charter members. Quickly added were others who became new members of the Lord's body at Rock Creek.

J. H. Srygley gave a summary of what took place at the Rock Creek church from the time the church was established in 1866 through September 1869. His letter continues below:

> He (Larimore) preached at Frankfort about the same time, when four others obeyed the Gospel and united with our congregation. Shortly after this time Bro. Joe Usry, son of our lamented Bro. Robert Usry, visited us. Under his defence of the truth, ten more were added to the cause, but being entirely from another neighborhood, they all united with another congregation. Bro. Taylor has visited and preached for us once a month most of the time, and by his faithful teaching, "the good seed or the kingdom" has been copiously sown. Bro. Taylor is a faithful soldier, but age has bleached his locks, dimmed his eye, made pale the cheek that once with health and vigor glowed, bowed down his manly form, and tells us that we must give him up. While these reflections trouble us, we rejoice to know that, as he approaches the grave, "land of the blessed." But as he declines someone must take his place, and we are very thankful to you and the Franklin College brethren for supplying this necessity by sending us our faithful young Bro. Larimore, whose heart and hands are in the cause, and who tells us that he is under many

lasting and great obligations to the brethren of Hopkinsville, Ky., and Franklin College, Tenn., for the position he now occupies as a defender of the truth once delivered to the saints.

At the time of Bro. Taylor's last monthly appointment, Saturday before the second Lord's day in July, Brother Larimore visited us again, and remained with us until the next Friday morning, during which time there were seventeen added to the Lord's cause—one from the Baptists, four from the Methodists, and twelve from the world. We believe that all who heard the series of discourses delivered are thoroughly convinced of the truth of the Gospel, which is "God's power unto salvation." Surely no candid man can fail to see the immovable power of God's Sacred Word, the Bible. It is a Fortress that never can be taken; built upon a "cornerstone" that never can be broken; and those who build upon it, and those who build upon the rock shall never be forsaken ... Rock Creek is six miles from Frankfort. We would be pleased for any of our preaching brethren to give us a call. Perhaps you may hear from me again soon. Fraternally, James H. Srygley. [358]

The following paragraph was written by F. D. Srygley concerning the people of Rock Creek:

The people were healthy, but poor. They were simple in customs, but honest of heart. They were not highly educated as the world count education, but they were strong in practical sense and trained by experience and observation in the matter of drawing conclusions from what they saw and heard."[359]

The first meeting house, after the group met in the Srygley

house, was the old log schoolhouse at Rock Creek. The old school building was in operation before the Civil War.[360] It was the meeting place used by all area denominations.[361] Andrew Jackson James was baptized at Rock Creek on July 14th, 1869, and sometime soon after he was baptized, he donated two acres of land on which a church building for the congregation at Rock Creek was erected.[362] It would be 1875 before the new church house was built. That year, a graduate—J. H. Holbrook— from Mars Hill College, near Florence, Alabama, came and labored in a meeting with the Rock Creek church. On August 30, 1875, he wrote about his trip to this church:

> I have just closed a very interesting meeting at this place, resulting in 16 additions to the body of Christ. This little band was organized in 1867, with but 7 members. Since that time 3 have been withdrawn from, 16 dismissed by commendation and 6 are sleeping beneath the clod of the valley, and there are still 100 members, as warmhearted as ever lived. The brethren have just built a good house of worship 30 by 36 ft. and the church meets every Lord's day and is in good working order. If any of our preaching brethren should pass this way, they will find a home among any of the brethren. Let us all be faithful in the discharge of duty and the cause of truth will triumph.[363]

F. D. Srygley also wrote about J. H. Holbrook's wife, Margaret, and the influence she had upon the Srygley boys during that meeting. This was included in her obituary. It was also a partial biographical sketch of F. D. Srygley and his search for the Lord. We give most of this article in full:

Margaret E. Vick was born November 13, 1841, baptized by Wade Barrett, of Tennessee, when in her sixteenth year and married to J. H. Halbrook Aug. 22, 1865. After seven months of patient, though almost painless, struggle against the steady ravages of wasting consumption, she died, at Bronson, Fla., Sept. 22, 1891. I first met her in the hill country of North Alabama in the summer of 1875. She was then the efficient and earnest helper of her ever-faithful husband in his labors as an evangelist in that rugged region. For more than a week my father's house was their home, and during that time they conducted a very successful meeting at Rock Creek church. The writer of these lines and F. B. Srygley, the well-known evangelist of Lebanon, Tennessee, were among those who were baptized during that memorable meeting. She knows now, what perhaps she never fully understood in this world, though I often tried to make her understand it, how much her steadfast faith, consuming zeal and earnest words of private admonition and exhortation during that meeting helped to decide me and others to turn to the Lord and trust him for salvation. I had long understood the way of the Lord, and for years had been deeply and seriously impressed with the importance of "so great salvation." From early childhood I had listened time after time to the matchless eloquence and inimitable pathos of the beloved Larimore. I loved him then as I love him now, for his godly walk, child-like faith, unfaltering friendship and brilliant talents, and often I felt, when listening to him, a wild desire and consuming anxiety to be a Christian, but somehow, I had never yet brought myself up to the supreme test of a complete submission to Christ. All the while there seemed to be a great gulf between what I really was and what I so earnestly longed to be, which I could not muster courage enough to attempt to cross. But when that godly woman came to me with the light of a purified heart shining in her face and the tear drops of a baptized soul trembling in her eyes, I began to see my way clearer. Somehow, she seemed to reach across the chasm, grasp my hand and nerve my heart for the leap. Others had explained to me how to become a Christian and had awakened in me a burning desire to be a Christian; but it remained for her to make me feel that I could be a Christian and to lead me to determine that I would be one. No, I cannot explain how she did it. I only know that she did it. It could hardly have been what she said or the way she said it. In truth she said but little, nor said that little well. She was not fluent of speech. Her vocabulary was meagre, her diction faulty, her grammar defective, her information limited. She was not even a good reader. In truth she read nothing but the Bible and religious books and papers, and it was with difficulty she spelled out the harder words in them. Her appearance was by no means prepossessing. Her dress was plain calico, made by her own hands and evidently cut with an eye to comfort and economy rather than gaudy display. She wore no jewelry, assumed no society airs, courted no homage. She always seemed prayerful, occasionally heart-burdened, rarely despondent and never frivolous. She talked constantly of the things pertaining to the kingdom of God and the name of Jesus Christ and never gossiped. Such was the sister Halbrook, who, as the handmaiden of the Lord, during that memorable meeting, gently led my weary soul into the joys of discipleship. She and her husband came to my father's house on horseback, and when they departed, they went on their way by the same conveyance over the hills to other appointments. Her mission with me did not end there. She assisted others in encouraging me to preach the gospel, and helped to keep alive in me that love of souls which made me feel, with Paul, "woe is me if I preach not the gospel," even to the time of her departure. She encouraged me to go to Mars Hill College, where her husband had prepared himself for the noble work in which they were engaged, and exhorted me often by letters during the weary years of anxious toil since those blessed days, to continue in the good work. The last time I met her was during a meeting near her humble home at New River, Alabama in the summer of 1889. I was then on a preaching tour, though sorely afflicted with disease. It was with much difficulty and in great suffering that I could stand on my feet long enough to preach a sermon, and all the time, when not in the pulpit, I was suffering intense pain and confined to my bed. My preaching must have been unusually poor, for it is never very brilliant even under favorable circumstances. But I shall never forget her enthusiasm during the meeting. Her ever ready and abundant sympathy brought tears freely from her eyes and gave a motherly tremor to her voice as she would say: "Thank the Lord, Bro. Srygley, for your afflictions. You never could have preached such a sermon as that or moved such hardened sinners as came forward to-day, if you had not been under the chastening hand of God." That was her way. She thanked the Lord for everything. She could see something good in everything. Once when her husband was riding over the hills on horseback to his appointments, his horse fell at an ugly place in the road, and one of Bro. Halbrook's legs was broken. A messenger was sent with the sad news to the faithful wife at home. Her first words, when the news was imparted, were: "Thank the Lord forever for his goodness. I am so glad it was not his neck instead of his leg that was broken." She had no appreciation at all of the ludicrous, and whatever of humor may seem to appear in such an expression was entirely lost to her. In truth, the ridiculousness of many of her sayings, as they appeared to others, consisted largely in the intense earnestness and reverent piety in which she habitually spoke.

When I was at New River in 1889, her husband was absent on a preaching tour as usual. She was staying at home alone, save the presence of her little niece, an orphan eight years of age whom they were bringing up, for they had no children of their own. She did her own cooking, washing and house work and worked her garden besides. A lonely time she had of it, to be sure, but she was full of joy at the thought that Joseph was winning souls to Christ. I shall not forget her hallowed influence, nor cease to thank the Lord that ever it was my good fortune to be a co-worker with her in the best of all causes, and if I but finish my course and keep the faith, not the least of my joys at the time of my departure will be the confident hope of meeting her in heaven. F. D. Srygley.[364]

This is a snapshot of the meeting at Rock Creek and the influence, behind the scenes, of a very devout woman and her love for lost souls, and how she encouraged young people. That was Margaret Holbrook, not only at this meeting, but the way her life was structured and lived.

J. H. Holbrook returned two years later and held another meeting for the church at Rock Creek. He wrote:

J. H. Holbrook writes from New River, Ala.: "I am again able to travel on horseback. I have just returned from Rock Creek, Colbert Co. Ala. At the meeting 8 were added besides 2 who took membership ....[365]

It would be two more years before we have another report in the *Gospel Advocate* on the Rock Creek work. That came in the form of a report about an area-wide Sunday School Convention at Rock Creek, and it was written by W. D. H. Harris of Mountain Mills, Alabama. It reads as follows:

> W. D. H. (Harris) writes from Mountain Mills, Ala.: The Christians and Methodist held their second Sunday-school Convention together at Rock Creek church Colbert county, Ala., Saturday August 2nd, 1879. The heavy fall of rain and the absence of T. B. Larimore greatly interfered with the programme of the day—causing some confusion and disappointment though the exercises were interesting the vocal music and F. W. Srygley examining the Bible class was the nicest thing I ever witnessed. There was supposed to be one thousand people on the grounds. Bro. J. W. Hudspeth then delivered six discourses closed with one addition, James Canady who forsook father, mother brother, and sister for the name of Christ. The people were highly pleased with Bro. Hudspeth's preaching.[366]

As one reads this report, he will notice that the Methodists met with our brethren for this convention. This was not an uncommon practice in those days. The denominations became more polarized against our brethren as the years passed. In this report, F. W. Srygley, a brother of F. D. and F. B. Srygley, taught the classes. J. W. Hudspeth, a Mars Hill student, did the preaching.

August 1880, F. D. Srygley conducted a meeting at Rock Creek with sixteen additions.[367] T. B. Larimore came and held a meeting that began July 23, 1881, in which he preached five sermons. W. D. Harris wrote of this meeting and its results:

> Bro. T. B. Larimore commenced a meeting here on Saturday night last; delivered five discourses. The immediate result was seven accessions, while several others were almost persuaded. Some believed that if the meeting could have continued a week, there would have been fifty additions. I never saw the Prospects better. But Bro. Larimore, having other engage-

ments, was compelled to leave. The church was organized here a few years ago with seven members. There was sixty-eight extended the hand of fellowship on Sunday; there was several outdoors we did not count; do not know whether the Lord will count them or not.[368]

The brethren at Rock Creek loved Larimore dearly and always received him with open arms. With the results that Larimore always seemed to get, one can understand the way they felt about him. The following year (1882), F. D. Srygley came and preached at Rock Creek. He wrote concerning this meeting:

> ... Preached three discourses at Rock Creek, my home congregation. One confession and baptism. I rejoice to see any one obey the Lord, more especially one with whom I have been associated since childhood... F. B. Srygley, Rock Creek Ala. [369]

He returned in September and baptized nine precious souls.

It was during this meeting that Lucy Malone was baptized and also her husband James Malone.[370] This was based upon what is contained in her obituary. W. T. Sandlin of Cherokee wrote the following in her obituary:

> Sister Lucy Malone died at her home, near Lile Academy, Feb. 25, 1892. She leaves a husband and seven children to mourn her exit, but their loss will be her gain. She left a young babe. Two of her children had gone before. She was thirty-five years old. Had been in the church about ten years. Came in while Bro. F. D. Srygley was holding a meeting at Rock Creek.[371]

Both Srygley brothers often came back to Rock Creek and held meetings for their old home church. They would continue this practice as long as they lived.

In June 17, 1883, T. E. Tatum came and preached at Rock Creek. He was paid $2.00 for holding a short meeting.[372] Tatum mentioned this visit also in the *Gospel Advocate*.[373]

In 1884 J. H. Holbrook[374] was hired to be their evangelist for that year. Apparently, his pay for the year, based on what is found in the records, was $120.00. He received $10.00 each time he was paid, which was one time each month.[375] Holbrook was a graduate of Larimore's Mars Hill Bible College. He was originally from Lewis County, Tennessee. F. D. Srygley wrote of Holbrook in his *Larimore and His Boys*:

> J. H. Halbrook, of Lewis county, Tenn., was at Mars' Hill two years, and on leaving school he settled at New River, Ala., where he still resides. He was somewhat advanced in years and was married when he entered school. He has preached extensively through Fayette, Lamar, Tuscaloosa, Walker, Marion, Lawrence, Franklin and Colbert counties, Alabama, and has also made preaching tours to Tennessee, Mississippi, Missouri, Arkansas and Texas. Except the tours to Missouri, Arkansas and Texas, he has traveled almost exclusively on horseback and in buggy. He has held two debates, and many very successful protracted meetings. He has baptized hundreds of people and has been instrumental in establishing many good churches. As a preacher he is earnest, Scriptural, original, argumentative, and ready in wit and repartee. It has been no unusual thing for him to baptize over forty people during a meeting. His leg was broken in 1877 by his horse falling on it while on his way to an appointment. He is a good financier, and when preaching does not support him, he turns his attention to something else that will and preaches what he

can. He is neither a profound scholar nor a finished orator, but a man of fair education and general information and a clear and forcible speaker.[376]

Srygley wrote the above biographical sketch of Holbrook only five years after his year's labor at Rock Creek. This was the man who worked so often and for the entire year of 1884.

During that year, a large gospel meeting was held at Rock Creek. The preachers who participated in the meeting were J. H. Holbrook, F. D. Srygley, F. B. Srygley, and John Taylor. This possibly could have been the last meeting in which John Taylor ever participated. He died on February 19, 1885. This meeting resulted in 25 additions whose names were entered into the Record Book.[377]

In 1895, F. D. Srygley returned and held a protracted meeting. He reported on his second day in the meeting as having only one response at that time.[378] In September—J. P. Smelser, a member at Rock Creek, reported on the entire meeting:

> Our dearly beloved F. D. Srygley, of the Gospel Advocate, delivered twelve sermons at Rock Creek, Colbert County, Ala., beginning the second Sunday in July. He was kindly and heartily received by all, and his preaching was in great simplicity, love, and power. He had large audiences and good attention and interest from beginning to close. There were eight added to the congregation—seven by baptism and one reclaimed. He went from here to Mountain Mills, where he preached ten sermons, beginning the third Sunday in July. Seven were added to the Lord by baptism there, and the faithful few were encouraged and persuaded to re-establish the worship on the first day of the week after the manner of New Testament teaching and precedent. The Lord help us to

work in his vineyard while we live, for the night cometh, when no man can work. J.P. Smelser.[379]

Smelser's report does not match the church records. The Record Book shows ten received by baptism.[380] A note is necessary here: Four of the dates were supposed to have been 1895, but somehow, the transcriber mistook a "5" for a "6." Since the report by Smelser was nearly six weeks after the meeting ended, he could have had a lapse in memory. Whatever the reason, Smelser's report was different than the church's records.

The following year F. D. Srygley's brother came to Rock Creek and held a meeting. Someone at the *Gospel Advocate* reported that meeting. It read:

> Brother F. B. Srygley begins a meeting at Rock Creek, Ala., on the third Lord's day in July. This is the place where Brother Srygley was raised.[381]

Nearly a month later, Srygley reported on the meeting himself. The report was still positive concerning the Rock Creek work. It read:

> Nashville, Aug. 1. On July 24 I closed a six-day meeting at Rock Creek, Ala., the place where my childhood days were spent, with six baptized. The church seems to be in very good condition. It was a pleasant meeting to me. I saw so many of my friends and acquaintances of former days ... F. B. Srygley. [382]

After Srygley's meeting, it would be two more years before the *Gospel Advocate* mentioned Rock Creek again. R. N. Moody of Albertville, Alabama, came into Colbert and

Franklin Counties and held several meetings, one of which was Rock Creek. The portion that pertained to Rock Creek was a short and simple message as can be seen here: "in a meeting at Rock Creek, in Colbert County" ... R. N. Moody.[383] On the next page of the *Gospel Advocate*, Moody gave another report. We give the entire note:

> F. D. Srygley will begin meetings at Bear Creek, Marion County, Ala., the second Sunday in July; at Crooked Oak, near Frankfort, Franklin County, Ala., third Sunday in July; at Rock Creek, Colbert County, Ala., fourth Sunday in July. At all these points he will be with friends and relatives among whom he lived and to whom he preached twenty years ago. He hopes to meet many of his relatives and old-time friends from other places at each appointment. Albertville, Ala., R. N. Moody.[384]

Moody also admired the work of both the Srygley boys and their work in the Lord's vineyard. At this time of Moody's reporting, he was on a tour of the two-county area—Colbert and Franklin. W. A. Kimbrough sent the next report concerning Moody's work in the area. The report read:

> There were eight additions to the Mount Zion congregation in the six-days' meeting there. His next meeting—at Rock Creek Church, the old home of Brothers F. D. and F. B. Srygley, resulted in one addition. W. A. Kimbrough, Frankfort, Ala.[385]

We keep hearing about meetings; but sometimes we need to take a look at the people at Rock Creek and how they deal with problematic questions that may arise, especially religious questions, and how they are solved. Here is an excerpt from a correspondence between W. A. Henry and David Lipscomb about a question from Revelation 21:1–2. It reads as follows:

> W. A. Henry, for "the brethren" at Rock Creek, Ala., asks for an explanation of Rev. 21:1, 2. The language is: "And I saw a new heaven and a new earth: for the first heaven and the first earth were passed away; and there was no more sea. And I John saw the holy city, new Jerusalem, coming down from God out of heaven, prepared as a bride adorned for her husband." This is understood by many people to teach that the heaven in which the righteous will live forever, after the resurrection, will be here on this earth, after the earth is purified and renovated by fire, in which the sea and the earth, as they now exist, will pass away. That the new Jerusalem will come down from God out of heaven and abide here on earth after this earth is changed and renewed is understood to mean that righteous semis, who have been with God, shall come as a city with whatever paraphernalia God provides them, and make their everlasting habitation on the renovated earth. If this theory is correct, it is a satisfactory explanation of the passage. I have had, and still have, some doubt whether this is what the passage means; but I have never heard any other explanation of it that is more satisfactory to my mind.[386]

This reveals to us that some of the people at that place were deep readers of the scriptures and wanted to be able to teach others. The church ledger gave a line that backs this statement: "The members studied the Bible and generally had an excellent knowledge of it."[387] This pretty well sums up the dedication to God and His word by the folks at Rock Creek.

Down toward the end of the summer, a new preacher shows up at Rock Creek. By new I mean he was new to the whole Northwest area. As a preacher, he was little known, but as a Christian, he was known for his Christian life. His name was A. P. Holtsford. He was new in the sense of being a novice in the pulpit. He wrote about holding a meeting at Rock Creek:

> Florence, October 16. I began a meeting on the first Lord's day in October at Rock Creek, closing on the following Lord's day. There were five additions. [388]

W. Michael Oldfield came to Rock Creek in December 1902 to hold a gospel meeting. He gave a report on three different congregations for which he held meetings. The report was taken from the *Firm Foundation*:

> Nashville, Tenn. —In the last month I have held three meetings, one at Dobbs, Tenn., with two baptisms, one at South Pittsburg, Tenn., with two baptisms and one at Rock Creek Ala., with eleven baptisms. Some of the brethren at Rock Creek read the Firm Foundation. —W. Michael Oldfield. [389]

Oldfield would have been at Rock Creek in December 1902. For some reason, these baptisms were not recorded in the church book. There were other baptisms that were overlooked in the record book. Maybe this was an oversight. One thing we learned from this report is that the journal—the *Firm Foundation* was being read by some members at Rock Creek. It was published in Austin, Texas by its founder—Austin McGary. That journal soon became a rival journal, in a good way, to the *Gospel Advocate* for about twenty years, throughout North Alabama. This happened in part after a new school was established at Berry, Fayette County, Alabama in 1912. It was known as Alabama Christian College. It was staffed by many Texas brethren, who brought the *Firm Foundation* along with them to Berry. Oldfield apparently was exposed to the journal shortly before coming to Rock Creek.

W. M. Oldfield returned to Rock Creek for another meeting July 1904. The report on this meeting was written by A. H. Taylor, of Rock Creek, Ala. He wrote:

> Brother W. M. Oldfield will begin a meeting at Rock Creek on the fourth Lord's day in July; he will begin a meeting at Pleasant Site on the fifth Lord's day in July.[390]

Oldfield baptized nine persons during that meeting, although it was not reported through the *Gospel Advocate*. It was, however, recorded in the Rock Creek Church Book.[391]

Brother E. C. L. Denton announced in the *Gospel Advocate* his intentions to come and hold a meeting at Rock Creek. He came and held the meeting in 1907, beginning on Sunday, July 28, 1907.[42] The Rock Creek Church Book recorded three baptisms as a result of the meeting. After the meeting he reported the results in the *Gospel Advocate*:

> Finger, Tennessee, October 12. Brother E. C. L. Denton has not been idle this year but has been very busy in the Master's cause ... Brother Denton held a meeting at Rock Creek, Ala. (Brother Srygley's old home) embracing the fourth Sunday in July, with six additions ....[393]

Only three baptisms were recorded during that meeting in the church record book.[394] We have found several discrepancies in the record book—many due to the recorders. Mistakes are made by men. These discrepancies between what is reported in the *Gospel Advocate* and the Rock Creek records could be because some of the people baptized during the meetings may be from other communities and their membership would be recorded at those congregations.

The next year in August I. B. Bradley came to Rock Creek and held a meeting. He gave a short statement on the results:

> ... I closed a fine meeting at Rock Creek last week, with eleven additions by primary obedience. Four of these were Missionary Baptists ... I. B. Bradley.[395]

For some reason, the years from 1908 to 1910 were not recorded in the records at Rock Creek. Perhaps these pages were lost through time. The *Gospel Advocate* is our only record of Bradley's meeting in 1908. It was two years later before any news about the church at Rock Creek was found and due to apparently lost pages in the record book these two years are silent to history.

William Behel (affectionately known as "Uncle Will") came to Rock Creek and preached in a meeting. He gave a good report on Belgreen, Frankfort, and Rock Creek, but mostly on Rock Creek. The report follows:

> St. Joseph, August 25. My meeting at Belgreen, Ala., closed with one baptism and one from the Baptists. From Belgreen I went to Frankfort, Ala., for eight days, and closed with five baptisms. On Saturday I went to Rock Creek, Ala., at the request of the elders of the Rock Creek church and preached two sermons, which resulted in five baptisms. So, the two weeks I spent in Alabama resulted in twelve additions—eleven baptized and one from the Baptists. I found much zeal among the majority of the brethren in those mountains, which demonstrates that churches can do a great deal, though they have been able to have preaching through only one protracted

meeting a year. But this is not their fault they have not been able to get a preacher. However, I have agreed to spend part of my time preaching there next year. William Behel.[396]

Behel's intentions were to work more in the Colbert-Franklin Counties area the next year. Until his death in 1939, he worked in this area often.

F. B. Srygley announced his intentions to hold a meeting at Rock Creek in July 1911.[397] He gave a very good description of what transpired during this meeting:

> ... I am now at Rock Creek, Ala., in an old-time, all-day meeting, with "dinner on the ground." It began last Sunday. There has only been one confession to date. This is my birthplace. Here I spent the first twenty years of my life, and here some thirty-seven years ago, at less than fifteen years of age, I made the good confession and was baptized into Christ by the late Joe Halbrooks (Holbrook). In the old graveyard near this church my grandfather and grandmother were buried. Most of the old people I knew here thirty years ago lie buried in the old churchyard. I am living in the past. I have been back to the old home and have drunk water out of the old well—the same old well I helped to water the soldiers from in 1865. The logs that are still in the old house were hewn by my father. Everything around here reminds me of the olden days, the happy days of my childhood and youth. May the God of our fathers be merciful to the children who constitute the men and women of the present day. F. B. Srygley. [398]

Srygley followed with another report seven days later:

> Brother F. B. Srygley's meeting at Rock Creek, Colbert

County, Ala., closed with seven baptized and one restored. He is now in a meeting at Flatwoods, Tenn.[399]

A Franklin County man—John T. Underwood, who lived at Spruce Pine, was a "rising star" throughout this region and was becoming a popular meeting preacher. He came to Rock Creek and held a meeting. The results were eight baptized.[400] He further reported in October concerning the same meeting:

> ... Brother John T. Underwood's experiences as detailed in the following report, sent under date of September 16: "I began a meeting at old Rock Creek, the Srygleys' old home, on the first Lord's day in August and closed it on the second Lord's day, with ten added to the one body and the church much edified ...."[401]

These numbers were also confirmed in the record book at Rock Creek.[402]

John T. Underwood, Spruce Pine, Ala., 5 additions; Tippecanoe, Miss., 3 additions; Beech Grove, Ala., 6 additions; Rock Creek, Ala., 8 additions.

William returned in the Fall of 1914 and held a week-long meeting with ten baptisms.[403] With Behel's report, this brings us to the end of our time allotted for this study of the congregation at Rock Creek. We do feel compelled, however, to close this study with a concise statement about the Srygley family, who were responsible for the Rock Creek Church's existence:

> Rock Creek was located in the rough mountain region of North Alabama. F. D. Srygley grew up in Rock Creek receiving the little education that such harsh frontier communities offered. F. D. had four brothers whose names were initials—F. W., F. B., F. G., and F. L. There were of course

curious questions raised. To the inquisitive, F. D. Srygley wrote in 1880 — "Those who are curious to know why all of our names commence with an "F" may write to our dear mother who lives at Rock Creek, Alabama enclosing stamp to pay return postage." There is no record that anyone wrote. J. E. Choate.[404]

There are so many other things that could be said about the Srygleys and the many other families—all who contributed to the success of that congregation lost to time. Our time does not permit it.

Mountain Mills—Barton Work

IN 1872 A GROUP of men organized the Mountain Mill Company. Their purpose was to build a cotton mill to make thread from cotton and maybe cloth and other items.[405]

In 1890 a local resident, J. B. Brendle, and a member of the Mountain Mills Church of Christ, gave a very good description of the village of Mountain Mills. His description was as follows:

> Mountain Mills is a little factory town in Colbert county, Ala., of about three hundred inhabitants. The houses etc., belong exclusively to the manufacturing company. Through their generosity, the people are furnished with a comfortable schoolhouse and a nice church-house, free to all. There are in this place and vicinity, about thirty-five disciples, who hold service here one Lord's day in each month, the second. Others generally occupying it the other Lord's days and sometimes the extra hours in the disciple's day. Bro. L. R. Sewell is now with us and began preaching Saturday night last., April 15, '90. J. B. Brendle.[406]

Brendle mentioned that L. R. Sewell was in a meeting at that place. Sewell had become a popular preacher in Northwest Alabama. He would return to this section and hold many gospel meetings.

The earliest report on the work, however, came from a "Larimore Boy"—J. C. McQuiddy. He reported that he had "three accessions, one over three score and ten."[407] He reported his intentions to hold another meeting in 1880.[408] The beginning of the demise of the village of Mountain Mills was brought on by what happened in 1883. That year the German National Bank foreclosed on the Mountain Mill Company. On April 7, 1883, W. N. Cherry bought out the owners of the Mountain Mills Company. The operation continued for about ten years at Mountain Mills. In 1892, it was decided to move the mill to Florence, Alabama. It would be four more years before the *Gospel Advocate* reported on any work at Mountain Mills. That report came from the pen of another "Larimore Boy"—T. E. Tatum. He was also a student at Mars Hill College. His report was more detailed than McQuiddy's report had been. He wrote:

> By request of one who is dear to me, I will give a report of my labors since Christmas. I have attended a flourishing school at this place, which has been a source of great pleasure to me. This school is worthy the patronage of all who desire to prepare for usefulness here, and happiness beyond. I have preached some since school closed, June 6, and occasionally before, at Bethabara, Stony Point, Bethel, Barton Station, on M. &. C. R. R., Mountain Mills, and Rock Creek, which has resulted in twelve additions. Others where I have been are almost persuaded to obey the Lord. I hope, they will soon be entirely persuaded. I meet sisters and brothers at the above-named places who are earnestly zealous and devoted. May

God bless them.— T. E. Tatum, Mars Hill, Ala, July 11, 1883.[409]

In this report Tatum mentions Barton Station which was a Railroad stop on the Memphis and Charleston Railroad. This little train stop would become the final location of the congregation that had begun at Mountain Mills, which was approximately five miles southwest of Barton.

The congregation at Mountain Mills was quite active in the early years and had several gospel meetings that were never reported, due to the lack of efforts of the preachers who came and preached. It was five years before John T. Underwood came and held a meeting and reported it. He reported that he was holding a meeting at Mountain Mills. He gave the following description:

> Held a meeting at Mountain Mills, with Bro. Irwin commencing Saturday night before the second Lord's day in September and closed Saturday night, preaching only at night. Result: Four noble young ladies made the good confession and were baptized.[410]

Underwood would return several more times and hold meetings for the church at that place. Some other preachers that preached at Mountain Mill were E. C. Fuqua and J. D. Tant.

Our next report on the Mountain Mills work came in the form of an obituary. J. B. Hamilton was a member at Mountain Mills. He died, January 23, 1891, near Barton, Ala. His obituary is filled with so many historical facts relating to his area we are compelled to give it in its entirety:

Died, Jan. 23, 1891, near Barton, Ala., Bro. J. B. Hamilton after many weeks of intense suffering. He was born near Russellville, Ala., Feb 21, 1829; was married in 1854 to Elizabeth, daughter of Gillington Chisholm, who was among the first in the reformation and who was a contemporary laborer with Bro. John Taylor years before the war. Much of the good seed sown about that time was harvested under the preaching of Bro. J. M. Pickens, after the war, at Frankfort, Ala., where over one hundred persons submitted to Christ during a two weeks' protracted meeting. In 1855 Bro. H. was baptized by Bro. John Taylor and lived a consistent member, meeting regularly with the disciples at Frankfort, until their dispersion caused by the war. Like many others he strayed from the fold but returned a few years before his death lamenting the lost years. He died exhorting and admonishing his children to live faithful to the end. The disciples with whom he worshipped last, together with his own family, now hold their Lord's day meetings at Mountain Mills. They laid him beside his dutiful Christian daughter who has gone before. My sympathies are with the bereaved family. Lebanon, Tenn. Mrs. N. Fuqua. [411]

From this obituary we learn that Hamilton was associated with the earliest pioneers in our movement in the Franklin-Colbert Counties. He was baptized by John Taylor. He was married to Elizabeth Chisholm, daughter of Gillington Chisholm and sister to L. C. Chisholm. This also shows that there was a connection to E. C. Fuqua and family. Remember we have already learned that E. C. Fuqua was one of the preachers who had preached at Mountain Mills. This obituary could be a key document to several people researching our Restoration History.

Following the obituary of J. B. Hamilton, we find a report of

Mountain Mills—Barton Work

one of "Larimore's Boys"— Eddie Blalock moving to Mountain Mills and teaching. This report gives the details:

> "Eddie" (Eddie Blaylock) graduated at the Florence State Normal College after Mars' Hill College suspended. He was one of the small boys then. He is now teaching successfully at Mountain Mills and making himself useful in the vineyard of the Lord as well. May the Lord bless him.[412]

Larimore came and held a meeting at Mountain Mills in 1892. It was reported by J. P. Brendle, a member at Mountain Mills. It was short and to the point. It reads as follows:

> T. B. Larimore began a meeting here the twenty-third of July at night and closed to-day. Preached seven discourses and read one from the Book on baptism. They had two additions: one a little boy of ten summers, the other a lady from the Episcopalians. J. P. Brendle, Mountain Mills, July 26. [413]

Our next reporter on the Mountain Mills' work was J. P. Smelser of Rock Creek. He reported that F. D. Srygley had preached at Rock Creek and then went to Mountain Mills and held a meeting. The results were as follows:

> He went from here to Mountain Mills, where he preached ten sermons, beginning the third Sunday in July. Seven were added to the Lord by baptism there, and the faithful few were encouraged and persuaded to re-establish the worship on the first day of the week after the manner of New Testament teaching and precedent. The Lord help us to work in his vineyard while we live, for the night cometh, when no man can work. J. P. Smelser.[414]

Srygley returned in 1896 and held another meeting at Mountain Mills. He first preached at Rock Creek, his old homeplace and then went to Mountain Mills and held a meeting of four days. His report on Mountain Mills follows:

> Nashville, Aug. 1: On July 24 I closed a six-day meeting at Rock Creek, Ala., the place where my childhood days were spent, with six baptized. The church seems to be in very good condition. It was a pleasant meeting to me. I saw so many of my friends and acquaintances of former days. I closed a four-day meeting last Wednesday night at Mountain Mills, Ala., with nine baptized. I think that they stopped meeting regularly there lately but hope now they will begin it again. F. B. Srygley.[415]

Possibly the reason the brethren were not meeting was that the "Candlestick" was being slowly removed to Barton. Our last bona fide report on any work at Mountain Mills came from the pen of W. A. Kimbrough. It simply read:

> We had eleven additions in the six days. From here (Rock Creek) he went to old Mount Mills Factory, near Barton Station, on the Memphis and Charleston Railroad. There are a few brethren there, and they have not been meeting on the first day of the week to worship God. I preached for them: five times monthly last year, their only meeting to break bread the day of preaching, which was the first Lord's day in each month. Here he immersed one. W. A. Kimbrough. Frankfort, Ala.[416]

By 1902, the transition had been made, and the Mountain Mills congregation was no more. Mountain Mills had relocated to the village of Barton, Colbert County. S. P. Copeland was holding a meeting at the newly organized congregation in Barton. The following is the first notice of the change of location in the *Gospel Advocate*:

> Our infant daughter, Etta Hester Copeland, was born on April 27. 1901, and died on August 21, 1902; being one year, three months, and twenty-four days old. When this child became ill, its father was at Barton, Ala., conducting a protracted meeting; and when the news reached him, he hastened home.[417]

Copeland received the news that his infant daughter had become ill. He cancelled the rest of his meeting at Barton and went home to be with his wife and sick child.

Van A. Bradley came in 1908 and conducted a meeting at Barton. He gave a lengthy report on this meeting:

> Dickson, October 14. Our meeting at Barton, Ala., began on the third Lord's day in September and continued nine days. The Methodist people invited us to use their new meetinghouse. Of course, we gladly agreed to go to their house for our meeting, since we had no house of our own. However, their "pastor" saw proper to change their plans, and the door was locked after some of the crowd had gathered for the first service. We then went to the schoolhouse and began at once. The house was well filled each night for more than a week. Interest increased from the beginning, and we trust that much good was accomplished. There were five baptisms during the meeting. At the conclusion of an effort I had made on the name "Christian" a Baptist came forward and expressed his desire to wear that name only. The Methodist people were so excited that their leader in the town walked the streets of the town with his little creed during the hour for

service in order that he might keep his brethren from the place of worship. I am to help them in a meeting again next year. Van A. Bradley.[418]

One may notice that there was no building mentioned at Barton; instead, a place to hold the meeting had to be borrowed. Bradley returned the next year in September and conducted his second meeting at Barton. On this second trip to Barton, Bradley had to use the schoolhouse. The report read:

> Cherokee, September 11. I recently closed a good meeting at Barton. The meeting was held in a very small schoolhouse, it being the only house available in town. We had very good crowds each day and a crowded house every night. The meeting continued nine days and resulted in eleven baptisms. One young lady united with us who had been baptized by a Methodist preacher simply to obey the Lord. This was my second meeting there. I am to help them in another meeting in July of next year. I am now in a meeting near this place. I am to begin a meeting on the third Lord's day in this month near Guntersville, where, as far as I can learn, we have only one sister. Van A. Bradley.[419]

Bradley returned in July of the next year for his third meeting at Barton. The church must have had their own building by this visit because nothing was said about borrowing a meeting place. Bradley wrote the following:

> Barton, July 20. — ... I am in a week's meeting with a few brethren at this place now. The meeting is three days old and we have had two baptisms. The house is crowded each night. The people are good hearers, and we are hoping for greater things. Van A. Bradley.[420]

Bradley had high expectations for his third meeting. He had a crowded house and the audiences were attentive. Everything was looking up for the future. In October of that year P. G. Wright came and held a meeting. It was published as follows:

> Brother P. G. Wright is in a meeting at Refuge, Tenn. He recently closed a meeting at Barton, Ala., with three baptized. [421]

The next report exceeds our time limit of 1914 by one year, but this is the most insightful report that we have for the next six years. It dealt with an inquiry concerning the use of proper song books. Obviously, someone in the congregation sent this report, perhaps just a concerned member. The report reads:

> Brother McQuiddy: We, a small band of members of the church of Christ, have been meeting at Barton, Ala., for a long time—fifteen years, I suppose. We have a neat, little house of worship. We have always used Christian hymn books—"Christian Hymns" and "Gospel Praise." Recently we bought two dozen of Brother Flavil Hall's new book, "Jesus in Song." If the hymns in the Baptist song book are scriptural and teach the truth, then it is not wrong to sing them; if they are unscriptural, then they should not be sung. It is wrong to sing error. We should have a scriptural hymnology and sing the truth, as well as preach the truth. When disciples meet and break bread on the first day of the week as did the early church, a Baptist song leader who believes in close communion cannot very consistently take a leading part in the worship. The elders of the church should not leave the selection of hymn books to a few young members, but, considering the needs of the flock, they them-

selves should see that scriptural hymn books are provided.
[422]

With this report, we close our discussion on the Mountain Mills—Barton work. The church at that place had good times and some bad times. It would be during one of these bad that the congregation at Barton closed their door and sold their building.

Christian Chapel—Maud

MAUD IS in the westernmost part of Colbert County, Alabama. It is located 11 miles southwest of Cherokee. It is located near the point that the Natchez Trace crosses the Mississippi state line. The Church of Christ had an unusual beginning at this place. It began with a neighbor trying to get another neighbor to read the *Gospel Advocate*. The Burns families lived in this community and owned much land. A man by the name of Bun Wallace was a reader of the *Gospel Advocate*. He lived as a sharecropper on the Burns's land. Wallace's nearest neighbor was Gus Burns, who was a Methodist. Wallace kept trying to get Gus to look at the *Gospel Advocate*, but Burns refused. So one day, Wallace threw a copy of the *Gospel Advocate* over the fence onto Gus's field. Gus finally read it and became interested in what the *Gospel Advocate* taught. Finally, Wallace invited W. H. Sandy to come to Maud and hold a meeting in 1907. When Sandy arrived there the denominations refused him the use of their buildings, which was very uncustomary in those days. He secured the schoolhouse for the first night, but the second night the schoolhouse was locked. Sandy was not to be stopped. He preached in front of the schoolhouse. The next day some men moved to the bottom of the hill and built a brush arbor. Sandy preached for several days. He baptized several, including Gus Burns, his wife Cassandra, and several others. The land on which the "brush arbor" was built was later donated by Doctor Finley—the community doctor. It was on this lot that the first building was constructed.[423]

In (Gus) Agustus H. Burns's obituary, his nephew, C. C. Burns wrote:

> Augustus H. Burns was born September 23, 1852; died June 28, 1934, being eighty-two years old. For a great number of years, he was loyal to the cause of Christ, and, with the aid of his brethren, established the congregation at Maud, Ala., of which he was a faithful member at his death. C. C. Burns, Florence, Ala.[424]

Gus Burns was involved in helping establish the congregation at Maud. With Sandy's help, the seed was tilled through the Burns and Wallace families. Sandy tells his own story concerning how the work began at Maud. It was published in the *Firm Foundation*:

> Brother W. H. Sandy writes from Maud, Ala., on my way to Scooba, Miss., I preached four discourses at Christian Chapel (Maud. Ala.), and baptized two. Two years ago, I did the first preaching here that was ever done by a Christian preacher in this section. It was done under the largest tent in the world (canopy of heaven), but where I stood on terre firma, now stands a splendid house of worship. I have held two meetings here and baptized some of the best citizens of the community. They now number twenty-five, as good loyal Christians as

Christian Chapel—Maud

can be found. Brother Peden will begin a meeting for them the 5th day of September.[425]

After Peden's meeting, the next meeting was held in 1910 by P. G. Wright of Corinth, Mississippi. It was reported in the *Gospel Advocate*. It read:

> Brother P. G. Wright, of Corinth, Miss., recently closed a meeting at Christian Chapel, Maud, Ala., with four baptized. [426]

In 1911, Wright returned for a second meeting. He reported the meeting while it was still in progress. Wright wrote on September 15 the following statement:

> I am now in a meeting at Christian Chapel, near Maud, Ala, We have had fine interest and two additions to date.[427]

From Wright's statement, we learn the exact date when he was at Maud. While Wright was at Maud, a preacher "in the making" was living there. He was G. T. Kay, who was also the school teacher at that place. Kay held a meeting at Maud in July of the following year. He wrote the editors of the *Gospel Advocate*, congratulating them on their work with the paper. It was published as follows:

> From Brother G. T. Kay, of Maud, Ala.: "I have noted with pleasure the improved features of the Gospel Advocate, especially the 'Cheerful Messages' and 'Serious and Timely Questions.' May you live long and prosper in the Lord! I am just beginning to contend for 'the faith once delivered unto the saints.' I am preaching to good congregations every Lord's day."[428]

Kay informs the readers of the *Gospel Advocate* that he was a novice in the preaching field. He proved to be an asset at Maud as a teacher and preacher. At the end of 1912, Kay took a temporary position as president of the Emmerson Bible School and Orphans' Home in Holland, Georgia.[429] In 1913, Kay was seeking to locate in some community where he could teach and preach. The *Gospel Advocate* gave this report:

> Brother G. T. Kay, of Maud, Ala., wishes to locate in some community to teach school during the week and preach on Lord's days.[430]

The next report comes two years after our 1914 boundary date. It gave such a detailed description of the congregation that we must allow it at this place:

> Brother Frank Baker writes from Belmont, Mississippi, date of March 15: We were with the faithful in Christ at Christian Chapel, Alabama, the second Lord's Day in March. They are a noble band of humble Christians and know how to treat a poor preacher royally, but no wonder for they have had that noble man of God—Brother J. T. Harris of Florence, Alabama has been preaching for them for some years.[431]

This information is valuable because it reveals characteristics that were present all the time, but no one had ever pointed them out. This writer has preached there many times through many years and can testify that those qualities are still imbedded there at Maud. Marvin Hastings wrote of the continued prejudice from the opposing religious group in Maud:

> The prejudice of the Maud community was great. The Methodist church finally died out, but the Presbyterian church still exists there and in Allsboro nearby. Families of those converted who remained denominationalists continue to show deep bias. The Burns families and members of other families who became Christians have experienced hurt. Their children in school were sometimes shunned and intolerance has marred relationships. While probably not as intense as earlier, there is still much prejudice and shunning evident on the part of many of the denominational people even today (1980). But, in spite of this, the church has grown. While there was a period when discouragement seemed to stifle growth, the congregation seems to have taken on new life in recent years. I was invited to hold a meeting in the summer of 1960, which I accepted. Improvements have been made on their building through the years, most recently classrooms have been added and the exterior bricked. The congregation employs a full-time preacher at this time.[432]

Hastings further wrote concerning his connection to the church at Maud:

> Mamie Hearn also lived in this same community. As a member of a strong Presbyterian family, she studied herself out of the Presbyterian church, having also come in contact with a copy of the Gospel Advocate. She married Thomas Burns, another of the brothers, and after moving from Mingo to Midway, south of Iuka, Mississippi (in the northeast corner of the state, adjoining Colbert County, Alabama), and attended the church services there (Maud). Thomas later obeyed the Gospel. One of their daughters, Susie, became my wife.[433]

The congregation retained the name "Christian Chapel" as late as 1932.[434] Just when the congregation completely dropped that name and began using "Maud," no one seemed to know. Even though Maud is deep into the hills and forests of western Colbert County—it is like a bright, shining star to the area south and west of Cherokee, Alabama. This is the conclusion of our study of the church at Maud.

Lyle Academy

We learn of the Lyle Academy congregation first through the pages of the *Gospel Advocate* in July 1890. The school house—meeting house was located about four miles west of Cherokee. One of its members, W. T. Sandlin, sent a very descriptive report. We give his report in full:

> Lile (Lyle) Academy is a neat frame house, painted white, with sufficient doors and windows, also belfry, with a good bell. About two miles south is the M & C. R. R. About the same distance north is the beautiful Tennessee river, on the west nearby is a nice stream of pure clear water. Along this beautiful valley are some fine lands, which are owned by a few. The people who cultivate this soil are poor, as far as this world is concerned, but some are rich in faith. About three-fourths of the soil in cultivation this year is cotton. About fifteen or twenty members meet every Lord's day to break the loaf. Bro. G.O.C. Srygley is superintendent, the writer assistant, and Bro. Oric teacher. Class meets at 3 p.m., to sing. We have as good vocal class as can be found in the country.

Bro. Underwood preaches for us first Lord's day in each month. Bro. Billingsley, of Mississippi, will begin a meeting here the first Lord's day in August. We have some very zealous members at this place, but there is a chance for much good to be done in the near future. The harvest truly is great, the laborers few. I see a card from my good sister and aunt of Coal Hill, Ark. Hope she will write again. We highly appreciate her sentiments. Glad the boys in Arkansas are so good and benevolent. Also Bro. Halbrook has been putting in some very interesting letters. I love to read them; write again Bro. Joe. W. T. Sandlin, Cherokee, June 17, 1890.[435]

It is obvious that the congregation had been meeting for some time due to Sandlin's letter. Just when the congregation was established, we do not know. From the estimated number given by Sandlin the congregation had been meeting for several months and maybe a few years. He mentioned that Bro. Billingsley, of Marietta, Mississippi, would begin a meeting there the first Lord's Day in August. That was J. B. Billingsley. Billingsley came but he was ill. He had called off his part of the meeting after Sunday and Monday mornings, and he returned to Mississippi. John T. Underwood gave the report on this meeting:

> I met Bro. J. B. Billingsley at the Billingsley schoolhouse in Tishomingo county, the first Lord's day in this month to assist him in a meeting. He left his wife sick and not well himself, prospects gloomy for a good meeting. So, he preached on Lord's day and I at night; he on Monday, I on Monday night again. I think he got somewhat discouraged, begged off Tuesday and went home for me to close out that night if no additions. (I) Had one addition that night which caused me to continue. Continued until Friday, resulting in seventeen

additions, having ten additions the last night of our meeting, which shows the meeting closed too soon. Barton, Sept. 16, '90. John T. Underwood.[436]

L. R. Sewell came to North Alabama and spent a month preaching in gospel meetings. The *Gospel Advocate* reported that Sewell would visit "Lyle Academy, Landersville, Moulton and other points in that region enroute to Northport."[437]

Sewell returned the next year and held another meeting at Lyle Academy. W. T. Sandlin wrote:

> Bro. L. R. Sewell preached for us last Lord's day and night to a large and attentive audience. Subject at 11 o'clock was "The travel of the children of Israel from Egyptian bondage, across the Red Sea into the wilderness." He made the analysis very clear. Subject at night was "Reconciliation." His argument was so clear that all could see no chance for union among those professing to be the children of God unless they be reconciled to his will. Bro. Sewell is doing some good work in North Ala. May the God of heaven spare him to do the great work so much needed in this field. The church at Lyle Academy meets every Lord's day to sing, pray and admonish each other; have been meeting one night in the week for prayer, think we have as good vocal class as can be found in the county. Have no regular preacher this year but would be pleased for any of our brethren to give us a call. Our whole desire is to learn our duty more perfectly. I would like to hear more from our dear brother J. H. Halbrook in Florida. Cherokee, March 7, '91. W. T. Sandlin.[438]

Sandlin must have had a special bond with J. H. Holbrook. He mentions him in his letters and never mentions other preachers of the past. Sandlin's mentioning of J. H. Holbrook in his letters is an indication that through the previous years, Holbrook must have preached many appointments at Lyle Academy. Could it have been that Holbrook may have helped establish the church?

Sandlin's letters were always very informative. He gave many facts that paint a picture of the congregation at that place. He had mentioned in his first letter that he was assistant superintendent of the Sunday School; thus, he seemed to be filling the position of secretary for the congregation. He had the unfortunate task of writing Lucy Malone's obituary for the *Gospel Advocate*. He wrote the following:

> Sister Lucy Malone died at her home, near Lile (Lyle) Academy, Feb. 25, 1892. She leaves a husband and seven children to mourn her exit, but their loss will be her gain. She left a young babe. Two of her children had gone before. She was thirty-five years old. Had been in the church about ten years. Came in while Bro. F. D. Srygley was holding a meeting at Rock Creek. She lived a devoted member always found on duty at Lord's day meeting; was cheerful and pleasant; did not murmur nor complain over the troubles of this life but bore it all with Christian patience. May her husband and oldest daughter be faithful unto death and the other motherless little ones come into the fold so soon as they realize they are sinners. Dear children, be cheerful and lead godly lives so you can meet mamma in the sweet by and by, for she can never come back to you, but you can go to her. W. T. Sandlin. [439]

She was a devoted member at Lyle Academy.

Our next report comes from Van A. Bradley in 1909. He informed the readers of the *Gospel Advocate* that he was going to preach at a congregation near Cherokee. This implies that he was going to preach at Lyle Academy, as that was the only congregation near Cherokee. His statement was: "August 30, ... Next week I shall be with a few brethren near Cherokee, Ala."[440]

Our next and final reports in the *Gospel Advocate* come in the 1930s and are all reported by J. H. Morris of Tuscumbia. We include them because they contain important information on the last years of Lyle Academy. In his first report, he wrote:

> May 9: "I preached at Lyle Academy, about four miles from Cherokee. Ala., last Lord's day at 3 P.M. There are a few brethren scattered around there who are not meeting, but who have expressed the desire to have monthly preaching and to begin meeting regularly upon the first day of the week. I will preach for them again the first Lord's day in June at 3 P.M., the Lord willing. This is purely mission work, and I am trusting the Lord for results."[441]

Notice he said: "There are a few brethren scattered around there who are not meeting." What had happened to the larger devoted congregation that had formerly met at that place?

In his second letter, he reveals more on the conditions at Lyle Academy:

> J. H. Morris, Tuscumbia, Ala., June 5: "I was at Lyle Academy, near Cherokee, Ala., last Lord's day afternoon, and will be with them again for two services on the first Lord's day in July. I understand that we had a congregation there a good many years ago and that several of our pioneer preachers preached there. It is purely mission work now, there being only a schoolhouse, used by any and all kinds of religious organizations, I understand, except Mormons and Catholics."[442]

Other religious groups were now strong enough to be rivals of the congregation that had formerly met there, and they all vied for the meeting place. Morris referred to Lyle Academy as a mission point. What had been a shining light before the Cherokee congregation came into existence was now growing very dim. Morris continued to preach there through 1932 and then the congregation went dark in the pages of the *Gospel Advocate*. Many families who had been connected with Lyle Academy were early members of the newly organized Cherokee Church of Christ. This closes our study of Lyle Academy.

Cherokee

In 1912, a report of a preaching effort in Cherokee, Colbert County, was reported in the *Gospel Advocate*.

> Brother P. G. Wright, of Rienzi, Miss., has done some effective preaching recently at Barton, Ala. He is now working with the church at Cherokee, Ala.[443]

Just what is meant by the phrase "He is now working with the church at Cherokee, Ala." is unclear. In 1923, J. H. Horton came to Cherokee and held a meeting. His report stated:

> ... Our next meeting was at Cherokee, Ala. This meeting resulted in four additions. We also found a few members of the one body here and set them to work. They meet in a rented hall over a store. Brother Shelton led the singing in this meeting...J. H. Horton.[444]

This sounds as though a congregation had been established prior to Horton's coming to Cherokee. To further confuse the facts, in 1933 Rollie B. Polk came and held a meeting at Cherokee. In his report, he wrote:

> In a recent report it was stated that I helped to establish a church in Cherokee, Ala. I neglected to explain that there were six members who had been meeting in the home of Lee Morris. They had been meeting regularly for three or four years, but they had no lot or church building. Since the meeting, a lot has been purchased, and a house of worship is to be erected in the near future. Rollie Polk.[445]

In this report, Polk took credit for establishing the church at Cherokee. Who exactly established the congregation at Cherokee and when was it established?

One explanation is that the 1912 reference to a church at Cherokee may have a similar situation as the one mentioned in F. D. Srygley's *Larimore And His Boys*. He wrote:

> Brother and sister Young live a way back—good preachers rarely go there; they will appreciate any kind of preaching; to them will we send him. They said to me: "We will take you to Bro. Young's; he and sister Young and Frank and another one or two are the church there; they are good people and will treat you well."[446]

Maybe it was a few people meeting in the home of someone —as was the case ten years later. Polk wrote about the "six members who had been meeting in the home of Lee Morris." [447] To make sense of these jumbled facts, we suggest that the early reports of a church in Cherokee were references to unorganized groups that were meeting sporadically but not organized with elders and deacons. Polk apparently organized the brethren at Cherokee by the New Testament pattern. That would be why Polk claimed that he established the church at Cherokee.

We realize we have jumped forward and backward with our timeline of 1914. That was the only way we could sort through the facts and arrive at any kind of conclusion.

Annapolis Avenue—Sheffield, Alabama

H. F. Williams gave us the first view of Sheffield and the church in that town. He painted a vivid and dismal word picture of the work in 1889 through the pages of the *Gospel Advocate*:

> A night and a day I have been in Sheffield. It far surpassed my preconceived notions. It has been laid out for a splendid city. The streets are so even and regular, the electric lights so brilliant, and the people so sanguine that one can easily imagine himself in a big, busy buzzing city. Mr. Solomon, a very genial gentleman, and popular land agent, kindly drove me over the whole city, showed me the new parks, the elegant drive, the grand Tennessee River scenery, the foundries, factories, etc., etc. Many very costly improvements are being made and several more talked of. Among the number is the project to build a female college. The gloomiest thing I saw in S. (Sheffield) was the cause of Christ. There are about thirty disciples there, but they seem cold, dead and indifferent. Those there talk like they would

like to do something but are so very poor or greatly in debt. The devil has a big mortgage on a man when he can get him to think that he is too poor or too badly situated to serve the Lord. These brethren have a lot offered them if they will build the house. They should utilize the offer at once. If they were faithfully reading, praying, teaching the word, praising and worshiping the Lord, it seems the house would be an easy thing. They need a good preacher to wake and work them up, but they should not depend on the preacher. Do your duty, brethren and all else will come up right. Some help may be needed on the house, but spend your last dollar, strike your last stroke before you whine and beg others to help you. So many in your situation I know who are sending out petitions, adverting through the papers and using every means to get money from others, and doing nothing themselves. They have decided they cannot build without help and so exhaust their zeal and energies simply hunting help.

When will Christians cease to advertise their own stinginess and lack of faith, love and loyalty by begging others for help. Any congregation doing its duty will find places within the radius of a few miles or within the scope of its own knowledge to spend every cent of its funds without being "drummed to death" by others who think it very hard that "Christians do not give liberally to every good work," especially to build "our meetinghouse." H. F. Williams.[448]

From this, we learn that the congregation was only about thirty strong and that they had no building of their own. To compound the problem, the Alabama Missionary Society tried to capitalize on this situation by sending one of their so-called "big guns" to solve the problem. The following excerpt is self-explanatory:

> Bro. A. R. Moore I see is behind the times. They have engaged their Alabama evangelist too late. He says that one purpose in engaging him is that he may visit the new Alabama cities, start the cause in each, secure lots, and build houses of worship. He mentions Decatur, Florence and Sheffield. I would like to inform him that Florence has a nice brick house, nearly completed. The Sheffield brethren have selected a lot worth nearly $2,000 and intend having a house by fall. North Alabama is by no means sleeping... H. G. Fleming. Tuscumbia, Ala.[449]

It will be seven more years before we see another report on the Sheffield work. John Hayes came and held a meeting sometime in November 1897. His note informs us of the results:

> Mooresville, Dec. 3. The writer held a meeting in Sheffield, Ala., last month. Visible results: five baptized into Christ (one a Methodist and one a Cumberland Presbyterian), much prejudice removed, and the brethren strengthened. I will preach for them once each month next year, and we hope to have Brother Harding hold a meeting next summer. John Hayes. [450]

The note also reveals that the next meeting would be held in the summer of 1897. James A. Harding would be the preacher for the meeting. The results to the meeting held by Hayes at Sheffield is given in the note below:

> Mooresville, April 15. At my regular appointment last Lord's day, in Sheffield, Ala., one young man made the good confession and was baptized in the Tennessee River. The cause of Christ is improving there, much prejudice has been removed,

and many more are expected to accept Christ during the year. John Hayes.[451]

Hayes believed that the Lord's work was improving at Sheffield. He had a bright outlook on that work. Hayes had begun a regular appointment schedule with the Sheffield brethren. John Hayes grew to manhood near Mooresville, Limestone County, Alabama. He spent most of his career preaching in North Alabama. Through the years he would return to Colbert and preach at various congregations.

Our next view of the Sheffield came when James E. Scobey held a week-long meeting with the church there. When Scobey left for Nashville, John Hayes continued the meeting. The report is given here:

> We enjoyed a visit last week from Brother James E. Scobey. He recently preached a week at Sheffield, Ala., with one addition. Brother John Hayes continued the meeting after he left. Brother Scobey expects to devote considerable time to preaching this summer.[452]

From the beginning, the brethren met from house to house. Later, they met in the old Atlanta Avenue Junior High School building. In 1904, the brethren purchased the old Episcopal Church building on Annapolis Avenue. Local preachers would occasionally stop by and preach for the brethren. There were some very diligent Bible students in the membership at Sheffield, as was demonstrated by the following inquiry to the *Gospel Advocate*:

> A question was sent to the Advocate. Brother Lipscomb: Please explain what is meant by "unbelievers" in 2 Cor. 6: 14. Does it mean people who are sectarians, or those who do not

believe in God or the one body? Is it a positive command not to marry out of the church? Laura Williams. Sheffield, Ala.

Answer: There were no sects when this scripture was written. An unbeliever was one who rejected Jesus as the Christ, the Son of God.[453]

We see several questions by members were sent to the *Gospel Advocate* through the years.

In April 1906, J. K. Hill came to Sheffield and preached two sermons.[454] He was asked to return and hold a meeting for them later that year. He returned in November of that year. The *Gospel Advocate* reported the results:

> Brother J. K. Hill began a meeting with the church at Sheffield, Ala., on last Lord's day. He recently closed a good meeting with the New Hope congregation, three miles north of Oakman, Ala., with eight baptisms.[455]

The first week in March of 1907 J. C. McQuiddy, along with other traveling companions, left Nashville for the Muscle Shoals area. McQuiddy spoke of this memorable trip:

> ... From Florence I went to Tuscumbia, Ala. There I met Brother Laffoon. He informed me that there were a number of believers there, but they were not active in the service of the Lord. The few faithful brethren of Tuscumbia meet with the church at Sheffield, I learned that there were only a few brethren at Sheffield, and that Brother Holt sometimes preaches for them. Either Sheffield or Tuscumbia is a good place for some faithful evangelist or preacher to locate. By an exemplary life and an earnest proclamation of the truth, he would doubtless be able to establish the cause of Christ in both places. He could make either place his radiating center,

reaching out into the territory around. The influence of an earnest, godly life is perfectly irresistible. It will melt stones of difficulty out of the way and add new converts to the Kingdom of God when and where the indifferent and faithless imagine it cannot be done. I would be glad to see some faithful, godly preacher locate in one of these towns ... J. C. McQuiddy.[456]

In August 1907, a student of the school in Bowling Green, Kentucky by the name of T. T. Pack came to Sheffield and managed to secure a preaching position with the church there. He worked with the scattered group in Tuscumbia and the small group meeting in Sheffield. Pack wrote a letter to the *Gospel Advocate* that read as follows:

Sheffield. July 29. Since my school closed at Bowling Green, Ky., I have been laboring with the church at this place. We have a fine congregation here. Our church house is in Sheffield, but we have a great many members in Tuscumbia. The two towns are just two miles apart. I am laboring in both places. We want to have our meeting later on. I have been here six weeks, and three persons have entered the fold by baptism, and many more are "almost persuaded." I want to hold a meeting in Tuscumbia, but we have no house to hold it in; so, I want to ask if anyone knows where I can get a tent for August and September. I would like to have one for two months, anyway. I think I can do great good here with it. If anyone knows of one that I can get, I would like to hear from him or her at once. We are commanded to carry the gospel to sinners, and that is what I am trying to do. The harvest is ripe, but laborers are few. T. T. Pack.[457]

Pack was not a good hire. After he remained in the city for

a while, things turned bad. He eloped with the wife and child of brother Dimit Lafoon of Tuscumbia. Ala., in November.[458] Pack nearly destroyed the work at Sheffield and Tuscumbia.

After this ordeal, C. E. Holt wrote a letter in which he paints a gloomy picture of the congregation at Sheffield. It was published in the *Gospel Advocate*:

> Brother C.E. Holt writes from Florence, Alabama under the date of March 30: ... I preach for the congregation at Sheffield, Ala., on every Sunday afternoon at three o'clock. I contemplate a protracted effort there in the very near future. It is regrettable fact that the work in Sheffield has been somewhat crippled by a corrupt preacher. Churches should be exceedingly careful along these lines. All men who have the "gift of gab" are not suitable for preachers. A preacher should be a clean man. Unfortunately, some preachers are intellectually and educationally strong, but morally weak. Churches too often seek for the former qualifications without giving much attention to the latter.[459]

Holt was one to not mince words. He always was what one would call a "straight shooter." He was also a protector of the Lord's church. If things did not seem right, he sounded the alarm, as he did about T. T. Pack.

After this horrible ordeal, J. Paul Hanlin was so discouraged that he moved from his work in Sheffield to Stearns, Kentucky.[460] Holt wrote the following article about another attempt to use the church for personal gain:

> LET ALL READ THIS.
> BY C. E. HOLT.
> Recently Florence and Sheffield, Ala., were visited by four Armenians, two of them in each city mentioned. They

Annapolis Avenue—Sheffield, Alabama

spent three or four days, including one Sunday, in drumming the cities for money with which, as they claimed, to assist in caring for orphan children in Armenia.

Their method is to first visit the resident preachers of a town, present what they call "credentials" from one in their own country whom they call their "bishop," and then ask the preachers to give them a certificate of approval and introduction to the people of their respective churches.

The men who came to Florence and Sheffield had letters of commendation from Brethren J. Paul Slayden, of Murfreesboro, Tenn., and Brother W. T. Boaz, of Columbia, Tenn. They also presented letters from a number of Christian preachers of the "digressive" type. I refused to give them a letter on the ground that they absolutely failed to satisfy me that they are worthy of the support for which they ask. Failing to get recognition from me and the elders of the church, they went to the Presbyterians, Methodists, and Baptists, but with what success I do not know ... immediately after receiving the foregoing, I addressed the following note to Brethren Slayden and Boaz: I have received an article from Brother C. E. Holt, of Florence, Ala., referring to two Armenians as frauds. They are exhibiting a letter of commendation, purporting to be from you. Do you know anything about them? The article that I have is for publication, but I do not care to publish it until I hear from you. Please let me hear from you by return mail.

To which I received the following replies:

Columbia, Tenn., January 28, 1909. Brother Shepherd: Your letter came. I know nothing of the men to whom you refer. I only saw their papers or credentials, and I wrote a statement that I only judged from the evidence presented and the appearance of the one I saw. Since considering the matter carefully, I fear they are impostors and maybe should be exposed. Yours truly, W. T. Boaz.

Murfreesboro, Tenn., January 27, 1909.—Brother Shepherd: There was an Armenian—Michael Jacobs—here two or three weeks ago, and I presented his case to the congregation and got seven dollars for him. I was impressed that he was one of the brethren but presented the matter to the brethren here as a claim of mercy, as I judged he was making an appeal that was rather general. However, I asked him about his worship, and he stated to me that he worshiped just as we do here in Murfreesboro. I feared that we might neglect a good work but was unable to fully satisfy myself of his merits because of his seeming inability to talk much English. I was disappointed later to learn that he claimed to be a member of some other religious body here. He presented a number of letters to me—among them, one from Brother Bradley, at Dickson, Tenn., one from the United States Consul to Turkey, etc. There was only one here, but he seems to have been enough. You have my best wishes in any effort to land on Sir Michael. Fraternally, J. Paul Slayden.

These men have been operating in this city (Nashville) during the last few days. Two of them called on Brother E. G. Sewell, but failed to convince him that he should render them any assistance. He told them that he had just read an account of their being in Florence and Sheffield, Ala., but they very promptly denied having been in Alabama. But in their interview with Brother McQuiddy, just before calling on Brother Sewell, they showed him a letter of commendation from someone at Athens, Ala. From these facts it seems that they are imposing on the people and should not be encouraged. J. W. Shepherd.[461]

C. E. Holt wrote the above article for the *Gospel Advocate,* and he included some of the responses he received when he investigated this Armenian fraud. It would be a little more than a year before we hear from Sheffield again.

This time it was R. H. Boll's reporting. Boll, a few years later, would openly teach premillennialism. That would cause the *Gospel Advocate* to break ties with him. The *Gospel Advocate* reported on the meeting he was holding at Sheffield. It read:

> Brother R. H. Boll writes from Sheffield, Ala., under the date of April 23: "The meeting at this place has been very good and helpful. Six have been baptized and two came in from the Baptists. The meeting will close on Sunday evening, April 24."[462]

The follow-up report on this meeting gave the results as "twenty added—seventeen baptized and three from the Baptists."[463] Sheffield seemed to be a place of "easy pickings." We compare the moral and spiritual condition of Sheffield to Rome when the Roman writer, Tacitus, said the following of Rome:

> (Christianity) a most mischievous superstition, again broke out not only in Judea, the first source of the evil, but even in Rome, where all things hideous and shameful from every part of the world find their centre and become popular.[464]

That sounds a lot like Sheffield at this point in time. Our brethren would survive, but not without many tough struggles. Our next report comes from the pen of J. Paul Hanlin:

> For several months, the Seventh Day Adventists have been making diligent efforts to build up their cause in Sheffield,

Ala., and have succeeded in making some headway. They became so bold that they boldly asserted publicly that no man had the courage to stand in their presence and deny what they taught. This they did so persistently that the brethren finally sent for Brother W. T. Boaz of Columbia, Tenn., who went to Sheffield and reviewed publicly the Advent doctrine. While there he gave them the opportunity to reply to his speech, but this they refused to do until they returned to their tent. After making an effort to reply, they refused to allow any response whatever to be made. This led to a long correspondence between Brother Boaz and Elder E. L. Maxwell, of Hammond, La.; but as they failed to reach an agreement, it seemed that nothing would come of It, and the matter dropped till just a few days before the debate began, when Brother Boaz received a note from Elder Maxwell stating that he would be in Sheffield on Sunday, March 19, at which time he would read the correspondence publicly, and if Boaz was not there he would take whatever course he esteemed proper. On receiving this information Brother Boaz called on his appointment and requested the editor of this page to accompany him to Sheffield. We reached there on Saturday evening, and Elder Maxwell was at our meeting on Sunday morning and announced that he would read the correspondence publicly that evening. He read the correspondence and endeavored to show that he was in no way responsible for the prospective discussion. When he closed, Brother Boaz reviewed the matter from the beginning, showing that the defiant way of Adventists had brought on the conflict; but as far as the challenging party was concerned, he freely admitted that he had challenged them to debate. Finally, it was agreed to begin the discussion on Monday evening, March 20, with Brother Boaz affirming the following proposition: "The Scriptures teach that the first day of the week is the Lord's day and was observed as such by early disciples." The discussion of this proposition continued for three evenings. On the fourth evening Elder Maxwell took the lead, affirming the proposition, "The Scriptures teach that the Sabbath of the fourth commandment was given for all men and is binding on people in the Christian age," the discussion of which also continued for three days. The attendance and interest throughout the whole discussion were good. Brother Boaz did fine work in the debate and great good will certainly result. Boaz is a strong debater and did splendid work in the discussion. Elder Maxwell made the very best defense he could, but was wholly unable to meet the strong, scriptural arguments of his opponent. Our space forbids further notice in this issue, but Brother Paul Hanlin of Sheffield has promised a report which we hope will reach us in time for our next issue.[465]

J. Paul Hanlin, you may remember, had moved away from Sheffield after the T. T. Pack scandal. One might ask, "Just who is J. Paul Hanlin"? He was born in Tennessee in 1884. By 1907, he was working in Sheffield. After the debacle of T. T. Pack, Hanlin moved to Stearns, Kentucky, to live and teach school. After a short stay in Kentucky, he moved back to Sheffield to work with the Christians in both Sheffield and Tuscumbia. This removal occurred by the end of 1910. J. Paul Hanlin immediately resumed teaching in the school system and working with the church. He was primarily a teacher who helped the churches in various ways. He led singing, taught classes, and preached when needed. He supported his family as a machinist. It seems Hanlin taught in some type of vocational school where he taught young men the machinist trade. He attended a meeting for machinists in Birmingham, where he led a prayer. This meeting occurred on February 27, 1911. Hanlin was a representative for the machinists in Sheffield.[466] He proved himself valuable wherever he might live. An important debate occurred in Sheffield in late March. Hanlin wrote a lengthy report on the Boaz-Maxwell Debate held in Sheffield:

> Late last summer two Adventist preachers pitched their tent in Sheffield, Ala., and began a meeting. In time they came to have a good hearing, and by means of their "Bible readings" had about persuaded some members of the church of Christ that they should "keep the Sabbath." At this point we sought to counteract their teaching and had some success. One of them said publicly that he had not yet found a man in Sheffield who had the courage to say they were wrong. The following day Brother W. T. Boaz, of Columbia, Tenn., came down, and we met with them in a "Bible reading" at a sister's house. Brother Boaz sought earnestly to arrange for a debate, but they would not; so, he spent three nights here and succeeded in showing up many of the inconsistencies of that faith. They finally agreed to try to make arrangements for a debate, and for the past three months Brother Boaz and Elder E. L. Maxwell, of Hammond, La., were in correspondence, but reached no agreement. Elder Maxwell wrote Brother Boaz that he would be in Sheffield on March 19, and that he would take the course be thought best if Boaz were not present. Brother Boaz came, the correspondence was read before the public, and propositions were signed. Six nights were spent upon two propositions. Brother J. W. Shepherd, of Nashville, Tenn., and Elder E. G. Hays, of Birmingham, Ala., were the moderators. For three nights Brother Boaz affirmed the following proposition: "The Scriptures teach that the first day of the week is the Lord's day and was observed as such by early disciples." In accepting the proposition as it is worded, Brother Boaz stated that he would do so with the under-

standing that the latter part of the proposition have this meaning: "The disciples for the first three hundred years after the apostles." He said that the Adventists had always claimed that the pope of Rome had changed the Sabbath from Saturday to Sunday, and that he wanted the proposition to cover that phase of the question. It was accepted and debated with this understanding. Brother Boaz showed that on the first day of the week Christ came forth from the grave and became the firstborn of all creation: that Pentecost came upon the first day of the week (Lev. 23:15, 16), thereby being the birthday of the church (Acts 2) as well as the birthday of Christ; that the disciples had a stated day for assembling (Heb. 10:25; 1 Cor. 11:20); that they met on the first day of the week to "break bread" (Acts 20:7); that they were commanded to lay by in store on the first day of the week (1 Cor. 16:1, 2); that these are all associated in Acts 2:42, the day upon which the church was established, the first day of the week; that "the Lord's day" (Rev. 1:10) was the Lord Jesus Christ's day, the day he arose from the dead, and the only day upon which we have any record of the disciples commemorating his death and sufferings; and that the early historians record the fact that the custom was to meet on this day for worship and that long before the time when the Adventists falsely claim that the pope of Rome changed the Sabbath from Saturday to Sunday. Elder Maxwell made every effort possible to break the force of the arguments but failed. He claimed that the "laying by in store" in 1 Cor. 16:2 was at home and not in the congregation. Brother Boaz read from Macknight's translation of the Epistles on this verse, which is as follows: "On the first day of every week, let each of you lay something by itself, according as he may have prospered, putting it into the treasury." Maxwell said that he did not know that Macknight said that, and claimed other translations read "at home," but did not have the translations with him. He also said that history showed that the disciples for the first two or three centuries did many things that Boaz would not accept. Brother Boaz replied by saying that he granted that, but that all were agreed that while the discipline of the church in those times was various, that there were some things on which all disciples agreed. He here quoted Mosheim (translated by Murdock, Book I., Century One, Part II.): "Yet there are a few regulations which may be considered as common to all Christians; and of these we shall give a brief account. The Christians in this century assembled for the worship of God, and for their advancement in piety, on the first day of the week, the day on which Christ reassumed his life: for that this day was set apart for religious worship by the apostles themselves, and that after the example of the church of Jerusalem it was generally observed, we have unexceptionable testimony." Ignatius to the Magnesians, chapter 9: "If, therefore, those who were brought up in the ancient order of things have come to the possession of a new hope, no longer observing the Sabbath, but living in the observance of the Lord's day, on which also our life has sprung up again by him and by his death." This was in A.D. 107. He also quoted Justin Martyr, Barnabas, and many others who lived in the first, second, and third centuries, showing that the claim of the Adventists that the pope changed the Sabbath is false. He had with him all the Ante-Nicene fathers and used them effectively against Maxwell. Challenge after challenge was made for the name of the pope who even claimed to have changed the Sabbath from Saturday to the first day, but it was never given. Brother Boaz in as much as the sowing of the seed of the kingdom is sure to produce sheaves for the Master's garner, we know that the cause has been strengthened here and much good will result.[467]

The debate hindered the Seventh Day Adventists's work for several years at Sheffield and Tuscumbia. A week later, R. H. Boll returned and preached at morning and evening services.[468] W. S. Long, Jr. announced that he would begin a meeting at Sheffield on April 24th.[469] He was hindered from coming at the appointed time, so he postponed the meeting until May 15th of that year.[470] The meeting finally happened, and it resulted in three baptisms and one person restored.[471]

There was an absence of information for the Sheffield work for a period of about six months—from June to December. Through the *Gospel Advocate,* we read that C. E. Coleman was coming to Sheffield to work with the church. Someone at the *Gospel Advocate* published this bit of news:

> Brother C. E. Coleman made us a pleasant visit during last week. He was on his way to Mississippi to visit his mother. About the first of January he will enter into the work at Sheffield, Ala.[472]

By the end of January 1912, Coleman sent his first report on the Sheffield work. It reads as follows:

> Brother C. E. Coleman writes from Sheffield, Ala.: "The work here is starting off well, considering the unfavorable weather and the great number of members who have not been attending the regular meetings. We have over one hundred names already and are sparing no efforts in the way of visiting and encouraging the work. Brother Paul Hanlin has been doing a splendid work here."[473]

Hanlin had been filling the pulpit until Coleman came to Sheffield. The first week of February Coleman returned to

Nashville and was married to a Miss Orlena Smith. We give the following:

> Married, at three o'clock Thursday afternoon, February 1, at the residence of Mr. W. H. Herbert, 1410 Arthur Avenue, this city, Brother C. E. Coleman to Sister Orlena Smith, Brother M. C. Cayce performing the ceremony. Only the immediate family and a few close friends were present. Immediately after the ceremony they boarded the train for Sheffield, Ala., their future home. The bride was a member of the congregation worshiping an Eighth Avenue North this city and was an efficient teacher in the Sunday school: For several years she had taught in the city public schools. Brother Coleman attended the Nashville Bible School for several years, and since leaving school has engaged in evangelistic work in East Tennessee, Colorado, and Alabama. He is now laboring with the church at Sheffield, Ala. We join their many friends in wishing them much happiness and usefulness in this life and eternal life in the world to come.[474]

Now Sheffield has a new preacher who has a new bride. Coleman would prove valuable in the work in Sheffield. With Handlin's help, the two men made a good team for the Lord's work. We learn through the *Gospel Advocate* that E. L. Jorgenson held a meeting in Sheffield during the month of July. The meeting report read:

> Brother E. L. Jorgenson called to see us while en route to Louisville from Sheffield, Ala., where he had a fine meeting. Six were baptized and four others were added to the congregation. Brother Jorgenson edits the first page of Word and Work and is one of the Gospel Advocate's staunchest supporters.[475]

Here, we learn a few facts about Jorgenson. He was the front-page editor of the journal *Word and Work,* who later became a strong advocate for the doctrine of premillennialism. Jorgenson was a close ally of R. H. Boll, who was the father of that teaching and caused much trouble in the church in later years. That doctrine grew so strong that it brought on a debate between R. H. Boll and H. Leo Boles. That debate is one of the most famous debates among our brethren during the twentieth century.

In January of 1913, C. E. Coleman gave an annual report on the work in Sheffield. It was published in the February 13th issue of the *Gospel Advocate*:

> Sheffield, Ala., January 22. The church here is doing much better than in former days. I have labored here one year. We have had one protracted meeting, given four missionary offerings, and recently put in and paid for nice new pews for the meetinghouse. Brother Paul Hanlin and I are doing some mission work around here as well. We expect to do some more repair work on the house and have another meeting soon. C. E. Coleman.[476]

During the first week of April, E. L. Jorgenson returned to Sheffield and held another meeting. It was a successful meeting. The result was a pleasing one for the church there. It read:

> Brother E. L. Jorgenson called to see us Saturday. His face was like a letter from home. He reported an unusually good meeting at Sheffield, Ala., which closed on April 9. There were eleven additions, including three baptisms. Brother Jorgenson stopped over at Lawrenceburg, Tenn., on the return trip.[477]

It was reported that there were three baptisms and eight other additions. Whether these were restorations, or people placing membership with that church or some other means, we do not know.

Jorgenson stopped over at Lawrenceburg, Tennessee, where he and R. H. Boll had worked with the church at that place. R. H. Boll had been in local work there and even had an infant child buried in May 1911 in the Mimosa Cemetery in Lawrenceburg.[478] It is understandable that Jorgenson would have friends there.

Our next note of the Sheffield was reported about J. Paul Hanlin in the *Gospel Advocate*:

> Brother J. Paul Hanlin, who lives at Sheffield, Ala., rendered fine service as song leader during their recent meeting. Brother C. E. Coleman was also an ardent co-worker. He preaches for this church regularly.[479]

Here we see a view into the teamwork of Coleman and Hanlin. Hanlin was a strong song leader, and Coleman was a strong gospel preacher. Teamwork was working to the advantage of the church at Sheffield.

Later in July John Hayes, of Texas, stopped over on the Lord's Day and preached twice. Hanlin wrote:

> Sheffield, Ala., July 14.—Brother John Hayes, of Cedar Hill, Texas, preached here twice yesterday to good audiences. He preached here a great deal several years ago and may be with us in a meeting this fall. He is a faithful worker and his preaching has the right ring. J. Paul Hanlin.[480]

John Hayes reported on a meeting in progress at Sheffield in September 1913. After having preached on that Lord's Day back in July, Hayes was asked to come back and do the meeting he was engaged in at the time he wrote this report:

> Sheffield, Ala., August 28, ... I am now in a meeting here, to continue as long as the interest demands. This is the home of Brethren Coleman and Hanlin; so, I have a good team to work with. John Hayes.[481]

The next report, which is the last report within our time boundary of 1914, came from C. E. Coleman. The report was about G. C. Brewer—who grew to manhood in Florence across the river from Sheffield. Brewer was just getting started in his ministry. He would eventually become one of the most popular preachers of his time. Coleman wrote:

> Sheffield, Ala., June 13. G. C. Brewer recently preached for us two weeks and a half and baptized eleven souls. Three were renewed and two others put in membership with us. The work is gradually growing here; much to be done yet. We expect to do some mission work in the county this summer. C. E. Coleman.[482]

Here, we have to hedge a little on our time parameter. One of the rocks in the work was moving to Berry, Alabama, to teach at the Alabama Christian College. J. Paul Hanlin moved to Berry in August 1915.[483] In December, Coleman moved to work in Trenton, Georgia,[484] leaving the Sheffield work in an almost helpless condition. After moving to Trenton, Georgia, Coleman reflected upon his four years at Sheffield:

> Trenton, January 22. My four years' work with the church at Sheffield, Ala., closed with December. The time was pleasantly and profitably spent, some success being attained for

the Master's cause. The growth was gradual, nothing exciting at any time. New members were added each year. We did not succeed in getting together enough to subtract any, which some thought should have been done. There was something over one thousand dollars paid out for improvements on the church property, besides my support for full time, except one day in each week which it was my pleasure to spend with the faithful and true band at Tuscumbia, in preparing a lesson in the forenoon, visiting and talking from house to house in the afternoon, and conducting the Bible study and prayer meeting at night. There were seven mission meetings held in the country around, one in South Florence, and one in South Sheffield. Some of the members gave monthly to missions, and a part of the time a monthly offering from the congregation was taken to help somewhere else. We also started a new congregation in South Sheffield that is doing well. They are meeting at present from house to house but planning to build a nesting house in the near future ... C. E. Coleman.[485]

Coleman's report gave a good picture of the work in Sheffield. The work was not very strong until much later in time. As Coleman wrote, "The growth was gradual, nothing exciting at any time." There would be new generations of preachers that would strengthen the church in Sheffield through the next hundred years.

Littleville

JUST WHEN THE gospel was first preached in the small community of Littleville is not known. We do know the brethren had helped build a union house for all religious groups to use for worship, and they were eventually barred from using it, though they had helped build it. So, they were forced to worship from house to house. The following report highlights this situation. In June 1913 L. S. Lancaster came to the Littleville community and held a "brush arbor meeting." He gave a report on this effort:

> Russellville, Ala., July 1. On the fifth Lord's day in June, I preached at Littleville, Ala., and baptized two who came from the Baptists. We have a few loyal members there who are laboring under very difficult circumstances and considerable persecution. Having been driven from the union meeting-house which they helped to build, they have erected an arbor in the grove nearby, under which they are now having their meetings. L. S. Lancaster.[486]

The next minister to come to Littleville was William Behel (more commonly known as Uncle Will Behel). He preached all over the northwestern part of Alabama for many years. His first report came the first week of September 1913:

> St. Joseph, Tenn., August 26. This summer's work so far is as follows: At Antioch, Ala., two baptized; Cherry Hill, Tenn., five baptized; Littleville, Ala., four baptized, four from the Baptists; Frankfort, Ala., six baptized, one restored; at Macedonia, Ala., seven baptized, one from the Baptists. I will begin near Barton, Ala., on August 31. William Behel.[487]

His report stated that he had baptized four from the Baptist Church. Behel returned again and held a meeting that summer. His report contained a lot of information, including the result of his meeting at Littleville. The result was eight additions.[488]

On February 19th of 1914, a debate was announced. The debate was to occur in a Baptist church house near Littleville It would be conducted between G. T. Kay of the Church of Christ and William Lindley of the Baptist Church. The notice was published and stated:

> There will be a discussion between G. T. Kay (Christian) and William Lindley (Baptist) sometime during the month of March near Littleville, Ala. The church propositions, apostasy, and the design of baptism will be discussed. The exact date will be announced later.[489]

Kay gave a follow-up on the debate. He wrote:

> Minor Hill, Tenn., February 27.—The debate booked to take place between myself and William Lindley (Baptist) will be

held at Mount Moriah Baptist Church, four miles from Littleville, Ala., beginning on Monday, March 16, at ten o'clock A.M. and continuing four days. Visiting brethren who wish to be met at Littleville may have conveyance by notifying Brother B. F. Martin, Russellville, Ala., Route No. 7. Littleville is situated on the Northern Alabama Railroad, between Sheffield and Russellville. G. T. Kay.[490]

B. F. (Ben) Martin was mentioned as a contact for the congregation at Littleville. Martin was described as one of the two strongest workers in the church at Littleville. John C. Graham said of Martin and his brother-in-law:

> I recently held a meeting at Littleville, Ala., with two baptisms. Ben Martin and Jim Weems are two of the faithful workers in the congregation at that place. John C. Graham, Sheffield, Ala.[491]

Ben Martin had been a truck driver for a mining company (1920 United States Federal Census). After mining ended in that region, he became a lumberman. His wife Clemmie Martin lived into the 1970s. This writer remembers her very well. She was a good student of the Word of God.

Our last report within our time frame was published in the *Gospel Advocate* on November 5, 1914. It was written by P. G. Wright. In this report, he wrote:

> Tuscumbia, October 26.—I have recently preached at the following places in Alabama: Hodges, two sermons; Bear Creek, three sermons; Haleyville, three sermons; Littleville, two sermons. I am now at Piney Grove. P. G. Wright.[492]

It would not be until 1939 that a church house of their own was ever mentioned. That was when the house in which they still meet was constructed. In 2025, the congregation is still shining a light for the Lord.

Littleville is dear to this writer's heart as he has had an interactive relationship with them since 1972.

Piney Grove

It is not known who preached in this community first, nor do we know what year this happened. We do know that one Mississippi preacher sent the first report on the work, to the *Gospel Advocate*. His name was Perry G. Wright. He was the first and only one to report on the work at Piney Grove within our time boundary. His first report was a brief mention of Piney Grove:

> Brother P. G. Wright will begin a meeting at Piney Grove, near Tuscumbia, Ala., on the fourth Lord's day in this month. [493]

From the meager information we only learn that the work at that place was already established when Wright came and preached in 1912. But when was it established? We do know that much of the work in our Restoration Movement went unpublished, due to the lack of reporting by the preachers or members. Our next comes from the same preacher and so will all the other reports. Just why this is so, we do not know. From the appearance, it seemed as though P. G. Wright was the only preacher coming to Piney Grove, until the 1930s. Others began to come and report on the work, but that was too far beyond our time limit.

In 1913 Wright comes again to Piney Grove and holds a meeting. The report was very brief. It simply read: "P. G. Wright, Piney Grove, eight miles south of Tuscumbia, Ala., 8 additions."[494] In 1914 he returned for a third reported meeting. The report was again brief on Piney Grove. It read much like the one given above. He did tell of preaching in Tuscumbia, while on this trip from Mississippi. Here we give the report:

> Rienzi, Miss., August 3. I closed a meeting at Piney Grove, in Alabama, last Friday, with eight additions and one restoration. I preached two sermons in Tuscumbia, Ala., last Lord's day. We were saddened by the death of Sister Ella Webb. She was, perhaps, the greatest church worker in Alabama. Perry G. Wright.[495]

Wright returns in October and preaches again.[496] His final report, before 1914 ends, reads as follows:

> Tuscumbia, November 2.—I preached eight sermons at Piney Grove last week, with six baptisms and one reclaimed. Interest good. I preached three sermons last Lord's day at Mount Olivet. I go from here to Oak Grove, where I baptized ten last September. P. G. Wright.[497]

The first report on Piney Grove given by anyone other than Wright, was given by C. L. Overturf, Sheffield, Ala., August 26.[498] The lack of reporting by anyone except Wright is the reason we suggested that Wright may have been the founder of

Piney Grove. He was still coming to Piney Grove and preaching as late as November 1932. This concludes our study of the Piney Grove church.

This also concludes our study of the Franklin and Colbert Counties' Restoration Movement among Churches of Christ. The work done here was among some of the very first congregations to be established in the state of Alabama. When Abner Hill came and established some early churches, he was a contemporary of Barton W. Stone and Alexander Campbell. It must be remembered, however, that he was not directly influenced by these men, but by men like Benjamin Lynn and John Mulkey. The two counties in this study should be proud of their religious heritage. May the Lord continue to bless them in their work in God's kingdom.

Endnotes

[1] *The Evangelist* (June 3, 1834), 132.

[2] (Francis Roberts, "County Seats in the Valley of the Tennessee," *Bulletin in the North Alabama Historical Association*, 1 (1956), 16.

[3] F. D. Srygley, *Larimore And His Boys* (Nashville, TN: Gospel Advocate Publishing, 1889).

[4] George M. and Mildred B. Watson, *History of the Christian Churches in the Alabama Area* (St. Louis, MO: Bethany Press, 1965).

[5] *The Christian Register* (1848).

[6] Terry Cowan and Harry Shetrone, *A Matthews History* (Wolfe City, TX: Henington Industries, 2002), 13.

[7] B. F. Hall, Unpublished Autobiography, 27.

[8] Abner Hill Journal, 18–20.

[9] Abner Hill Journal, 18–20.

[10] L. C. Chisholm, *Gospel Advocate* (May 9, 1872), 454.

[11] *Gospel Advocate* (August 22, 1888), 14.

[12] *Christian Messenger* (December 1831), 280–281.

[13] Abner Hill Journal, 24–25; The Third and Fourth

Annual Reports of the Officers of the Tuscumbia, Courtland & Decatur Railroad Company, (1836), 26–27.

[14] The Third and Fourth Annual Reports of the Officers of the Tuscumbia, Courtland & Decatur Railroad Company (1836), 26–27.

[15] Abner Hill Journal, 38.

[16] Abner Hill Journal, 38.

[17] Terry Cowan and Harry Shetrone, *A Matthews History* (Wolfe City, TX: Henington Industries, 2002), 13.

[18] The Third and Fourth Annual Reports of the Officers of the Tuscumbia, Courtland & Decatur Railroad Company (1836), 26–27.

[19] *Gospel Advocate* (August 22, 1888), 14.

[20] Abner Hill Journal, 38.

[21] Earl Kimbrough, *The Restoration In Russell's Valley And Northwest Alabama 1842–1945* (Monroe, GA: Book Production Resources, 2013).

[22] *Christian Messenger* (June 1828), 178–188.

[23] *Christian Messenger* (November 1828), 43.

[24] *Christian Messenger* (November 25, 1826), 21–22; (December 1831), 280–281.

[25] The Mansell W. Matthews Papers held in a collection at the Texas Christian University Library.

[26] Abner Hill Journal, 28.

[27] *Christian Review* (May 1844), 117–118.

[28] Dr. William Henry Wharton, "An unsigned, undated sketch," p. 1. It belongs to the "Dickson Letters," owned by Sadie Dickson Shrader of Tuscumbia, Alabama.

[29] Dr. William Henry Wharton, "An unsigned, undated sketch," p. 1. It belongs to the "Dickson Letters," owned by Sadie Dickson Shrader of Tuscumbia, Alabama.

[30] Dr. William Henry Wharton, "An unsigned, undated

sketch," p. 1. It belongs to the "Dickson Letters," owned by Sadie Dickson Shrader of Tuscumbia, Alabama.

[31] *The Evangelist* (June 3, 1834) 132.
[32] *The Evangelist* (June 3, 1834) 132.
[33] *The Evangelist* (June 3, 1834), 132.
[34] *Millennial Harbinger* (December 1834), 605.
[35] B. F. Riley, *History of the Baptists of Alabama* (Birmingham: Roberts and Son, 1895), 79.
[36] *Millennial Harbinger* (December 1834) 605.
[37] *The Evangelist* (July 1835), 167.
[38] *Christian Messenger* (November 1834), 346.
[39] Alexander Campbell, "Ledger, 1830-37," 241.
[40] *Christian Messenger* (November 1834) 346.
[41] *The Evangelist*, July 6, 1835), 167
[42] Crisler B. Ransom, *History of the First United Methodist Church of Tuscumbia, Alabama* (No publisher given, 1976), 16.
[43] *The Evangelist*, August 1835), 191.
[44] *The Evangelist*, August 3, 1835), 191.
[45] *Millennial Harbinger* (January 1837), 43.
[46] *Millennial Harbinger* (January 1837), 43.
[47] Josephus Shackelford, "Reminiscences of Tuscumbia Baptist Church, One of Its Old Pastors," (Tuscumbia, AL, July 11, 1911), 1.
[48] *Christian Monthly* (August 1870), 241.
[49] *Christian Monthly* (August 1870), 241.
[50] *Millennial Harbinger* (May 1837), 239–40.
[51] *The Christian Monthly* (August 1870), 242.
[52] *The Christian Preacher* (November 1839), 218–19.
[53] *Millennial Harbinger* (April 1842), 186.
[54] *Christian Magazine* (July 1852), 213.
[55] *The Christian Register* (December 1848), preface.
[56] *Gospel Advocate* (December 1860), 375–376.

[57] Nina Leftwich was in error about Alexander Campbell coming to Tuscumbia. He never set foot in Alabama, north of Tuscaloosa. That is confirmed by Campbell's own documents.

[58] Nina Leftwich, *Two Hundred Years at Muscle Shoals* (North Port, AL: American Southern Printers, 1965, 149–150.

[59] Cora Bales Sevier and Nancy S. Madden, *Sevier Family History* (Washington, D.C.: private publication, 1961), 265.

[60] Dr. William Henry Wharton, (no date) p. 4, Found in the Dickson Letters.

[61] Nina Leftwich, *Two Hundred Years at Muscle Shoals* (North Port, AL: American Southern Printers, 1965), 153.

[62] *The Oaks*, A historical booklet about the Ricks's Plantation House, 7.

[63] Mrs. Thurmon Kimbrough, owner of "The Oaks," the Abraham Ricks's Plantation House, February 24, 1978.

[64] Mrs. Thurmon Kimbrough, owner of "The Oaks," the Abraham Ricks's Plantation House, February 24, 1978.

[65] Mrs. Thurmon Kimbrough, owner of "The Oaks," the Abraham Ricks's Plantation House, February 24, 1978.

[66] *Millennial Harbinger* (September 1848), 534.

[67] *Millennial Harbinger* (September 1848), 534.

[68] *Christian Monthly* (June 1870), 179–181.

[69] *Christian Monthly* (August 1870), 241–242.

[70] *World Evangelist* (August 1980), 1; 21.

[71] L. C. Chisholm, "Russellville, Alabama," *Millennial Harbinger* (February 1850) 114.

[72] Cora Bales Sevier and Nancy S. Madden, *Sevier Family History* 263.

[73] Tolbert Fanning, "News from the Churches," *Millennial Harbinger* (April 1842), 186.

[74] Tolbert Fanning, "The Church at Russellville, Alabama," *Christian Review* (February 1845), 47.

[75] Tolbert Fanning, *Christian Review* (February 1845), 47.

[76] Tolbert Fanning, *Millennial Harbinger* (April 1842), 186.

[77] Tolbert Fanning, *Millennial Harbinger* (April 1842), 186.

[78] *Millennial Harbinger* (April 1842), 186.

[79] *Millennial Harbinger* (April 1842), 186.

[80] Tolbert Fanning, *Christian Review* (February 1845) 47.

[81] James E. Scobey, *Franklin College and Its Influences* (Nashville, TN: Gospel Advocate Company, 1954) 217.

[82] George W. Dehoff, *The Russellville Christian* (March 25, 1945), 1.

[83] Alexander Campbell, "Ledger, 1830-37," 241.

[84] Alexander Campbell, "Ledger, 1830-37," 241.

[85] Alexander Campbell, "Ledger, 1830-37," 382.

[86] J. H. Dunn, *Bible Advocate* (April 1843), 143.

[87] J. H. Dunn, *Gospel Advocate* (October 25, 1877), 660.

[88] Abner Hill, *Christian Review* (May 1844), 118.

[89] Tolbert Fanning, *Christian Review* (December 1844), 265.

[90] J. H. Dunn, *Christian Review* (February 1845), 46–47.

[91] Alexander Campbell, "Ledger, 1846-50," 382.

[92] N. R. Ladd, *Christian Review* (January 1846), 22.

[93] J. H. Dunn, *Christian Review* (August 1846), 190.

[94] Tolbert Fanning, *Christian Review* (August 1846), 190–191.

[95] Alexander Hall, *Christian Register* (1848), 38.

[96] L. C. Chisholm, *Millennial Harbinger* (February 1850), 114.

[97] *Gospel Advocate* (December 18, 1913), 1245.

[98] W. T. Crenshaw, *Christian Magazine* (December 1851), 375.

[99] J. J. Trott, *Christian Magazine* (January 1852), 29.

[100] J. J. Trott, *Christian Magazine* (January 1852), 29.

[101] Tolbert Fanning, *Gospel Advocate* (January 1858), 3.

[102] Eld Dunn, *Christian Register* (1848), 38.

[103] John Taylor, *Gospel Advocate* (October 1860), 319–320.

[104] Tolbert Fanning, *Gospel Advocate* (May 1861), 149.

[105] John Taylor, *Millennial Harbinger* (June 1859), 349.

[106] John Taylor, *Millennial Harbinger* (June 1859), 349.

[107] Thomas B. Trotter, *Gospel Advocate* (December 1860), 375–376.

[108] Thomas B. Trotter, *Gospel Advocate* (December 1860), 375–376.

[109] J. M. Downs, *Bible Advocate* (September 1845), 213.

[110] J. H. Dunn, *Bible Advocate* (September 1845), 213.

[111] L. C. Chisholm, "Russellville, Alabama," *Millennial Harbinger* (February 1850) 114.

[112] L. C. Chisholm, *Gospel Advocate* (June 8, 1882), Front Page.

[113] L. C. Chisholm, *Gospel Advocate* (June 8, 1882), Front Page.

[114] A. C. Henry, (June 20, 1883), 395.

[115] A. C. Henry, (August 29, 1883), 552.

[116] A. C. Henry, *Gospel Advocate* (September 19, 1883), 599.

[117] A. C. Henry, *Gospel Advocate* (October 31, 1883), 694.

[118] A. C. Henry, *Gospel Advocate* (January 6, 1886), 11.

[119] A. C. Henry, *Gospel Advocate* (October 13, 1886), 654.

[120] J. H. Holbrook, October 20, 1886), 670.

[121] Lee Jackson, *Gospel Advocate* (January 30. 1889), 74.

[122] *Gospel Advocate* (January 30. 1889), 74.

[123] R. W. Norwood, *Gospel Advocate* (September 25, 1889), 611.

[124] W. D. Harris, *Gospel Advocate* (May 28, 1890), 350.

[125] J. H. Holbrook, *Gospel Advocate* (July 9, 1890), 437.

[126] J. H. Holbrook, *Gospel Advocate* (July 9, 1890), 437.

[127] J. H. Holbrook, *Gospel Advocate* (July 9, 1890), 437.

[128] J. H. Holbrook, *Gospel Advocate* (August 20, 1890), 542.

[129] J. H. Holbrook, *Gospel Advocate* (September 10, 1890), 578.

[130] Handwritten letter in the old church records at Russellville.

[131] L. R. Sewell, *Gospel Advocate* (August 11, 1892), 505.

[132] F. D. Srygley, *T. B. Larimore And His Boys* (Nashville, TN: Gospel Advocate Publishing, 1889), 172.

[133] Brown Godwin, *Gospel Advocate* (October 27, 1892), 686.

[134] O. P. Barry, *Gospel Advocate* (August 24, 1893), 533.

[135] *Gospel Advocate* (October 4, 1894), 630.

[136] O. P. Barry, *Gospel Advocate* (September 5, 1895), 572.

[137] *Gospel Advocate* (March 26, 1896), 200.

[138] I. B. Bradley, *Gospel Advocate* (September 24, 1896), 620.

[139] *Gospel Advocate* (December 10, 1896), 792.

[140] *Gospel Advocate* (December 24, 1896), 828.

[141] *Gospel Advocate* (December 9, 1897), 776.

[142] *Gospel Advocate* (December 23, 1897), 809.

[143] *Gospel Advocate* (February 24, 1898), 117.

[144] R. N. Moody, *Gospel Advocate* (February 3, 1898), 75.

[145] I. B. Bradley, *Gospel Advocate* (July 28, 1898), 483.

[146] M. H. Northcross, *Gospel Advocate* (September 8, 1898), 576.

[147] We could find no reference that would explain what Bradley meant by this statement.

[148] *Gospel Advocate* (September 22, 1898), 608.

[149] Earl Kimbrough, *The Restoration In Russell's Valley And Northwest Alabama 1842–1945* (Monroe, GA: Book Production Resources, 2013), 286.

[150] *Gospel Advocate* (May 29, 1902), 340.

[151] *Gospel Advocate* (June 5, 1902), 357.

[152] *Gospel Advocate* (June 5, 1902), 362.

[153] *Gospel Advocate* (August 4, 1904), 492.

[154] *Gospel Advocate* (April 13, 1905), 229.

[155] *Gospel Advocate* (June 15, 1905), 373; *Gospel Advocate* (July 6, 1905), 421.

[156] *Gospel Advocate* (February 7, 1907), 85.

[157] *Gospel Advocate* (July 4, 1907), 421.

[158] *Gospel Advocate* (July 4, 1907), 421.

[159] *Gospel Advocate* (September 5, 1907), 574.

[160] *Gospel Advocate* (October 3, 1907), 636.

[161] *Gospel Advocate* (October 28, 1909), 1360.

[162] *Gospel Advocate* (June 30, 1910), 764.

[163] *Gospel Advocate* (November 3, 1910), 1212.

[164] *Gospel Advocate* (June 16, 1911), 660.

[165] *Gospel Advocate* (June 29, 1911), 708.

[166] *Gospel Advocate* (July 11, 1912), 812.

[167] *Gospel Advocate* (November 6, 1913), 1072.

[168] *Gospel Advocate* (September 3, 1914), 940.

[169] *Gospel Advocate* (March 11, 1891), 147.

[170] J. B. Hamilton, *Gospel Advocate* (May 23, 1867), 418.

[171] *Gospel Advocate* (September 1, 1904), 554.

[172] *Gospel Advocate* (March 11, 1891), 147.

[173] *Gospel Advocate* (June 7, 1900), front page, 353; Rock Creek Record Book, 10.

[174] *Gospel Advocate* (June 7, 1900), front page, 353.

[175] *Gospel Advocate* (June 6, 1867), 453.

[176] F. B. Srygley, *Gospel Advocate* (May 16, 1929), 470.

[177] F. D. Srygley, *T. B. Larimore And His Boys* (Nashville, TN: Gospel Advocate Publishing, 1889), 34.

[178] Bethel Berry Church Book, 1.

[179] James H. Srygley, *Gospel Advocate* (September 9, 1869), 834–835.

[180] F. B. Srygley, *Gospel Advocate* (May 16, 1929), 471.

[181] F. B. Srygley, *Gospel Advocate* (May 16, 1929), 470.

[182] *Gospel Advocate* (April 1, 1869), 297.

[183] F. B. Srygley, *Gospel Advocate* (July 30, 1890), 487.

[184] Dr. William Henry Wharton, "An unsigned, undated sketch," 1. It belongs to the "Dickson Letters," owned by Sadie Dickson Shrader of Tuscumbia, Alabama. Sadie Dickson Shrader was Wharton's great-niece.

[185] *Gospel Advocate* (May 8, 1930), 444.

[186] J. H. Srygley, *Gospel Advocate* (September 9, 1869), 834.

[187] A. C. Henry, *Gospel Advocate* (October 13, 1886), 654.

[188] W. A. Kimbrough, *Gospel Advocate* (January 26, 1899), 62.

[189] *Gospel Advocate* (November 13, 1902), 733.

[190] *Gospel Advocate* (September 5, 1907), 572.

[191] *Gospel Advocate* (September 24, 1908), 618.

[192] *Gospel Advocate* (October 7, 1909), 1280.

[193] *Gospel Advocate* (August 25, 1910), 976.

[194] *Gospel Advocate* (October 21, 1912), 1173.

[195] *Gospel Advocate* (September 4, 1913), 852.

[196] *Gospel Advocate* (October 30, 1913), 1037.

[197] *Gospel Advocate* (September 20, 1917), 925.

[198] *Gospel Advocate* (August 8, 1929), 753.

[199] *Gospel Advocate* (July 27, 1882), 473.

[200] W. A. Kimbrough, *Gospel Advocate* (January 26, 1899), 62.

[201] W. A. Kimbrough, *Gospel Advocate* (January 26, 1899), 62.

[202] W. A. Kimbrough, *Gospel Advocate* (January 26, 1899), 62.

[203] *Gospel Advocate* (August 28, 1902), 556.

[204] *Gospel Advocate* (July 21, 1904), 457.

[205] (*Gospel Advocate* (August 24, 1906), 621.

[206] *Gospel Advocate* (September 26, 1907), 621.

[207] F. B. Srygley, *Gospel Advocate* (July 27, 1882), 473.

[208] *Gospel Advocate* (August 20, 1908), 540.

[209] *Gospel Advocate* (October 16, 1913), 989.

[210] *Gospel Advocate* (March 19, 1914), 338.

[211] *Gospel Advocate* (November 21, 1883), 743.

[212] *Gospel Advocate* (December 19, 1883), 811.

[213] See page 75.

[214] *Gospel Advocate* (October 6, 1886), 631.

[215] *Gospel Advocate* (October 29, 1903), 703.

[216] *Gospel Advocate* (May 26, 1886), 331.

[217] *Gospel Advocate* (October 3, 1888), 3.

[218] *Gospel Advocate* (October 3, 1888), 3.

[219] *Gospel Advocate* (October 27, 1892,) 686.

[220] *Gospel Advocate* (October 15, 1896), 664.

[221] W. A. Kimbrough. *Gospel Advocate* (January 26, 1899), 62.

[222] *Gospel Advocate* (September 14, 1899), 588.

[223] *Gospel Advocate* (September 6, 1906), 565.

[224] *Gospel Advocate* (September 20, 1906), 597.

[225] *Gospel Advocate* (September 17, 1914), 988.

[226] *Gospel Advocate* (March 18, 1909), 338.

[227] *Gospel Advocate* (December 23, 1909), 1611.

[228] *Gospel Advocate* (August 25, 1910), 976.

[229] *Gospel Advocate* (October 6, 1910), 1120.

[230] *Gospel Advocate* (July 27, 1911), 815.

[231] *Gospel Advocate* (November 2, 1911), 266–1267.
[232] R. N. Moody, Eunice Loyd, *Gospel Advocate* (April 5, 1909).
[233] *Gospel Advocate* (February 1, 1912), 134.
[234] *Gospel Advocate* (March 13, 1913), 258.
[235] *Gospel Advocate* (August 7, 1913), 757.
[236] *Gospel Advocate* (August 21, 1913), 801.
[237] *Gospel Advocate* (August 21, 1913), 801.
[238] *Gospel Advocate* (August 27, 1914), 919–920.
[239] *Gospel Advocate* (July 8, 1915), 679–680.
[240] Earl Kimbrough, *The Restoration In Russell's Valley And Northwest Alabama 1842–1945*, Monroe, GA: Book Production Resources, 2013), 308.
[241] *Gospel Advocate* (August 14, 1902), 524.
[242] *Gospel Advocate* (August 28, 1902), 556.
[243] *Gospel Advocate* (August 16, 1906), 525.
[244] *Gospel Advocate* (August 27, 1908), 558.
[245] *Gospel Advocate* (November 12, 1908), 735.
[246] *Gospel Advocate* (November 2, 1911), 1278.
[247] *Gospel Advocate* (April 2, 1914), 386.
[248] *Gospel Advocate* (August 2, 1917), 748.
[249] *Gospel Advocate* (September 22, 1921), 932.
[250] Earl Kimbrough, *The Restoration In Russell's Valley And Northwest Alabama 1842–1945* (Monroe, GA: Book Production Resources, 2013), 352.
[251] *Franklin County Times* (September 29, Oct. 13, 1932).
[252] Paralee Annie Gassaway, Interview by Earl Kimbrough, July 28, 1965; Earl Kimbrough, *The Restoration In Russell's Valley And Northwest Alabama 1842–1945* (Monroe, GA: Book Production Resources, 2013), 225.
[253] Earl Kimbrough, *The Restoration In Russell's Valley And Northwest Alabama 1842–1945* (Monroe, GA: Book Production Resources, 2013), 225.

[254] *Gospel Advocate* (October 3, 1888), 3.

[255] *Gospel Advocate* (September 18, 1889), 595.

[256] Earl Kimbrough, *The Restoration In Russell's Valley And Northwest Alabama 1842–1945* (Monroe, GA: Book Production Resources, 2013), 308.

[257] *Gospel Advocate* (Oct. 4, 1894), 630.

[258] *Gospel Advocate* (February 3, 1898), 75.

[259] *Gospel Advocate* (September 8, 1898), 579.

[260] *Gospel Advocate* (January 26, 1899), 49.

[261] *Gospel Advocate* (September 7, 1899), 571.

[262] *Gospel Advocate* (October 4, 1923), 972.

[263] Earl Kimbrough, *The Restoration In Russell's Valley And Northwest Alabama 1842–1945* (Monroe, GA: Book Production Resources, 2013), 308.

[264] Earl Kimbrough, "John Taylor—The Life And Times Of A Backwoods Preacher, 1807–1885." *Alabama Restoration Journal*, (2010), 9–10.

[265] *Gospel Advocate* (December 1860), 375–376.

[266] *Gospel Advocate* (December 1860), 375-376.

[267] Earl Kimbrough, "John Taylor—The Life And Times Of A Backwoods Preacher, 1807–1885." *Alabama Restoration Journal*, (2010), 177.

[268] Ernest A. Clevenger, Jr., *@ Any Age: An Autobiographical Memoir With Genealogical and Historical Records*. s.l.: Clevenger Publications, 2011.

[269] Earl Kimbrough, *The Restoration In Russell's Valley And Northwest Alabama 1842–1945* (Monroe, GA: Book Production Resources), 308.

[270] Earl Kimbrough, *The Restoration In Russell's Valley And Northwest Alabama 1842–1945* (Monroe, GA: Book Production Resources), 308.

[271] *Gospel Advocate* (September 9, 1885), 571.

[272] *Gospel Advocate* (September 16, 1885), 583.

[273] *Gospel Advocate* (September 30, 1891), 617.
[274] F. D. Srygley, *Larimore And His Boys* (Nashville, TN: Gospel Advocate Publishing Company, 1889), 155.
[275] *Gospel Advocate* (October 23, 1889), 675.
[276] *Gospel Advocate* (August 11, 1892), 505.
[277] *Gospel Advocate* (April 20, 1893), 253.
[278] *Gospel Advocate* (August 24, 1893), 533.
[279] *Gospel Advocate* (November 9, 1893), 708); *Gospel Advocate* (December 28, 1893), 820.
[280] *Gospel Advocate* (March 26, 1896), 200.
[281] *Gospel Advocate* (August 20, 1896), 540.
[282] *Gospel Advocate* (October 29, 1903), 700.
[283] *Gospel Advocate* (October 13, 1904), 656.
[284] *Gospel Advocate* (April 13, 1905), 229.
[285] *Gospel Advocate* (October 3, 1907), 636.
[286] *Gospel Advocate* (October 10, 1907), 653.
[287] *Gospel Advocate* (May 1, 1924), 425.
[288] *Gospel Advocate* (April 13, 1905), 229.
[289] Earl Kimbrough, *The Restoration In Russell's Valley And Northwest Alabama 1842–1945* (Monroe, GA: Book Production Resources, 2013), 289.
[290] *Gospel Advocate* (September 11, 1919), 896–897.
[291] *Gospel Advocate* (September 20, 1906), 597.
[292] *Gospel Advocate* (August 20, 1908), 540.
[293] *Gospel Advocate* (October 1, 1908), 629.
[294] *Gospel Advocate* (September 30, 1909), 1233.
[295] *Gospel Advocate* (November 24, 1910), 1310–1311.
[296] *Gospel Advocate* (August 22, 1912), 961.
[297] *Gospel Advocate* (August 22, 1912), 961.
[298] *Gospel Advocate* (October 9, 1913), 973.
[299] *Gospel Advocate* (November 6, 1913), 1072.
[300] *Gospel Advocate* (September 3, 1914), 940.
[301] *Gospel Advocate* (September 17, 1914), 988.

[302] *Gospel Advocate* (May 26, 1910), 644.

[303] *Gospel Advocate* (October 3, 1907), 636.

[304] *Gospel Advocate* (September 9, 1909), 1136.

[305] *Gospel Advocate* (January 19, 1911), 71.

[306] *Gospel Advocate* (September 12, 1912), 1028.

[307] *Gospel Advocate* (August 21, 1913), 805.

[308] *Gospel Advocate* (September 2, 1909), 1112.

[309] *Gospel Advocate* (September 30, 1909), 1282.

[310] *Gospel Advocate* (December 30, 1909), 1662.

[311] *Gospel Advocate* (June 2, 1910), 672.

[312] *Gospel Advocate* (August 1, 1912), 884.

[313] *Gospel Advocate* (June 15, 1916), 605.

[314] *Gospel Advocate* (June 21, 1917), 606.

[315] *Gospel Advocate* (March 24, 1921), 280.

[316] *Gospel Advocate* (September 25, 1924), 940.

[317] Earl Kimbrough, *The Restoration In Russell's Valley And Northwest Alabama 1842–1945* (Monroe, GA: Book Production Resources, 2013), 354–355.

[318] Earl Kimbrough, *The Restoration In Russell's Valley And Northwest Alabama 1842–1945* (Monroe, GA: Book Production Resources, 2013), 352.

[319] *Gospel Advocate* (August 19, 1920), 817.

[320] J. M. Pickens, *Gospel Advocate* (May 8, 1866), 300–301.

[321] *Gospel Advocate* (September 11, 1866), 588–589.

[322] *Gospel Advocate* (April 11, 1867), 296–297.

[323] Francis Roberts, "County Seats in The Valley of the Tennessee," *Bulletin in the North Alabama Historical Association,* 1 (1956), 16.

[324] *Christian Monthly* (June 1870), 179–181.

[325] Captain A. H. Keller, *History of Tuscumbia,* (1888), 10.

[326] *Christian Monthly* (August 1870), 241–242.

[327] *Gospel Advocate* (January 11, 1883), 26.
[328] *Gospel Advocate* (November 21, 1883), 739.
[329] *Gospel Advocate* (May 14, 1890), 314.
[330] *Gospel Advocate* (July 2, 1890), 421.
[331] *Gospel Advocate* (August 8, 1907), 508.
[332] *Gospel Advocate* (November 14, 1907), 725.
[333] *Gospel Advocate* (March 5, 1908), 147.
[334] *World Evangelist* (August 1980), 1, 21.
[335] *Gospel Advocate* (March 31, 1910), 403.
[336] *Gospel Advocate* (March 31, 1910), 403.
[337] *Gospel Advocate* (August 7, 1913), 766.
[338] *Gospel Advocate* (July 4, 1912), 794.
[339] *Gospel Advocate* (August 7, 1913), 766.
[340] *Gospel Advocate* (December 18, 1913), 1248.
[341] *Gospel Advocate* (May 6, 1915), 454.
[342] *Gospel Advocate* (May 6, 1915), 454.
[343] Abraham Ricks's family papers.
[344] *The Oaks*, a journal about the Ricks family, 7.
[345] Abe Ricks—the grandson, *The Oaks*, 7.
[346] *Gospel Advocate* (January 2, 1868), 24.
[347] *Gospel Advocate* (January 2, 1868), 24.
[348] Abraham Ricks's family papers.
[349] *Gospel Advocate* (April 29, 1885), 203.
[350] *The Leighton News* (Friday, 1 January 1909), 8.
[351] Sandra Sockwell, *The Place Names of Colbert and Lauderdale Counties, Alabama, 1985*. Diss., 1988.
[352] Sandra Sockwell, *The Place Names of Colbert and Lauderdale Counties, Alabama, 1985*. Diss., 1988.
[353] *Gospel Advocate* (June 7, 1900), front page 353; Rock Creek Record Book, 10.
[354] *Gospel Advocate* (June 7, 1900), front page 353.
[355] *Gospel Advocate* (August 30, 1900), 545.
[356] *Gospel Advocate* (June 7, 1928), 539.

[357] Rock Creek Record Book, 1.

[358] *Gospel Advocate* (September 9, 1869), 834–835.

[359] F. D. Srygley, *Larimore & His Boys*, (1889), 20.

[360] Sandra Sockwell, *The Place Names of Colbert and Lauderdale Counties, Alabama, 1985*. Diss., (1988), 490–491.

[361] Jesse Clopton James, *Natchez Trace Traveler*, 12.2 (May 1992), 49.

[362] Jesse Clopton James, *Natchez Trace Traveler*, 11.1 (Feb. 1991), 12.

[363] *Gospel Advocate* (September 30, 1875), 936.

[364] *Gospel Advocate* (October 7, 1891), 626.

[365] *Gospel Advocate* (October 11, 1877), 635.

[366] *Gospel Advocate* (August 28, 1879), 555.

[367] *Gospel Advocate* (August 26, 1880), 556.

[368] *Gospel Advocate* (August 11, 1881), 505.

[369] *Gospel Advocate* (July 13, 1882), 438.

[370] Rock Creek Record Book, 23.

[371] *Gospel Advocate* (May 12, 1892), 297.

[372] Rock Creek Record Book, part 2, p. 6.

[373] *Gospel Advocate* (July 27, 1883), 473.

[374] J. H. Holbrook was the way J. H. wrote his name. In the *Gospel Advocate,* they always spelled it as Halbrook. On Holbrook's tombstone and his wife Margret's also, who preceded him in death, the name is spelled Holbrook.

[375] Rock Creek Record Book, 42.

[376] F. D. Srygley, *Larimore & His Boys* (1889), 153–154.

[377] Rock Creek Record Book, 24–26.

[378] *Gospel Advocate* (July 25, 1895), 472.

[379] *Gospel Advocate* (September 12, 1895), 588.

[380] Rock Creek Record Book, 26–27.

[381] *Gospel Advocate* (July 16, 1896), 456.

[382] *Gospel Advocate* (August 13, 1896), 525.

[383] *Gospel Advocate* (September 8, 1898), 578.

[384] *Gospel Advocate* (September 8, 1898), 579.
[385] *Gospel Advocate* (January 26, 1899), 49.
[386] *Gospel Advocate* (May 25, 1899), 321.
[387] Rock Creek Record Book, 57.
[388] *Gospel Advocate* (October 26, 1899), 684.
[389] *Firm Foundation* (January 6, 1903), 5.
[390] *Gospel Advocate* (July 21, 1904), 457.
[391] Rock Creek Church Book, 33–34.
[392] *Gospel Advocate* (July 18, 1907), 453.
[393] *Gospel Advocate* (October 31, 1907), 700.
[394] Rock Creek Church Book, 33–34.
[395] *Gospel Advocate* (August 20, 1908), 540.
[396] *Gospel Advocate* (October 6, 1910), 1120.
[397] *Gospel Advocate* (July 20, 1911), 785.
[398] *Gospel Advocate* (August 3, 1911), 862.
[399] *Gospel Advocate* (August 10, 1911), 880.
[400] *Gospel Advocate* (August 21, 1913), 805.
[401] *Gospel Advocate* (October 16, 1913), 989.
[402] Rock Creek Church Book, 36–37.
[403] *Gospel Advocate* (September 10, 1914), 967.
[404] *Gospel Advocate* (July 21, 1966), 455.
[405] Lewis C. Gibbs, Jr., *The History of Mountain Mills*.
[406] *Gospel Advocate* (April 23, 1890), 271.
[407] *Gospel Advocate* (October 23, 1879), 683.
[408] *Gospel Advocate* (November 13, 1879), 731.
[409] *Gospel Advocate* (July 18, 1883), 458.
[410] *Gospel Advocate* (October 3, 1888), 3.
[411] *Gospel Advocate* (March 11, 1891), 147.
[412] *Gospel Advocate* (October 14, 1891), 649.
[413] *Gospel Advocate* (August 25, 1892), 535.
[414] *Gospel Advocate* (September 12, 1895), 588.
[415] *Gospel Advocate* (August 13, 1896), 525.
[416] *Gospel Advocate* (January 26, 1899), 62.

[417] *Gospel Advocate* (September 18, 1902), 602.

[418] *Gospel Advocate* (October 23, 1908), 685.

[419] *Gospel Advocate* (September 23, 1909), 1204.

[420] *Gospel Advocate* (July 28, 1910), 880.

[421] *Gospel Advocate* (November 3, 1910), 1212.

[422] *Gospel Advocate* (May 11, 1916), 474.

[423] This information is found in a document written by Pauline Burns and Beatrice Wear. It was prepared for Marvin W. Hastings, *Saga of a Movement: Story of the Restoration Movement* (Manchester, TN: Christian Schoolmaster Publications, 1981).

[424] *Gospel Advocate* (January 24, 1935), 95.

[425] *Firm Foundation* (Sept. 14, 1909), 5.

[426] *Gospel Advocate* (October 27, 1910), 1188.

[427] *Gospel Advocate* (September 28, 1911), 1105.

[428] *Gospel Advocate* (July 11, 1912), 812.

[429] *Gospel Advocate* (September 5, 1912), 1104.

[430] *Gospel Advocate* (July 24, 1913), 708.

[431] *Firm Foundation* (March 26, 1916), 6.

[432] Marvin W. Hastings, *Saga of a Movement: Story of the Restoration Movement* (Manchester, TN: Christian Schoolmaster Publications, 1981), 214–215.

[433] Marvin W. Hastings, *Saga of a Movement: Story of the Restoration Movement* (Manchester, TN: Christian Schoolmaster Publications, 1981), 214–215.

[434] *Gospel Advocate* (December 8, 1932), 1315.

[435] *Gospel Advocate* (July 2, 1890), 430.

[436] *Gospel Advocate* (September 24. 1890), 610.

[437] *Gospel Advocate* (January 8, 1890), 26.

[438] *Gospel Advocate* (March 25, 1891), 179.

[439] *Gospel Advocate* (May 12, 1892), 297.

[440] *Gospel Advocate* (September 9, 1909), 1137.

[441] *Gospel Advocate* (May 15, 1930), 465.

[442] *Gospel Advocate* (June 12, 1930), 565.

[443] *Gospel Advocate* (May 9, 1912), 592.

[444] *Gospel Advocate* (September 13, 1923), 900.

[445] *Gospel Advocate* (September 14, 1933), 885.

[446] F. D. Srygley, *Larimore And His Boys* (Nashville: Gospel Advocate Publishing, 1889), 34.

[447] *Gospel Advocate* (September 14, 1933), 885.

[448] *Gospel Advocate* (August 14, 1889), 515.

[449] *Gospel Advocate* (July 2, 1890), 421.

[450] *Gospel Advocate* (December 16, 1897), 797.

[451] *Gospel Advocate* (April 21, 1898), 260.

[452] *Gospel Advocate* (August 18, 1898), 521.

[453] *Gospel Advocate* (December 1, 1904), 756.

[454] *Gospel Advocate* (April 12, 1906), 229.

[455] *Gospel Advocate* (November 15, 1906), 725.

[456] *Gospel Advocate* (March 14, 1907), 169.

[457] *Gospel Advocate* (August 8, 1907), 508.

[458] *Gospel Advocate* (March 5, 1908), 147.

[459] *Gospel Advocate* (April 9, 1908), 229.

[460] *Gospel Advocate* (November 26, 1908), 757.

[461] *Gospel Advocate* (February 18, 1909), 218–219.

[462] *Gospel Advocate* (April 28, 1910), 529.

[463] *Gospel Advocate* (May 12, 1910), 592.

[464] Tacitus, *Annals*, Book XV, section 44.

[465] *Gospel Advocate* (March 30, 1911), 297.

[466] *The Birmingham News* (February 27, 1911), 2.

[467] *Gospel Advocate* (April 13, 1911), 452–453.

[468] *Gospel Advocate* (April 20, 1911), 468.

[469] *Gospel Advocate* (April 20, 1911), 468.

[470] *Gospel Advocate* (April 27, 1911), 492.

[471] *Gospel Advocate* (June 22, 1911), 681.

[472] *Gospel Advocate* (December 28, 1911), 1520.

[473] *Gospel Advocate* (January 25, 1912), 112.

[474] *Gospel Advocate* (February 8, 1912), 177.
[475] *Gospel Advocate* (July 18, 1912), 836.
[476] *Gospel Advocate* (February 13, 1913), 156.
[477] *Gospel Advocate* (April 17, 1913), 372.
[478] Tombstone of little Mabelle Boll.
[479] *Gospel Advocate* (April 17, 1913), 372.
[480] *Gospel Advocate* (July 24, 1913), 708.
[481] *Gospel Advocate* (September 11, 1913), 878.
[482] *Gospel Advocate* (June 18, 1914), 676.
[483] *Gospel Advocate* (September 2, 1915), 877.
[484] *Gospel Advocate* (December 30, 1915), 1916.
[485] *Gospel Advocate* (February 3, 1916), 126–127.
[486] *Gospel Advocate* (July 10, 1913), 660.
[487] *Gospel Advocate* (September 4, 1913), 660.
[488] *Gospel Advocate* (October 30, 1913), 1037.
[489] *Gospel Advocate* (February 19, 1914), 280.
[490] *Gospel Advocate* (March 5, 1914), 280.
[491] *Gospel Advocate* (August 18, 1921), 788.
[492] *Gospel Advocate* (November 5, 1914), 1166.
[493] *Gospel Advocate* (July 18, 1912), 836.
[494] *Gospel Advocate* (September 18, 1913), 901.
[495] *Gospel Advocate* (August 13, 1914), 876.
[496] *Gospel Advocate* (November 5, 1914), 1166.
[497] *Gospel Advocate* (November 12, 1914), 1194.
[498] *Gospel Advocate* (September 15), 1932, 1026.

Bibliography

Books

Clevenger, Ernest A., Jr., *@ Any Age: An Autobiographical Memoir With Genealogical and Historical Records*. s.l.: Clevenger Publications, 2011.

Cowan, Terry and Harry Shetrone. *A Matthews History*. Wolfe City, TX: Henington Industries, 2002.

Gibbs, Lewis C., Jr. *The History of Mountain Mills*.

Hastings, Marvin W. *Saga of a Movement: Story of the Restoration Movement*. Manchester, TN: Christian Schoolmaster Publications, 1981.

Kimbrough, Earl. *The Restoration In Russell's Valley And Northwest Alabama 1842–1945*. Monroe, GA: Book Production Resources, 2013.

Leftwich, Nina, *Two Hundred Years at Muscle Shoals* (North Port, AL: American Southern Printers, 1965

Ransom, Crisler B. *History of the First United Methodist Church of Tuscumbia, Alabama*. No publisher given, 1976.

Riley, B. F. *History of the Baptists of Alabama*. Birmingham: Roberts and Son, 1895.

Scobey, James E. *Franklin College and Its Influences*. Nashville, TN: Gospel Advocate Company, 1954.

Sevier, Cora Bales and Nancy S. Madden. *Sevier Family History*. Washington, D.C.: private publication, 1961.

Sockwell, Sandra. *The Place Names of Colbert and Lauderdale Counties, Alabama, 1985*. Diss., (1988).

Srygley, F. D. *Smiles and Tears: or Larimore and His Boys*. Nashville, TN: Gospel Advocate Company, 1889.

Tacitus, *Annals*, Book XV, section 44.

Watson, George M. and Mildred B. Watson, *History of the Christian Churches in the Alabama Area*, St. Louis, MO: Bethany Press, 1965.

Periodicals

Alabama Restoration Journal
Bible Advocate
The Birmingham News
Bulletin in the North Alabama Historical Association
Christian Magazine
Christian Monthly
Christian Preacher
Christian Reformer
Christian Register
Christian Review
The Evangelist
Franklin County Times
Gospel Advocate
The Leighton News
Millennial Harbinger
Natchez Trace Traveler
The Russellville Christian
World Evangelist

Name Index

Alabama Christian xi, 238
Alabama Christian College 175, 225
Albertville, Alabama 52, 54, 79, 93
Allen, James C. 46
Anderson, Frank 145
Apple Grove, Alabama 109–110
Armenians 212–213
Armstrong, J. H. 21
Baker, Frank 194
Baptists 15–16, 18–19, 22–27, 30–31, 36–37, 42, 48–49, 51, 53, 55, 68. 76, 81–82, 84–85, 100, 107–108, 119–120, 139–142, 144, 162, 177, 213, 215, 227–228, 237, 255
Barnes, Justus M. 148
Barry, O. P. 48, 111–112, 241
Barton Station (Barton), Alabama (Colbert County) 92, 182–183, 186
Barton Warren Stone xvi, 1, 8, 11, 38, 132, 233
Bear Creek 36–37, 49, 87, 111–112, 173, 229
Behel, William 70–71, 85, 133, 177–179, 229
Belgreen, Alabama 71, 79–90, 92–93, 96, 99,

101, 109, 118–119, 121–122, 177
Benson, John A.   81, 87, 89, 118–119
Berea church   19, 60, 103–104
Billingsley, J. B.   98–99, 108, 198
Birmingham, Alabama   132, 217–218, 237, 253
Blackburn, W. B.   65–66
Boles, H. Leo   223
Boll, R. H.   215, 221, 223–224
Bradley, I. B.   48–52, 54, 56, 75–76, 84, 89–90, 94, 96, 101, 112–113, 117–123, 177, 241
Bradley, Minnie (Young)   51
Bradley, Van   101, 188
Bradley's Chapel   84, 117–123, 130
Brown, George L.   36, 104
Brown, John T.   xi
Bunker Hill, Alabama   91, 106, 133–134
Burns, C. C.   192
Butler, James A.   17–18
Campbell, Alexander   ix, xvi, xviii, 1, 3, 16–17, 20, 154, 233, 237–239
Campbell, Thomas   ix
Campbellism   16, 22, 25, 139, 142
Caskey, Thomas W.   80
Catholics   201
Cherokee, Alabama   xv, 146, 169, 188, 191, 196–205
Chickasaw Indian Nation   103
Chisholm, Ed   20, 155
Chisholm, Gillington   7–8, 21, 184
Chisholm, John   viii
Chisholm, Lewis C.   8, 21, 31, 35, 39, 62, 137–138, 184, 235, 238–240
Chisholm, Obediah   61
Christian Baptist   xviii, 3
Christian Church   4, 24, 46, 52, 91, 141, 154
Christian Messenger   11, 17, 235–237
Christian Monthly   25, 143, 237–238, 248
Christian Review   13, 34, 236, 238–239
Civil War   xiii, xvii, 1, 19–22, 35, 38–39, 62, 68, 99, 104, 131–132,

136–137, 154, 159, 163
Colbert County, Alabama xiii, xv, xvii, 1–2, 4, 13–14, 19–21, 27, 38, 60–61, 69–70, 74, 83, 85, 92, 100, 117, 139, 148, 156, 159–161, 167–168, 170–173, 178, 181, 184, 186, 191, 195–196, 202, 209, 233, 249
Crooked Oak 92, 107, 158, 173
Cypress Creek viii, 64, 105
Dale, John H. 132
DeSpain, Marshall viii, 5–6, 10
Dickson, Priscilla 14, 20
Dickson, Tennessee 84, 118, 120, 122, 187, 214
Dies, A. D. 130
Disciples of Christ xi–xii
Dunn, G. A., Sr. 58, 88, 149–150
Dunn, John E. 148
Dunn, J. H. 32–35, 37, 239–240
Episcopalians 19, 22, 26, 140, 144, 185
Ezell, Alice 86

Ezell, J. Petty 95–96
Fanning, Tolbert ix, 11–12, 19, 28–29, 31, 33–35, 39–40, 55, 62, 136, 155, 238–240
Firm Foundation xiii, 175, 192, 251–252
Florence, Alabama vi, viii, 14, 29, 52, 145–146, 149–150, 153–154, 163, 175, 182, 192, 194, 208, 210, 212–214, 225–226
Frankfort, Alabama 19, 36–37, 42, 44–45, 61–73, 83, 85, 91, 96, 98, 101, 103–104, 106, 108, 158, 161–162, 173, 177, 184, 186, 228
Franklin, Tennessee 46–47, 53
Franklin College 8, 155–156, 161–162, 239
Franklin County, Alabama 8, 33, 40
Franklin County Times 96, 245
Fuqua, E. C. 183–184
Gassaway, Paralee Annie 98–99, 103, 245
Godwin, Brown 47, 81–83, 88, 107, 241

Gospel Advocate xii, 10, 36, 43–44, 48, 50–51, 56, 58–59, 61–62, 64, 77, 79, 81–82, 85–89, 93, 96, 99–100, 103–104, 107–109, 112–114, 117–119, 121–122, 124–126, 128–129, 131, 136, 138, 145–147, 152, 154, 156, 167, 170–173, 175–177, 182, 187, 191, 193–195, 197, 199203, 206, 209–212, 214–215, 221–224, 229, 231, 235–254
Graham, Alexander, (A.) 18
Graham, John C. 229
Griffin, Thacker 9
Gum Fork, Mississippi 104
Hackleburg 111
Halbrook, Joseph H. (Joe) 46, 164, 166, 170, 178, 198–199, 250
Halbrook, Margaret 165
Hall, B. F. 4, 8, 235
Hall, Dorinda G. viii
Hall Town, Alabama 95
Harding, James A. 208
Harris, J. T. 194

Harris, W. D. 43–46, 51–52, 168, 241
Hayes, John 48, 92, 100, 110–111, 208–209, 224–225
Hayes, Paul 48
Henry, A. C. 40–42, 69, 79–80, 88, 240, 243
Henry, J. Waller xi
Hill, Abner 2, 4–13, 17, 27, 233, 235–236, 239
Hodges, Alabama 126, 229
Holt, C. E. 212–214
Howard, John R. 36
Huntsville, Alabama viii, xvi, 14
Illinois Central Railroad 128–129
Isbell, Alabama 48–49, 57, 109–115, 125
Jackson, Lee 42–43, 79–80, 240
Jackson County, Alabama xv–xvi, 105
James, Richard L. xi
Kendrick, Allen ix
Kendrick, Carroll 18–19
Kidwill, W. T. 82
Kimbrough, Earl 11, 54, 74, 91, 96–99, 103–

106, 117, 132–133,
    236, 242, 245–248
Kimbrough's Chapel   96,
    106–108
Ladd, Noble R.   32, 34,
    239
Lancaster, L. S.   58–59,
    96, 122, 149, 151,
    227
Landersville, Alabama
    40–41, 43, 57, 125,
    199
Lard, Moses E.   21
Larimore, T. B.   xvii, 2,
    41, 52, 64–66, 79,
    110, 144, 156, 158–
    162, 164, 168–169,
    185
Lauderdale County,
    Alabama   vi, viii, xv,
    xviii, 12, 17, 29, 64,
    70, 105, 249–250
Lawrence County,
    Alabama   xv, 10,
    40, 55, 170
Liberty, Alabama   xviii,
    36, 104–105
Limestone County,
    Alabama   xv, 209
Lipscomb, David   10,
    62–63, 136, 155, 174,
    209

Lloyd, Eunice   86–87,
    245
Lost Creek   91, 103–
    106
Lynn, Benjamin   viii,
    xvii–xviii, 4, 17, 233
Madison County, Alabama
    viii, xv–xvi, xviii, 6,
    10
Manire, B. F.   61
Marietta, Mississippi   70,
    198
Marion County, Alabama
    xv, 128, 170, 173
Mars Hill College   163,
    166, 182, 185
Matthews, James E.   ix,
    9, 13
Matthews, Mansel W.   8,
    10, 12–13
McDonald, Crockett   18
McGarvey, J. W.   21
McQuiddy, J. C.   50,
    182, 189, 210–211,
    214
Methodists   30–31,
    36, 42, 49–50, 69, 81,
    107–108, 162, 168,
    213
Millennial Harbinger   ix,
    17, 34, 131
Mississippi   xv–xvi,
    6, 13, 29, 33, 42, 61,

69–71, 79, 98, 108, 110, 120, 128, 130, 136, 170, 191, 193–195, 198, 221, 231–232
Montgomery, Alabama 148
Moody, R. N. 52, 54, 69, 73–74, 79, 83, 92–97, 100–101, 172–173, 241, 245
Moore, A. R. xi, 208
Moore, Ephraim D. 9, 13
Mooresville, Alabama 48, 100, 110, 208–209
Morgan County, Alabama xv
Morris, James Harvey 27, 114, 148, 201–202
Moulton, Alabama 34, 43, 66, 111, 145, 199
Mountain Home School 64, 66
Mount Hope, Alabama 51, 58, 120, 125
Mount Mills (Mount Mills Factory), Alabama 92, 186
Mount Olivet church 232
Mount Pleasant church 74, 91–97, 106, 120–122

Mount Zion, Alabama 100–101
Mulkey, John 8, 10, 233
Nance, Mrs. Louisa 31
Nance, Mrs. Rufus 31
Nance, W. H. 41, 46
Newburg, Alabama 106–107
New Hope church 210
Northcross, M. H. 52–54, 241
Norwood, R. W. 43, 240
Nunnelly, Donald A. xi
O'Kelly, James xvi, 1
Old Philadelphia church (Viola, Tennessee) xvii
Pack, T. T. 146–148, 211–212, 217
Patton, J. D. 92, 146
Peden, F. E. 57–58, 114, 125, 193
Pickens, James Madison (J. M.) 20–22, 25, 62–64, 136–137, 139, 142–145, 158–159, 184, 248
Piney Grove, Alabama 92, 107, 229, 231–233
Pleasant Site, Alabama 73–78, 80, 93, 120, 176

Potter Bible College   57, 114, 125
Presbyterian   ix, 8, 14–15, 17–18, 22, 26, 30–31, 50, 107–108, 140, 143, 159, 195, 208, 213
Red Bay, Alabama   77, 124
Rickard, James Henry   85–86
Ricks, Abe   154
Ricks, Abraham   21, 152–154, 238, 249
Ricks, George.   153–156
Ricks, Percy   154
Ricks, T. L.   21
Rock Creek, Alabama   42–44, 54, 62–65, 71, 73, 75–76, 83, 92–93, 100–101, 120, 127, 158–180, 182, 185–186, 200, 242, 249–251
Rocky Springs Church   xvi–xvii, 105
Russell's Valley   91, 102, 106, 133, 236, 242, 245–248
Russellville Church of Christ   11, 35, 41, 46, 114

Sandlin, W. T.   169, 197–200
Scott, Walter   xvii, 8, 15–17
Sevier, Daniel V., Sr.   31
Sevier, John   28
Sevier, Samuel   21, 28, 30, 32, 34
Sewell, E. G.   111, 126, 214
Sewell, L. R.   44, 46–47, 56–57, 110–111, 146, 181–182, 199, 241
Shady Grove, Alabama   67, 71–72, 96
Slayden, J. Paul   150, 213–214
Smith, E. A.   17–18
Smith, F. W.   46–47, 56
Smith, G. Dallas   58–59
Spiegel, O. P.   xi
Spout Spring   19, 36–37, 103–105
Spring Creek   8–10, 12, 27
Spruce Pine, Alabama   58, 125–127, 179
Srygley, F. B.   55–56, 63–68, 71, 73, 101, 164, 168–173, 178, 186

Srygley, F. D. xvii, 2, 44–45, 63–64, 82–83, 101, 109, 160, 162–163, 167–173, 179, 185, 200, 204
Srygley, F. W. 168
Srygley, James H. 62–63, 66, 68, 158–159, 161–162
Stone, Barton Warren xvi, 1, 8, 11, 38, 132, 233
Stony Point xvii, 104–105, 182
Stout, Chester 92, 106, 133
Sunday School 167, 200
Tant, J. D. 183
Taylor, James A. (J. A.) 36, 104
Taylor, John 19, 35–36, 44–46, 61–62, 67–69, 73, 79–80, 98–99, 103–105, 161–162, 171, 184, 240, 246
Taylor, John Abraham 36, 104
Tennessee vii, xvi–xvii, 1, 7–13, 19, 23, 28–30, 32, 39, 46, 55–56, 59, 81–82, 84, 110, 114, 117, 120, 136, 141, 164, 170, 176, 217, 222, 224, 235, 248
Tennessee River xi, xv, 2, 5, 14, 197, 206, 208,
Tennessee Valley vi, 14, 42
Trotter, Thomas B. 61, 103–104, 240
Tuscaloosa, Alabama 20, 170, 238
Tuscumbia, Alabama xvii, 2, 6, 8–14, 16–25, 27, 29, 38–39, 62, 67, 114, 136–155, 157, 201, 208, 210–212, 217, 221, 226, 229, 231–232, 236–238, 243, 248
Underwood, John T. 69–70, 76–77, 79–81, 88, 98–99, 124, 126–131, 146, 179, 183, 198–199
Union, Alabama 104
Vina, Alabama 128–132
Walker County, Alabama 170
Waterloo, Alabama viii, 12, 91, 107
West, Earl Irvin vii

Wharton, William H.
    xvii, 8, 14–27, 29, 32,
    66, 143–144
Wilson Mercantile
    Company   54
Wolf Creek, Alabama 104
Wright, P. G.   130, 189,
    193, 203, 229, 231–
    232

Also by C. Wayne Kilpatrick

An Early History of the Mars Hill Church of Christ: With a Collection of Memories by Members of the Congregation (2024)

J. R. Bradley: A Forgotten Larimore Boy (2019)

John Chisholm Church History Series

including

A Faithful Band of Workers: The Beginnings of Churches of Christ in Jackson County, Alabama

A Humble Band of People: The Beginning of Churches of Christ in Franklin and Colbert Counties, Alabama

A Little Band of Disciples: The Beginnings of Churches of Christ in Madison County, Alabama

A Noble Band of Worshipers: The Beginnings of Churches of Christ in Lauderdale County, Alabama

A Small Band of Brethren: The Beginnings of Churches of Christ in Limestone County, Alabama

To see the full catalog of Heritage Christian University Press
and its imprint, Cypress Publications, visit
www.hcu.edu/publications

www.ingramcontent.com/pod-product-compliance
Lightning Source LLC
Chambersburg PA
CBHW030447100526
44580CB00002B/26